AAKAR BOOKS CLASSICS

THE DIALECTICS OF THE ABSTRACT AND THE CONCRETE IN MARX'S CAPITAL

E.V. Ilyenkov

Translated by
Sergei Syrovatkin

The Dialectics of the Abstract and the Concrete in Marx’s Capital
E.V. Ilyenkov

First Published 1960
Indian Edition 2008
Reprinted 2013, 2017, 2022
Reprinted 2025

ISBN 978-81-89833-38-1

Published by
AAKAR BOOKS
28 E Pocket IV, Mayur Vihar Phase I
Delhi 110 091, India
www.aakarbooks.com

Printed at
D.K. Fine Art Press, Delhi

CONTENTS

AUTHOR'S PREFACE FOR THE GERMAN EDITION

This book was written almost twenty years ago and published in Russian in 1960. Experience has shown, however, that the interest for the ideas expounded in it is still alive. The book has been translated and continues to be translated into foreign languages. It has been published in full in Italy (Feltrinelli Publishers, 1961), Japan (1969), Yugoslavia (1975), and in part, in France (1962) and Mexico (1966). In 1973, preparations were made for its publication in Chile, later cancelled for well-known reasons. In German, there is a translation of a small excerpt from it (an abridged version of Chapter 3) done from French and published by Alfred Schmidt in the collection *Beiträge zur marxistischen Erkenntnistheorie*, Suhrkamp, 1969.

This fact, as well as constant references to the book, permit me to hope that its publication may prove to be useful for the reader interested in problems of dialectics and epistemology. Regrettably I have been unable to add to it an analysis of the literature on the subject covering the recent years, for carrying out this task would have required, in fact, an independent study. This omission may be justified by the fact that the principal theoretical propositions of the book have not become obsolete and do not require emendation on the basis of the achievements of Marxist thought in recent years. As for the criticism in this book, it is mostly levelled at widely spread trends (neopositivism, existentialism, neo-Hegelianism, and their varieties) whose conceptual tenets have not undergone any significant changes in recent times, while the Marxist view of the problem has obviously not been presented to the West fully enough.

Taking this into account, I deemed it possible to restrict myself to minor corrections of the old text and interpolation of materials from an article in the collection *Forms of Thought* (Moscow, 1961), which complement the historico-philosophical part of the book and add to the scope of treatment of the problem.

Author

PREFACE

This book is devoted to problems of dialectical logic. It is hardly necessary to go into the importance of research in this major field of Marxist philosophy. Both the needs of further development of the natural and social sciences and the requirements of present-day social practice bring dialectical logic into the foreground. This was pointed out already by V. I. Lenin, who insisted that Marxist philosophers ought to give their greatest attention to these problems. Lenin it was who left in his *Philosophical Notebooks* and other works most valuable hints as to the lines along which such studies should proceed.

Most significant among Lenin's directions is the idea that Marx's *Capital* ought to be maximally used for further development of dialectical logic and epistemology. We know that Lenin believed that in this great work of scientific socialism Marx had applied dialectics in all its richness to the study of political economy of capitalism and substantiation of the inevitability of revolutionary transformation of society. That was why Lenin insistently recommended to undertake an allround study of the dialectics of *Capital*—the classical model of interpretation and application of the Marxist method of cognition.

E. V. Ilyenkov's book studies one of the most essential and interesting aspects of the dialectical method, which Marx himself described as the method of ascending from the abstract to the concrete. In our view, the author's work in this field is worthy of the attention of readers interested in Marxist philosophy, and will take a proper place in the literature studying the philosophical significance of *Capital*.

On the whole, the author takes a correct approach to the

problem of the dialectics of the abstract and the concrete; at the same time the book contains propositions which will require further discussion. Creative debate and scientific discussion on these problems, based on the study of the great heritage of the classics of Marxism-Leninism and modern data of the natural sciences and social practice, will undoubtedly be of great use, exerting favourable influence on further development of dialectical logic.

Professor *M. Rosental*

Moscow, 1960

Chapter 1

THE DIALECTICAL AND METAPHYSICAL CONCEPTION OF THE CONCRETE

THE CONCEPTION OF THE ABSTRACT AND THE CONCRETE IN DIALECTICS AND IN FORMAL LOGIC

The terms 'the abstract' and 'the concrete' are employed both in everyday speech and in the special literature rather ambiguously. Thus, one hears of 'concrete facts' and 'concrete music', of 'abstract thinking' and 'abstract painting', of 'concrete truth' and 'abstract labour'. This usage is in each case apparently justified by the existence of shades of meanings in these words, and it would be ridiculously pedantic to demand a complete unification of the usage.

However, things are different when we are dealing not merely with words or terms but with the content of scientific categories that have become historically linked with these terms. Definitions of the abstract and the concrete as categories of logic must be stable and unambiguous within the framework of this science, for they are instrumental in establishing the basic principles of scientific thought. Through these terms, dialectical logic expresses a number of its fundamental principles ('there is no abstract truth, truth is always concrete', the thesis of 'ascending from the abstract to the concrete', and so on). Therefore the categories of the abstract and the concrete have quite a definite meaning in dialectical logic, which is intrinsically linked with the dialectico-materialist conception of the truth, the relation of thought to reality, the mode of theoretical reproduction of reality in thinking, and so on. As long as we deal with categories of dialectics connected with words, rather than with words themselves, any licence, lack of clarity or instability in their definition (let alone incorrectness) will necessarily lead to a distorted conception of the essence of the matter. For this reason it is necessary to free the categories of the abstract and the concrete from the connotations that have been associated with them throughout centuries in many works by tradition, from force of habit or simply because of an error, which has often interfered with correct interpretation of the propositions of dialectical logic.

* * *

The problem of the relationship of the abstract and the concrete in its general form is not posed or solved in formal logic, for it is a purely philosophical, epistemological question, quite outside its sphere of competence. However, when it is a matter of classifying concepts, namely, of dividing concepts into 'abstract' and 'concrete', formal logic necessarily assumes a quite definite interpretation of the corresponding categories. This interpretation appears as the principle of division and may therefore be established analytically.

On this point, most authors of books on formal logic apparently give a rather unanimous support to a certain tradition, albeit with some reservations and amendments. According to this traditional view, concepts (or ideas) are divided into abstract and concrete in the following manner:

'Concrete concepts are those that reflect really existing definite objects or classes of objects. Abstract concepts are those that reflect a property of objects mentally abstracted from the objects themselves.' [1]

'A concrete concept is one relating to groups, classes of things, objects, and phenomena or to separate things, objects, or phenomena.... An abstract concept is a concept of properties of objects or phenomena, when these properties are taken as an independent object of thought.' [2]

'Concrete concepts are those whose objects actually exist as things in the material world.... Abstract concepts are those that reflect a property of an object taken separately from the object, rather than the object itself.' [3]

The examples cited to illustrate the definitions are mostly of the same type. *Concrete* concepts are usually said to include such concepts as 'book', 'Fido', 'tree', 'plane', 'commodity', whereas *abstract* ones are illustrated by 'whiteness', 'courage', 'virtue', 'speed', 'value', etc.

---

[1] N. I. Kondakov, *Logika* (Logic), Moscow, 1954, p. 300.
[2] M. S. Strogovich, *Logika* (Logic), Moscow, 1949, p. 87.
[3] V. F. Asmus, *Logika* (Logic), Moscow, 1947, p. 36.

Judging from the examples, the division is in fact the same as in the well-known textbook on logic by G. I. Chelpanov. Improvements on the Chelpanov definition are mostly concerned not with the division itself but with its philosophico-epistemological foundation, for Chelpanov was, philosophically, a typical subjective idealist.

Here is his version of the division of concepts into abstract and concrete ones:

'Abstract terms are those that serve for designating *qualities* or *properites*, *states*, or *actions* of things. They denote qualities considered by themselves, without the things. . . . Concrete concepts are those of *things*, *objects*, *persons*, *facts*, *events*, *states of consciousness*, if we regard them as having definite existence. . . .'[4]

The distinction between 'term' and 'concept' is a matter of indifference for Chelpanov. 'States of consciousness' are in his view in the same category as facts, things, and events. 'Having definite existence' is for him the same as 'having definite existence in the individual's immediate consciousness', that is, in his contemplation, conception, or at least imagination.

Chelpanov therefore regards as concrete anything that may be conceived (imagined) as a separately existing single thing, or image, and he regards as abstract anything that cannot be so imagined, that can only be thought of as such.

The individual's ability or inability to conceive something graphically is, in fact, Chelpanov's criterion for the division into the abstract and the concrete. This division, however shaky it may be from the philosophical standpoint, is rather definite.

Inasmuch as some authors endeavoured to correct the philosophico-epistemological interpretation of the classification without changing the actual type of examples concerned, the classification proved to be open to criticism.

If one includes among concrete concepts only those that pertain to *objects of the material world*, a centaur or Athena Pallas will apparently be regarded as abstract concepts along with courage or virtue, while Fido will be included among concrete ones along with value.

---

[4] G. I. Chelpanov, *Uchebnik Logiki* (Textbook on Logic), Moscow, 1946, pp. 10-11.

What is the use of such a classification for logical analysis? The traditional classification is destroyed or confused by this kind of amendment introducing a completely alien element into it. On the other hand, no new strict classification is obtained.

Attempts by certain authors to oppose a new principle or basis of division to the one suggested by Chelpanov can hardly be regarded as apt, too.

Kondakov believes, for instance, that the division of concepts into abstract and concrete should express a 'difference in the content of concepts' [5]. That means that concrete concepts must reflect *things*, and abstract ones, *properties and relations* of these things. If the division is to be complete, neither properties nor relations of things can be conceived in concrete concepts, according to Kondakov. It remains unclear how one can conceive of a thing or a class other than through a conception of their properties and relations. In fact, any thought about a thing will inevitably prove to be a thought about some property of this thing, for conceiving a thing means forming a conception about the entire totality of its properties and relations.

If one frees the thought of a thing from all thoughts of properties of this thing, there will be nothing left of the thought other than the name. In other words, the division of concepts according to their content means, in actual fact, this: a concrete concept is a concept without content, while an abstract one does have some content, though very meagre. Otherwise the division will not be complete and will thus be incorrect.

The principle of division suggested by Asmus, 'actual existence of the objects of these concepts', [6] is just as unfortunate.

How is one to understand this formula? Do the objects of concrete concepts actually exist, while the objects of abstract concepts are nonexistent? But the category of abstract concepts embraces not only virtue but also value, weight, speed, that is, objects whose existence is no less real than that of a plane or a house. If one means to say that extension, value, or speed actually do not exist outside a house, a tree, a plane, or some other individual things, clearly the

---

[5] See N. I. Kondakov, *op. cit.*, pp. 300-01.

[6] See V. F. Asmus, *op. cit.*, p. 36.

individual things also exist without extension, weight and other attributes of the material world only in the head, only in subjective abstraction.

Real existence is consequently neither here nor there, the more so that it cannot be made into a criterion of division of concepts into abstract and concrete. That can only create the false impression that individual things are more real than universal laws and forms of existence of these things.

All of this shows that the amendments to the Chelpanov division introduced by some authors are extremely inadequate and formal, and that the authors of books on logic have failed to make a critical materialist analysis of this division, restricting themselves to corrections of particulars, which merely confused the traditional classification without improving it.

We shall therefore have to undertake a small excursion into the history of the concepts of the abstract and the concrete to introduce some clarity there.

FROM THE HISTORY OF THE CONCEPTS OF THE ABSTRACT AND THE CONCRETE

The definition of abstract concepts shared by Chelpanov was clearly formulated by Christian Wolff. According to Wolff, abstract concepts have for their content properties, relations, and states of things mentally isolated from things and represented as an independent object. [7]

Wolff is not the original source. He merely reproduces the view taken in the logical treatises of medieval scholastics. All names/concepts (they did not distinguish name from concept) denoting properties and relations of things they called abstract, whereas names of things were called concrete. [8]

This usage was originally determined by mere etymology. In Latin '*concretus*' means simply 'mixed', 'fused', 'composite', compound; while the Latin word '*abstractus*' means 'withdrawn', 'taken out of', 'extracted' (or 'isolated'), or 'estranged'. That is all that is contained in the original ety-

---

[7] See *Wörterbuch der philosophischen Begriffe,* Historisch-Quellenmässig bearbeitet von Dr. Rudolf Eisler, 3. Auflage, Bd. 1, Ernst Siegfried Mittler und Sohn, Berlin, 1910, S. 5.

[8] See Carl Prantl, *Geschichte der Logik im Abendlande,* Bd. 3, Akademie-Verlag, Berlin, 1957, S. 363.

mological meaning of these words. The rest pertains to the philosophical conception that is expressed through them.

The opposition of medieval realism and nominalism is not relevant to the direct etymological meanings of the words 'abstract' and 'concrete'. Both nominalists and realists equally apply the term 'concrete' to separate sensually perceived and directly observed 'things', individual objects, while the term 'abstract' is applied to all concepts and names designating or expressing their general 'forms'. The difference lies in that the former believe names to be merely subjective designations of individual concrete things, whereas the latter believe that these abstract names express eternal and immutable 'forms' having their existence in the womb of divine reason, the prototypes in accordance with which the divine power creates individual things.

Contempt for the world of sensually perceived things, for the 'flesh', that is characteristic of the Christian worldview in general and is particularly clearly expressed in realism, determines the fact that the abstract (estranged from the flesh, from sensuality, the purely cognitive) is believed to be much more valuable (both on the ethical and epistemological planes) than the concrete.

The concrete is here a full synonym of the sensually perceived, individual, carnal, mundane, transient ('composite' and therefore doomed to disintegration, to disappearance). The abstract is a synonym of the eternal, imperishable, indivisible, divinely instituted, universal, absolute, etc. An individual 'round body' will disappear, but the 'round body' in general exists eternally as form, as entelechy creating new round bodies. The concrete is transient, elusive, fleeting. The abstract exists immutably, constituting the essence, the invisible scheme upon which the world is built.

It is the scholastic conception of the abstract and the concrete that is at the bottom of the antiquarian respect for the abstract which Hegel later so caustically ridiculed.

The materialist philosophy of the 16th and 17th centuries which, forming an alliance with natural science, commenced to destroy the foundations of the religious and scholastic worldview, in effect re-interpreted the categories of the abstract and the concrete.

The direct sense of these terms remained the same: the term 'concrete' referred, just as in scholastic doctrines, to individual, sensually perceived things and their graphic images, while the term 'abstract' was used to refer to the general forms of these things, to immutably recurring properties and law-governed relations of these things expressed in terms, names, and numbers. However, the philosophico-theoretical content of these categories became the opposite of the scholastic one. The concrete, that which is given to man in sensual experience, came to be understood as the only reality worthy of attention and study, and the abstract, as a mere subjective psychological shadow of that reality, its meagre mental schema. The abstract became a synonym for expression of sensual empirical data in words and figures, a synonym for a sign description of the concrete.

But this interpretation of the relationship between the abstract and the concrete, characteristic of the first steps in natural science and materialist philosophy, very soon came into contradiction with the practice of natural-historical research. Natural science and materialist philosophy of the 16th-18th centuries tended more and more towards mechanistic views, and that meant that temporal and spatial characteristics and abstract geometrical forms became recognised as the only objective qualities and relations of things and phenomena. The rest appeared as mere subjective illusion created by man's sense organs.

In other words, everything 'concrete' was conceived as a *product of the activity of the sense organs,* as a certain psychophysiological state of the subject, as a subjectively coloured replica of the colourless abstract geometrical original. The prime task of cognition was also viewed in a new light: to obtain the truth, one had to erase or wash off all the colours superimposed by sensuality upon the sensually perceived image of things, baring the abstract geometrical skeleton, the schema.

So the concrete was interpreted as subjective illusion, merely as a state of the sense organs, while the object outside consciousness was transformed into something entirely abstract.

The picture thus obtained was as follows: outside man's consciousness there exists nothing but eternally immutable abstract geometrical particles combined according to identical, eternal, and immutable abstract mathematical schemes, while the concrete is within the subject only, as a form of sensory perception of the abstract geometrical bodies. Hence the formula: the only correct way to truth is through soaring away from the concrete (the fallacious, false, subjective) to the abstract (as the expression of eternal and immutable schemes for constructing bodies).

This determines the strong nominalistic bias in the philosophy of the 16th-18th centuries. Any concept, except for the mathematical ones, was simply interpreted as an artificially invented sign, a name serving as an aid to memory, to ordering the varied data of experience, to communication with other men, etc.

George Berkeley and David Hume, the subjective idealists of those times, directly reduced concepts to names, to designations, to conventional signs or symbols, beyond which, they believed, it would be absurd to look for any other content except for a certain similarity of series of sensual impressions, the common element in experience. This tendency became particularly firm-rooted in England and is still living out its days in the shape of neopositivist conceptions.

The weaknesses of this approach, that was in its perfect form characteristic of subjective idealism, were also peculiar to many materialists of that age. Particularly striking in this respect were the studies of John Locke. Hobbes and Helvétius were no exception either. In their work this approach was present as a tendency obscuring their basically materialist positions.

Taken to an extreme, this view results in logical categories being dissolved in psychological and even linguistic, grammatical ones. Thus Helvétius defines the method of abstraction as a means to fix 'a great number of objects in our memory'.[9] He regards 'abuse of words' as one of the most important causes of error.[10] Hobbes follows a similar line of reasoning: "Wherefore, as men owe all their True Ratiocination to the right understanding of Speech; So also they owe their Errors to the misunderstanding of the same".[11]

Since rational cognition of the external world was reduced to a purely quantitative, mathematical processing of data, and for the rest, to ordering and verbal recording of sensual images, the place of logic was naturally taken, on

---

[9] C. A. Helvétius, *De l'Esprit; or Essay on the Mind and Its Several Faculties*, J. M. Richardson, *et al.*, London, 1809, p. 10.

[10] Ibid., p. 8.

[11] Thomas Hobbes, *Elements of Philosophy, the First Section Concerning Body*, R. & W. Legbourn, London, 1656, p. 27.

the one hand, by mathematics, and on the other, by the science of combination and division of terms and propositions, the science of the correct usage of words created by men.

This nominalistic reduction of the concept to the word, the term, and of thinking, to the ability for correct usage of words that we ourselves create, undermined the materialist principle itself. Locke, the classical representative and the originator of this view, found already that the concept of *substance* could neither be explained nor justified as simply 'the general in experience', as the broadest possible universal', as an abstraction from individual things. Naturally Berkeley rushed into this breach, using the Lockean theory of concept formation against materialism and against the very concept of substance. He declared it to be a meaningless name. Continuing his analysis of the basic concepts of philosophy, Hume proved that the objective character of such a concept as causality could also be neither proved nor verified by reference to the fact that it expressed 'the general in experience', for abstraction from the sensually given individual objects and phenomena, from the concrete might just as well express the identity of the psychophysiological structure of the subject perceiving things rather than an identity of the things themselves.

The narrow empirical theory of the concept reducing it to a mere abstraction from individual phenomena and perceptions, reflected only the superficial psychological aspects of rational cognition. On the surface, thought indeed appears as abstraction of the 'identical' from individual things, as ascending to increasingly comprehensive and universal abstractions. Such a theory, however, may equally well serve diametrically opposite philosophical conceptions bypassing as it does the most important point—the question of the objective truth of universal concepts.

Consistent materialists realised the weakness of the nominalistic view of the concept, its vulnerability to idealist speculations and errors. Spinoza stressed that the concept of substance, expressing the 'first principle of nature', 'cannot be conceived abstractedly or universally, and cannot extend further in the understanding than it does in reality'. [12]

---

[12] Benedict de Spinoza, *Improvement of the Understanding, Ethics and Correspondence,* translated from the Latin by R. Elwes, M. Walter Dunne Publisher, Washington and London, 1901, p. 26.

There is an idea running through Spinoza's entire treatise—that simple 'universals', simple abstractions from the sensually given multiformity recorded in names and terms are merely a form of vague imaginative cognition. Genuinely scientific, 'true ideas' do not emerge in that way. The establishment of 'the differences, the agreements, and the oppositions of things' is, according to Spinoza, the mode of 'chaotic experience' uncontrolled by reason. 'Moreover its (of the mode of perception—*Ed.*) results are very uncertain and indefinite, for we shall never discover anything in natural phenomena by its means, except accidental properties, which are never clearly understood, unless the essence of the things in question be known first.' [13]

To begin with, the 'chaotic experience' forming universals is never completed, so that any new fact may overthrow the abstraction. Second, it contains no guarantees that the given universal really expresses a genuine universal form of things rather than a merely subjective fiction.

In opposition to 'chaotic experience' and its philosophical justification in empiric conceptions, Spinoza sets up a higher mode of cognition based on strictly verified principles and concepts expressing 'the adequate essence of a thing'. These are no longer 'universals', no longer abstractions from the sensually given multiformity. How are they formed and where do they come from?

Comments on this point often run as follows: these ideas (principles, universal concepts) are contained in the human intellect a priori and brought out by an act of intuition or self-contemplation. In this interpretation Spinoza's position becomes very much like that of Leibniz or Kant and has very little to do with materialism. But in reality it is all rather different—quite different, in fact. The thinking of which Spinoza treats is by no means the thinking of a human individual. This concept is by no means fashioned in his theory after the model of individual consciousness, but is actually oriented at mankind's theoretical self-consciousness, at the spiritual-theoretical culture as a whole. Individual consciousness is here taken into account only insofar as it embodies this thinking, that is, thinking which agrees with the nature of things. An individual's intellect does not necessarily contain the ideas of reason at all, and

[13] Benedict de Spinoza, op. cit., pp. 8-9.

no self-contemplation, however thorough it may be, can discover them in it.

They mature and crystallise in the human intellect only gradually, through reason's indefatigable work aimed at its own perfection. These concepts are by no means self-obvious to an intellect that is not developed through this kind of work. They are simply absent in it. It is only reasonable knowledge taken as a whole that, as it develops, works out such concepts. Spinoza firmly asserts this view by an analogy with the perfection of instruments of material labour.

As far as the 'method for finding out the truth' is concerned, 'the matter stands on the same footing as the making of material tools.... For, in order to work iron, a hammer is needed, and the hammer cannot be forthcoming unless it has been made; but, in order to make it, there was need of another hammer and other tools, and so on to infinity. We might thus vainly endeavour to prove that men have no power of working iron.' [14]

'But as men at first made use of the instruments supplied by nature to accomplish very easy pieces of workmanship, laboriously and imperfectly, and then, when these were finished, wrought other things more difficult with less labour and greater perfection.... So, in like manner, the intellect, by its native strength, makes for itself intellectual instruments, whereby it acquires strength for performing other intellectual operations, and from these operations gets again fresh instruments, or the power of pushing its investigations further, and thus gradually proceeds till it reaches the summit of wisdom.' [15]

Try as one might, this argument can hardly be made to resemble the view of Descartes, according to whom the higher ideas of intuition are directly contained in the intellect, or to that of Leibniz, according to whom these ideas are something like the viens in marble. According to Spinoza, they are innate in quite a specific sense—as natural, that is inherent from nature, intellectual capabilities, in precisely the same way as man's hand is originally a 'natural instrument'.

Here Spinoza attempts a fundamentally materialist interpretation of the innateness of 'intellectual instruments', de-

[14] Ibid., p. 9.
[15] Ibid., pp. 9-10.

ducing it from man's natural organisation rather than from the 'God' of Descartes or Leibniz.

What Spinoza failed to understand was the fact that the originally imperfect 'intellectual instruments' are products of material labour rather than of nature. He believed them to be products of nature, and in this, and only this, point lies the weakness of his position. But this weakness is shared by Feuerbach even. This defect can by no means be regarded as idealist wavering. That is merely an organic shortcoming of the entire old materialism.

Spinoza's rationalism should therefore be strictly distinguished from the rationalism of both Descartes and Leibniz. His contention is that man's ability to think is inherent in man's *nature* and is explained from substance interpreted in a clearly materialist manner.

When Spinoza calls thinking an *attribute*, that means precisely this: the essence of substance should not be reduced to extension only; thinking pertains to that very nature to which extension belongs—it is a property just as inseparable from nature (or substance) as extension and corporeality. It cannot be conceived of separately.

It is precisely this view that motivated Spinoza's criticism of 'abstract universals', of those ways in which scholastics, occasionalists, and nominalist empiricists attempt to explain substance. That is the reason why Spinoza held a low view of the path from concrete existence to an abstract universal. This mode is incapable of solving the problem of substance, always leaving a gap for scholastic and religious constructions.

Spinoza rightly believed that the way leading from concrete existence to an empty universal, the way explaining the concrete by a reduction to an empty abstraction, was of little value from the scientific standpoint.

'Thus, the more existence is conceived generally, the more is it conceived confusedly, and the more easily can it be ascribed to a given object. Contrariwise, the more it is conceived particularly, the more is it understood clearly, and the less liable is it to be ascribed, through negligence of Nature's order, to anything save its proper object.' [16]

No comments are needed to realise that this view is much closer to the truth than the view of narrow empiricism in-

---

[16] Benedict de Spinoza, op. cit., p. 17.

sisting that the essence of rational cognition of things lies in regular ascents to increasingly more general and empty abstractions, in moving away from the concrete specific essence of things under study. According to Spinoza, this way does not lead from the vague to the clear but, on the contrary, it leads away from the goal.

The way of rational cognition is precisely the reverse. It begins with a clearly established general principle (but not with an abstract universal, by any means) and proceeds as a step-by-step mental reconstruction of a thing, as reasoning which deduces the thing's particular properties from its universal cause (ultimately from substance). A genuine idea, as distinct from a simple abstract universal, must contain necessity, following which one can explain all the directly observable properties of the thing. As for 'universals', they reflect one of the more or less accidental properties out of which no other properties are deducible.

Spinoza explains this conception of his by citing an example from geometry—a definition of the essence of a circle. If we define a circle as a figure in which 'all straight lines drawn from the centre to the circumference are equal, every one can see that such a definition does not in the least explain the essence of a circle, but solely one of its properties'. According to the correct mode of definition, a circle is 'the figure described by any line whereof one end is fixed and the other free'. This definition, indicating the *mode of the origin* of a thing and a comprehension of the 'proximate cause', and thereby containing a mode of its mental reconstruction, enables one to deduce all the other properties of it, including the one pointed out above.[17]

One should thus proceed not from a 'universal' but rather from a concept expressing the actual, real cause of the thing, its concrete essence. Therein lies the gist of Spinoza's method.

'...We may never, while we are concerned with inquiries into actual things, draw any conclusions from abstractions; we shall be extremely careful not to confound that which is only in the understanding with that which is in the thing itself.'[18]

It is not the 'reduction of the concrete to the abstract' or explanation of the concrete through including it into a

[17] Ibid., pp. 32-33.
[18] Ibid., p. 31.

universal that leads to the truth but, on the contrary, deduction of the particular properties from the actual universal cause. In this connection Spinoza distinguishes between two kinds of general ideas: *notiones communes*, or concepts expressing the really universal cause of the origin of a thing, and the simpler abstract universals expressing simple similarities or differences of many individual things, *notiones generalis universales*. The former include substance, the latter, for instance, existence in general.

To bring any thing under the head of the general 'universal' of the *existing* means to explain absolutely nothing about it. This used to be the vacuous preoccupation of scholastics. Worse still is the deduction of the properties of things according to the formal rules of syllogistics *ex abstractis*—'from the universal'.

It is difficult to study and mentally reconstruct the entire process of the emergence of all the particular specific properties of a thing from one and the same really universal actual cause expressed in the intellect by the *notiones communes*. This 'deduction' is merely a form of reconstructing in the intellect of the real *process of emergence of a thing* out of nature, out of 'substance'. This deduction is not performed according to the rules of syllogistics but according to the 'truth norm', the norm of agreement, unity of thinking and extension, of the intellect and the external world.

It would hardly be appropriate to discuss here the shortcomings of Spinoza's conception, as they are well known: Spinoza failed to understand the connection between thinking and practical activity with objects, between theory and practice, the role of practice as the only objective criterion of the truth of a concrete concept. From the formal standpoint Spinoza's view is, of course, incomparably deeper and closer to the truth than Locke's.

Locke's theory afforded an easy transition to Berkeley or Hume without any essential alterations, merely through interpreting its propositions. Spinoza's position is not amenable to such an interpretation in principle. It is not for nothing that contemporary positivists brand this theory as 'rank metaphysics', whereas Locke sometimes rates a polite bow.

Spinoza's conception of the nature and formal composition of concretely universal concepts (that seems to be the best way of rendering his term *notiones communes*), as opposed to simple abstract universals, abounds in brilliant anticipations of dialectics. For instance, the concept of 'substance', a typical and principal example of such a concept, is obviously viewed as a unity of two mutually exclusive and at the same time mutually assuming definitions.

Thinking and extension, two attributes and two modes of realisation of substance, have nothing *abstract-general* in common and neither can they have anything of the kind in common. In other words, there is no abstract feature that would simultaneously form part of the definition of thinking and of the definition of the external world ('extended world').

This feature would be a universal that would be broader than the definition of the external world and of thinking. Such a feature would not be compatible either with the nature of thinking or that of extension. It would not reflect anything real outside intellect. The conception of 'God' characteristic of scholastics, is constructed precisely out of such features.

According to Malebranche, both extended and ideal things are 'contemplated in God'—in that general element that mediates between the idea and the thing as a middle term, as a feature common to both. And such a common element (in the sense of an abstract universal) between thinking and extension does not exist. What is common to both of them is their primordial unity. Spinoza's God therefore equals nature plus thinking, a unity of opposites, of two attributes. But in this case there is nothing left of the traditional God. What is called God is actually the extended nature as a whole with thought as an aspect of its essence. Only nature as a whole possesses thinking as its attribute, as an absolutely necessary property. A separate, limited part of the extended world does not necessarily have this property. For instance, a stone as a mode does not 'think' at all. But it does form part of 'substance' that thinks, it is its mode, its particle—and it may well think if it forms part of an appropriate structure becoming, e.g., a particle of the human body. (That was exactly the way in which Diderot decoded the main idea of Spinoza's teaching: can a stone feel?—It can. All you have to do is pound it, grow a plant on the powder, and eat the plant, transforming the matter of the stone into the matter of a sentient body.)

However, these brilliant gleams of dialectics in Spinoza

combined with a fundamentally materialist view of the human intellect, were buried in the general flow of metaphysical thinking in the 17th and 18th centuries, being deluged by it. The Lockean theory of abstraction with its bias towards nominalism, for some reasons proved to be more acceptable for the natural and social sciences of the times. The rational kernels of Spinoza's dialectics came to the surface only in German classical philosophy late in the 18th and early in the 19th century and were developed on a materialist basis only by Marx and Engels.

Immanuel Kant, endeavouring to reconcile the principles of rationalism and empiricism on the basis of subjective-idealist views of cognition, was driven to the conclusion that a hard and fast division of concepts into two classes, abstract and concrete, was in general impossible. As Kant puts it, it is absurd to ask whether a separate concept is abstract or concrete, if it is considered outside its links with other concepts, outside its usage.

'The expressions *abstract* and *concrete* refer not so much to the concepts themselves—for any concept is an abstract concept—as to their *usage*. And this usage can again have different grades;—according as one treats a concept now more, now less abstract or concrete, that is, takes away from or adds to it now more, now fewer definitions', writes Kant in his *Logic.*[19]

According to Kant, a concept, if it is really a *concept* rather than an empty appellation, a name of an individual thing, always expresses something in general, a generic or specific definiteness of a thing, and is thus always abstract, whether it be substance or chalk, whiteness or virtue. On the other hand, any such concept is in some way or other defined 'within itself', through a number of its features. The more such features-definitions are added to a concept the more concrete it is, in Kant's view, that is, the more definite, richer in definitions. The more concrete it is, the fuller it characterises the empirically given individual things. If a concept is defined through inclusion in 'higher genera', through 'logical abstraction', it is used *in abstracto*; it is applicable to a greater number of individual things and species, but the number of definitions in its composition is fewer.

[19] *Immanuel Kant's Logik,* 2. Auflage. F. Meiner, Leipzig, 1876, S. 109.

'Through abstract usage a concept approaches a higher genus, through concrete usage, on the contrary, it approaches the individual.... Through very abstract concepts, we learn *little* about *many* things; through very concrete concepts, we learn *much* about *few* things;—thus what we win on one side, we lose again on the other.' [20]

The limit of concreteness is thus a sensually contemplated individual thing, a separate phenomenon. A concept, however, never reaches this limit. On the other hand, the highest and most abstract concept always retains in its composition a certain unity, a certain synthesis of different definitions that one cannot break up (through formulating the ultimate definition) without making the concept senseless, without destroying it as such. For this reason even the highest generic concept has a measure of concreteness.

Here the empiric tendency, the Lockean tradition apparently makes itself felt. However, Kant combines with it an extremely rationalistic view of the nature of 'synthesis of definitions of a concept'. This synthesis or combining of definitions in the concept (that is, the concreteness of the concept) naturally cannot be simply oriented at the sensually given empirical multiformity of phenomena. To claim a *theoretical* significance, this synthesis must be based on another principle—the ability to combine definitions a priori, independently of empirical experience. The concreteness of a concept (that is, that unity in diversity, the unity of different definitions that has a universal and necessary significance) is thereby explained and deduced by Kant from the nature of human consciousness which allegedly possesses original unity, the transcendental unity of apperception. This latter is precisely the genuine basis of the concreteness of a concept. In this way, the concreteness of a concept has no firm links with 'things-in-themselves', with the sensually given concreteness.

Hegel also assumed that any concept was abstract, if abstractness is to be interpreted as the fact that a concept never expresses in its definitions the sensually contemplated reality in its entirety. Hegel was in this sense much closer to Locke than to Mill or medieval nominalism. He realised quite well that definitions of concepts always include an expression of something general, if only because concepts

[20] Ibid.

are always embodied in words, and words are always abstract, they always express something general and are incapable of expressing the absolutely individual and unique.

Therefore anyone thinks abstractly, and the thinking is the more abstract the poorer in definitions those concepts that one uses. Abstract thinking is by no means a virtue but, on the contrary, a shortcoming. That is the whole point—thinking concretely, expressing through abstractions the concrete and specific nature of things rather than mere similarity, merely something that different things have in common.

The concrete is interpreted by Hegel as unity in diversity, as unity of different and opposing definitions, as mental expression of the organic links, of syncretism of the separate abstract definitenesses of an object within the given specific object.

As for the abstract, Hegel interpreted it (just as Locke did, but not Mill or the scholastics) as anything general, any similarity expressed in word and concept, a simple identity of a number of things with one another, whether it be house or whiteness, man or value, a dog or virtue.

The concept 'house' is in this sense in no way different from the concept 'kindness'. Both register in their definitions the common elements inherent in a whole class, series, genus, or species of individual things, phenomena, spiritual states, etc.

If a word, term, symbol, name express only that—only the abstract similarity of a number of individual things, phenomena or images of consciousness—that is not yet a *concept*, according to Hegel. That is merely an abstractly general *notion* or representation *(Vorstellung)*, a form of empirical knowledge, of the sensual stage of consciousness. This pseudo-concept always has a certain sensually given image for its meaning or sense.

As for concepts, they express not merely the general, but the general that contains the richness of particulars, comprehended in their unity. In other words, a genuine concept is not only abstract (Hegel, of course, does not negate that), but also concrete—in the sense that its definitions (what old logic calls features) are combined in it in a single complex expressing the unity of things, rather than merely joined according to the rules of grammar.

The concreteness of a concept lies, according to Hegel, in

the unity of definitions, their meaningful cohesion—the only means of revealing the content of a concept. Out of context, an individual verbal definition is abstract and abstract only. Immersed into the context of a scientific theoretical discourse, any abstract definition becomes concrete.

The genuine sense, genuine content of each abstract definition taken separately is revealed through its links with other definitions of the same kind, through a *concrete unity of abstract definitions*. The concrete essence of a problem is therefore always expressed through unfolding all the necessary definitions of the object in their mutual connections rather than through an abstract 'definition'.

That is why a concept, according to Hegel, does not exist as a separate word, term, or symbol. It exists only in the process of unfolding in a proposition, in a syllogism expressing connectedness of separate definitions, and ultimately only in a system of propositions and syllogisms, only in an integral, well-developed theory. If a concept is pulled out of this connection, what remains of it is mere verbal integument, a linguistic symbol. The content of the concept, its meaning, remains outside it—in series of other definitions, for a word taken separately is only capable of *designating* an object, naming it, it is only capable of serving as a sign, symbol, marker, or symptom.

Thus the concrete meaning of a separate verbal definition is always contained in something else—whether it be a sensually given image or a well-developed system of theoretical definitions expressing the essence of the problem, the essence of the object, phenomenon, or event.

If a definition exists in the head separately, in isolation from the sensually contemplated image, unconnected with it or with a system of other definitions, it is ratiocinated abstractly. There is certainly nothing commendable about this way of ratiocination. Thinking abstractly merely means thinking unconnectedly, thinking of an individual property of a thing without understanding its links with other properties, without realising the place and role of this property in reality.

'Who thinks abstractly?' asks Hegel; and his answer is, 'An uneducated person, not an educated one.' A market-woman thinks abstractly (that is, one-sidedly, in accidental and unconnected definitions) in regarding all men exclusively from her own narrow pragmatic viewpoint, seeing them only as objects of swindling; a martinet thinks abstractly in regarding a private only as someone to be beaten up; an idler in the street thinks abstractly in seeing a person being taken to execution only as a murderer and ignoring all of his other qualities, not interested in the history of his life, the causes of his crime, and so on.

Contrariwise, a 'knower of men' thinking concretely will not be satisfied with tagging phenomena with abstract indices—a murderer, a soldier, a buyer. Still less will the 'knower of men' view these general abstract tags as expressions of the *essence of an object,* phenomenon, man, event.

A concept revealing the essence of the matter is only unfolded through a system, through series of definitions expressing separate moments, aspects, properties, qualities, or relations of the individual object, all these separate aspects of the concept being linked by a logical connection, not merely concatenated in some formal complex grammatically (by means of such words as 'and', 'or', 'if ... then', 'is', etc.).

The idealism of Hegel's conception of the abstract and the concrete consists in that he regards ability for synthesising abstract definitions as a primordial property of thinking, as a divine gift rather than the universal connection, expressed in consciousness, of the actual, objective, sensually perceived reality independent of any thinking. The concrete is in the final analysis interpreted as the product of thought.

That is also idealism, of course, but a much more 'intelligent' one than Kant's subjective idealism.

Late 19th-century bourgeois philosophy, that was gradually sliding towards positivism, proved incapable of remembering even the views of Kant and Locke, let alone Spinoza or Hegel. To take a particularly clear example—Mill believed Locke's theory of abstraction and its relation to concreteness to be an 'abuse' of those concepts that in his view were conclusively established by medieval scholastics.

'I have used the words concrete and abstract in the sense annexed to them by the schoolmen, who, notwithstanding the imperfections of their philosophy, were unrivalled in the construction of technical language, and whose definitions, in logic at least, ... have seldom, I think, been altered but to be spoiled.' The Locke school, in Mill's view, committed an unforgivable sin in extending the expression 'abstract name' to all 'general names', that is, to all 'concepts' 'which are the result of abstraction or generalisation'.[21]

Summing up, Mill declares: 'By *abstract*, then, I shall always, in Logic proper, mean the opposite of *concrete*; by an abstract name, the name of an attribute; by a concrete name, the name of an object.'[22]

This 'usage' is in Mill closely linked with his subjective-idealist conception of the relation between thought and objective reality.

Mill does not like Locke's view that all concepts (except for individual names) are abstract, all of them being products of abstracting an identical property, the general form of many individual things.

In Mill's opinion, this usage deprives a whole class of words of a brief specific designation, namely the class of names of attributes. By attributes or properties Mill means general properties, qualities or relations between individual things that may and must be conceived abstractly, that is, separately from the individual things, as specific objects.

Thus, concepts like 'house' or 'fire', 'man' or 'chair' cannot be thought of in any other way than as a common property of individual things. 'House', 'fire', 'whiteness', 'roundness' always pertain to some individual thing or other as their characteristic. One cannot conceive 'fire' as something existing separately from individual fires. 'Whiteness', too, cannot be conceived as something existing separately, outside individual things and independent from them. All of these general properties exist only as general forms of individual objects, only in the individual and through the individual. Therefore, conceiving them abstractly would mean conceiving them incorrectly.

Abstract names, names of 'attributes', are quite a different matter. Abstract names (or concepts, which is one and the same thing according to Mill) express general properties, qualities and relations that not only may but even must be conceived independently from individual objects, as separate objects, although in direct contemplation they appear to be the same kind of general properties of individual things as 'whiteness', 'woodenness', 'fire', or 'gentleman'.

---

[21] J. S. Mill, *A System of Logic Ratiocinative and Inductive*, Longmans, Green and Co., London, 1900, pp. 17-18.

[22] Ibid., p. 18.

Among such concepts Mill includes 'whiteness', 'courage', 'equality', 'similarity', 'squareness', 'visibleness', 'value', etc. These are also general names but the objects of these names (or what in formal logic is referred to as the content of these concepts) should not be conceived as general properties of individual things. All these properties, qualities or relations are only erroneously taken to be the general properties of the (individual) things themselves, says Mill. In actual fact all these 'objects' exist not in the things but outside them, independently from them, though they are merged with them in the act of perception, appearing as general properties of individual things.

Where do such objects exist, then, if not in the individual things?

Mill's answer is: in our own spirit. These are either 'Feelings, or States of Consciousness', or 'the Minds which experience these feelings', or 'the Successions and Co-existences, the Likenesses and Unlikenesses, between feelings or states of consciousness'.[23]

All these objects should also be conceived abstractly, that is, separately from things, precisely because they are no properties, qualities, or relations of these things. Conceiving them separately from things means conceiving them correctly.

The fundamental defect of this delimitation lies in it stipulating that some concepts should be linked in the mind with individual things (phenomena), given in contemplation, while others should be considered outside this connection, as specific objects conceived quite independently from any individual phenomena whatsoever.

For example, value in general, value as such, may according to Mill be conceived in abstraction, without analysing any of the types of its existence outside the head. This may and must be done precisely for the reason that it does not exist as a real property of objects outside the head. It only exists as an artificial method of assessment or measurement, as a general principle of man's subjective attitude to the world of things, that is, as a certain moral attitude. It cannot therefore be considered as a property of things themselves, outside the head, outside consciousness.

According to this kind of logic, of which Mill is a classic representative, that is precisely why value should be re-

[23] J. S. Mill, op. cit., p. 49.

garded only as a concept, only as an a priori moral phenomenon independent from the objective properties of things outside the head and opposing them. As such, it exists only in self-consciousness, in abstract thinking. That is why it can be conceived 'abstractly', and that will be the correct mode of considering it.

We have dealt with Mill's views in such detail only because they represent, more consistently and clearly than others, the antidialectical tradition in the interpretation of the abstract and the concrete as logical categories. This tradition is manifested not only as an antidialectical one but also as generally antiphilosophic. Mill consciously rejects the arguments developed in world philosophy during the past few centuries. For him, not only Hegel or Kant never seem to have existed—even Locke's studies appear in the light of unwanted sophistication in dealing with things that were established absolutely rigorously and for all time to come by the medieval Schoolmen. That is why everything seems so simple to him. The concrete is that which is immediately given in individual experience as an 'individual thing', an individual experience, and a concrete concept is a verbal symbol that may be used as a name of an individual object. That symbol which cannot be used as a direct name of an individual thing is 'the abstract'. One may say, 'That is a red spot'. One cannot say, 'That is redness'. The former is therefore concrete, the latter abstract. That is all there is to it.

All neopositivists retain the same distinction, the only difference being that the abstract and the concrete (just as all philosophical categories) are here treated as linguistic categories, and the question of whether phrases expressing 'abstract objects' are permissible or impermissible is reduced to that of fruitfulness or expediency of their utilisation in building 'language frames'. 'The abstract' is here consistently treated as everything that is not given in individual experience as an individual thing and cannot be defined in terms of those types of objects that are given in experience, cannot be a direct name of individual objects that are moreover interpreted in subjective-idealist manner.

This interpretation of the terms 'abstract' and 'concrete' is refuted by the entire heritage of the history of philosophy and by Marxist philosophy; we are now passing on to the exposition of the treatment of these questions in the latter.

THE DEFINITION OF THE CONCRETE IN MARX

Marx defines the concrete as 'the unity of diverse aspects'.[24] This definition may appear paradoxical from the standpoint of traditional formal logic: the reduction of the sensually given diversity to unity appears at first sight to be the task of abstract knowledge of things rather than of concrete one. From the point of view of this logic, to realise unity in the sensually perceived diversity of phenomena means to reveal the abstractly general, identical elements that all of these phenomena possess. This abstract unity, recorded in consciousness by means of a general term, appears at first sight to be that very 'unity' which is the only thing to be treated in logic.

Indeed, if one is to interpret the transition from living contemplation and notion to the concept, from the sensual stage of cognition to the rational, only as reduction of the sensually given diversity to abstract unity, Marx's definition will certainly seem hardly justifiable in 'logical' terms.

The whole point is, however, that Marx's views are based on a conception of thinking, its goals and tasks, quite different from those on which old, non-dialectical logic built its theory. This is reflected not only in the substance of the solution of logical problems but in terminology as well. And that is inevitable: 'Every new aspect of a science involves a revolution in the technical terms of that science.'[25]

When Marx defines the concrete as unity of diverse aspects, he assumes a dialectical interpretation of unity, diversity, and of their relationship. In dialectics, unity is interpreted first and foremost as connection, as interconnection and interaction of different phenomena within a certain system or agglomeration, and not as abstract likeness of these phenomena. Marx's definition assumes exactly this dialectical meaning of the term 'unity'.

If one unfolds somewhat Marx's aphoristically laconic formula, his definition of the concrete means literally the following: the *concrete, concreteness,* are first of all syn-

---

[24] Karl Marx, *A Contribution to the Critique of Political Economy,* Progress Publishers, Moscow, 1978, p. 206.

[25] Karl Marx, *Capital,* Vol. I, Progress Publishers, Moscow, 1974, p. 14.

onyms of the real links between phenomena, of concatenation and interaction of all aspects and moments of the object given to man in contemplation and in a notion. The concrete is thereby interpreted as an internally divided totality of various forms of existence of the object, a unique combination of which is characteristic of the given object only. Unity thus conceived is realised not through similarity of phenomena to each other but, on the contrary, through their difference and opposition.

This conception of unity in diversity (or concreteness) is not merely different from the one which old logic proceeded from, but is its direct opposite. The conception approaches that of the concept of integrity or wholeness. Marx uses this term in those cases when he has to characterise the object as an integral whole unified in all its diverse manifestations, as an organic system of mutually conditioning phenomena in contradiction to a metaphysical conception of it as a mechanical agglomeration of immutable constituent parts that are linked with each other only externally, more or less accidentally.

The most important aspect of Marx's definition of the concrete is that the concrete is treated first of all as an objective characteristic of a thing considered quite independently from any evolutions that may take place in the cognising subject. The object is concrete by and in itself, independent from its being conceived by thought or perceived by sense organs. Concreteness is not created in the process of reflection of the object by the subject either at the sensual stage of reflection or at the rational-logical one.

In other words, 'the concrete' is first of all the same kind of objective category as any other category of materialist dialectics, as 'the necessary' and 'the accidental', 'essence' and 'appearance'. It expresses a universal form of development of nature, society, and thinking. In the system of Marx's views, 'the concrete' is by no means a synonym for the sensually given, immediately contemplated.

Insofar as 'the concrete' is opposed to 'the abstract', the latter is treated by Marx first and foremost objectively. For Marx, it is by no means a synonym of the 'purely ideal', of a product of mental activity, a synonym of the subjectively psychological phenomenon occurring in man's brain only. Time and again Marx uses this term to characterise real phenomena and relations existing outside consciousness, irrespective of whether they are reflected in consciousness or not.

For instance, Marx speaks in *Capital* of abstract labour. Abstractness appears here as an objective characteristic of the form which human labour assumes in developed commodity production, in capitalist production. Elsewhere he stresses that the reduction of different kinds of labour to uniform simple labour devoid of any distinctions 'is an abstraction which is made every day in the social process of production'. It is 'no less real (an abstraction) than the resolution of all organic bodies into air'.[26]

The definition of gold as material being of abstract wealth also expresses its specific function in the organism of the capitalist formation and not in the consciousness of the theoretician or practical worker, by any means.

This use of the term 'abstract' is not a terminological whim of Marx's at all: it is linked with the very essence of his logical views, with the dialectical interpretation of the relation of forms of thinking and those of objective reality, with the view of practice (sensual activity involving objects) as a criterion of the truth of the abstractions of thought.

Still less can this usage be explained as 'a throwback to Hegelianism': it is against Hegel that Marx's proposition is directed to the effect that 'the simplest economic category, e.g., exchange value ... cannot exist except as an abstract, *unilateral* relation of an already existing concrete organic whole'.[27]

'The abstract' in this kind of context, very frequent in Marx, assumes the meaning of the 'simple', undeveloped, one-sided, fragmentary, 'pure' (i.e., uncomplicated by any deforming influences). It goes without saying that 'the abstract' in this sense can be an objective characteristic of real phenomena, and not only of phenomena of consciousness.

'It is precisely the predominance of agricultural peoples in the ancient world which caused the merchant nations—Phoenicians, Carthaginians—to develop in such purity (ab-

---

[26] Karl Marx, *A Contribution to the Critique of Political Economy*, p. 30.
[27] Ibid., p. 206.

stract precision)'[28]; it was not, of course, the result of predominance of the 'abstractive power of thought' of Phoenicians or the scholars writing the history of Phoenicia. 'The abstract' in this sense is by no means the product and result of thinking. This fact is just as little dependent on thinking as the circumstance that 'the abstract law of multiplying exists only for plants and animals'.

According to Marx, 'the abstract' (just as its counterpart, 'the concrete') is a category of dialectics as the science of universal forms of development of nature, society and thought, and on this basis also a category of *logic*, for dialectics is also the *Logic* of Marxism.

This objective interpretation of the category of the abstract is spearheaded against all kinds of neo-Kantian logic and epistemology which oppose, in a crudely metaphysical way, 'pure forms of thought' to forms of objective reality. For these schools in logic, 'the abstract' is only a form of thought, whereas 'the concrete', a form of a sensually given image. This interpretation, in the Mill-Humean and Kantian traditions in logic (e.g., Chelpanov and Vvedensky in Russia), is alien and hostile to the very essence of dialectics as logic and theory of knowledge.

The narrow epistemological (that is, essentially psychological, in the final analysis) interpretation of the categories of the abstract and the concrete became firmly rooted in modern bourgeois philosophy. Here is a fresh example—definitions from the *Philosophical Dictionary* by Max Apel and Peter Ludz:

'*abstract*: divorced from a given connection and considered by itself only. Thus abstract acquires the meaning of conceptual, conceived, in opposition to given in contemplation.

'*abstraction*: the logical process for ascending, through omission of features, from that given in contemplation to a general notion and from the given concept to a more general one. Abstraction decreases the content and extends the volume. Opposed to determination.

'*concrete*: the immediately given in contemplation; concrete concepts denote that which is contemplated, individual objects of contemplation. Opposed to abstract.'[29]

---

[28] Ibid., p. 213.

[29] *Philosophisches Wörterbuch*, von Dr. Max Apel, Dr. Peter Ludz, de Gruyter, Berlin, 1958, S. 4-5, 162.

This one-sided definition (abstraction is, of course, mental separation, among other things, but it is by no means reducible to it) varies but insignificantly from dictionary to dictionary. It has been polished in dozens of editions and has become generally accepted among philosophers in capitalist countries. That is certainly no proof of its correctness.

A 'concrete concept' is reduced by these definitions to 'designating' the sensually contemplated individual things, to a mere sign, or symbol. In other words, 'the concrete' is only nominally present in thought, only in the capacity of the 'designating name'. On the other hand, 'the concrete' is made into a synonym of uninterpreted, indefinite 'sensual givenness'. Neither the concrete nor the abstract can, according to these definitions, be used as characteristics of theoretical knowledge in regard of its real objective content. They characterise only the 'form of cognition': 'the concrete', the form of sensual cognition, and 'the abstract', the form of thought, the form of rational cognition. In other words, they belong to different spheres of the psyche, to different objects. There is nothing abstract where there is something concrete, and vice versa. That is all there is to these definitions.

The problem of the relation of the abstract to the concrete appears in quite a different light from Marx's point of view, the point of view of dialectics as logic and theory of knowledge.

It is only at first sight that this question might seem a merely 'epistemological' one, a question of the relation of a mental abstraction to the sensually perceived image. In actual fact its real content is much wider and deeper than that, and it is inevitably supplanted by quite a different problem in the course of analysis—the problem of the relation of the object to itself, that is, relationship between different elements of the objective reality within a certain concrete whole. That is why the problem is solved, first and foremost, within the framework of objective dialectics—the teaching of the universal forms and laws of development of nature, society and thought itself, and not on the narrow epistemological plane, as neo-Kantians and positivists do.

Insofar as Marx treats the epistemological aspect of the problem, he interprets the abstract as any one-sided, incomplete, lopsided reflection of the object in consciousness, as opposed to concrete knowledge which is well developed, all-round, comprehensive knowledge. It does not matter at all in what subjective psychological form this knowledge is 'experienced' by the subject—in sensually perceived images or in abstract verbal form. The logic (dialectics) of Marx and Lenin establishes its distinctions in regard of the objective sense and meaning of knowledge rather than in regard of the subjective form of experience. Poor, meagre, lopsided knowledge may be assimilated in the form of a sensual image. In this case, logic will have to define it as 'abstract' knowledge, despite its being embodied in a sensually given image. Contrariwise, abstract verbal form, the language of formulas, may express rich, well-developed, profound and comprehensive knowledge, that is, concrete knowledge.

'Concreteness' is neither a synonym for nor a privilege of the sensual-image form of reflection of reality in consciousness, just as 'abstractness' is not a specific characteristic of rational theoretical knowledge. Certainly we speak, as often as not, of the concreteness of a sensual image and of abstract thought.

A sensual image, an image of contemplation, may just as often be very abstract, too. Suffice it to remember a geometric figure or a work of abstract painting. And vice versa, thinking in concepts may and even must be concrete in the full and strict meaning of the word. We know that there is no abstract truth, that truth is always concrete. And that does not mean at all that only the sensually perceived image, the contemplation of an individual thing may be true.

The concrete in thinking also appears, according to Marx's definition, in the form of combination (synthesis) of numerous definitions. A logically coherent system of definitions is precisely that 'natural' form in which concrete truth is realised in thought. Each of the definitions forming part of the system naturally reflects only a part, a fragment, an element, an aspect of the concrete reality—and that is why it is abstract if taken by itself, separately from other definitions. In other words, the concrete is realised in thinking through the abstract, through its own opposite, and is impossible without it. But that is, in general, the rule rather than an exception in dialectics. Necessity is in just the same kind of relation with chance, essence with appearance, and so on.

On the other hand, each of the numerous definitions forming part of the conceptual system of a concrete science, loses its abstract character in it, being filled with the sense and meaning of all the other definitions connected with it. Separate abstract definitions mutually complement each other, so that the abstractness of each of them, taken separately, is overcome. In short, herein lies the dialectics of the relation of the abstract to the concrete in thinking which reflects the concrete in reality. The dialectics of the abstract and the concrete in the course of theoretical processing of the material of living contemplation, in processing the results of contemplation and notions in terms of concepts is the subject-matter of study in the present work.

Of course, we cannot claim to offer an exhaustive solution to the problem of the abstract and the concrete at all the stages of the process of cognition in general, in all forms of reflection. The formation of the sensually perceived image of a thing involves its own dialectics of the abstract and the concrete, and a very complicated one, and that is even more true of the formation of the notion connected with speech, with words. Memory, which also plays an enormous role in cognition, contains in its structure a no less complex relation of the abstract to the concrete. These categories also have a bearing on artistic creativity. We are compelled to leave all of these aspects out of consideration, as subject-matter of a special study.

The path of cognition leading from living contemplation to abstract thought and from it to practice, is a very complicated path. A complex and dialectically contradictory transformation of the concrete into the abstract and vice versa takes place in each link of this path. Even sensation gives a rougher picture of reality than it actually is, even in direct perception there is an element of transition from the concrete in reality to the abstract in consciousness. The transition from living contemplation to abstract thought is by no means the same thing as the movement 'from the concrete to the abstract'. It is by no means reducible to this moment, although the latter is always present in it. It is the same thing only for those who interpret the concrete as a synonym of an immediate sensual image, and the abstract, as a synonym of the mental, the ideal, the conceptual.

ON THE RELATION OF THE NOTION TO THE CONCEPT

Pre-Marxian logic, alien to the dialectical approach to the relation of the sensually empirical stage or form of cognition to the rational one, was unable, despite all its efforts, to provide a clearcut solution to the problem of relation of notions to concepts.

The concept was defined as verbal designation of the general in a number of simple ideas (notions), as a name/term (Locke, Hobbes), or simply as any notion of a thing in our thought (Christian Wolff), or as something opposed to contemplation, inasmuch as it is a general notion or a notion of what is common to many objects of contemplation (Kant), or as a notion of definite, unambiguous, stable, generally accepted meaning (Sigwart), or a notion about a notion (Schopenhauer). Nowadays, too, widely current is the definition of concept as simply 'the semantic meaning of a term', whatever the latter might mean. Neopositivists often refuse to deal at all with the relationship between concept and notion, proceeding to purely formal definitions of the concept—specifying the concept as 'the function of an utterance', 'propositional function', and so on. Generally speaking, this question has remained extremely confused in modern bourgeois philosophy and logic. Very typical is the view expressed in Heinrich Schmidt's *Philosophical Dictionary*. The concept is here defined as 'the meaningful content of words', and in the stricter 'logical sense' as a meaningful content of a word that is 'freed from momentaneous perception in such a way that it may be transferred to other similar perceptions as their designation'.[30] The Kirchner-Michaëlis' *Dictionary of Basic Philosophical Concepts* attempts to avoid the identification of concept and notion: 'The concept is therefore not just a closed general notion, it emerges out of notions through their comparison and extraction of that which is common to them.'[31]

The Russian logician Vvedensky, a follower of Kant, proceeds from the assumption that a notion differs from a con-

---

[30] Heinrich Schmidt, *Philosophisches Wörterbuch*, 9. Auflage, Kröner, Leipzig, 1934, S. 67.

[31] *Kirchner's Wörterbuch der philosophischen Grundbegriffe*, 6. Auflage, Dritte Neubearbeitung von Dr. Carl Michaëlis, Verlag von Felix Meiner, Leipzig, 1911, S. 130.

cept not in the 'psychological mode of experience' but in the fact that in the notion things are considered 'with regard to any features whatsoever', while in the concept, only 'with regard to the essential features'. On the next page, however, he discards this distinction in a characteristic argument that 'something may be essential from one viewpoint, and quite a different thing, from another'. But the question of whether certain features are 'essential' or 'inessential' is solved somewhere outside logic as a formal discipline, somewhere in epistemology, ethics, or some such discipline. Therefore logic, according to Vvedensky, is quite right in artlessly considering any verbally recorded 'general' entity, any term regarded from its meaningful aspect, as a concept.

These arguments (highly typical of non-Marxist, antidialectical logic) lead in the final analysis, in a more or less roundabout way, to one and the same denouement: the term 'concept' is taken to mean *any verbally expressed 'general'*, any terminologically recorded abstraction from the sensually given multiformity, any notion of what is common to many objects of direct contemplation.

In other words, all the antidialectical versions of the concept ultimately go back to one and the same classical source —the definition of Locke and Kant, and at times even further back, to the definition of medieval nominalism which did not distinguish between word and concept at all.

The fundamental weakness of the conception of Locke and Kant lies in that its attempts to distinguish between notion as a form of sensual empirical knowledge and concept as a form of rational knowledge are firmly based on a Robinson Crusoe model of epistemology, in which the subject of cognition is a separate human individual isolated from the concatenation of social links and opposed to 'all the rest'. That is why the relation of consciousness to objective reality is given a very narrow interpretation here—only as the relation of the individual consciousness, many times repeated, to everything that lies outside this consciousness and does not depend on its existence and will.

But it is not only material nature that exists outside of and independently from the consciousness and will of the *individual*—so does the extremely complex and historically shaped sphere of the material and spiritual culture of *mankind*, of society. Rising to conscious life within society, the individual finds pre-existing 'spiritual environment', objectively implemented spiritual culture. The latter is opposed to individual consciousness as a specific object which the individual has to assimilate taking into account its nature as something quite objective. A system of forms of social consciousness (in the broadest possible sense, including forms of political organisation of society, law, morality, everyday life, and so on, as well as forms and norms of actions in the sphere of thought, grammatical syntactic rules for verbal expression of notions, esthetic tastes, etc.) structures from the very outset the developing consciousness and will of the individual, moulding him in its own image. As a result, each separate sensual impression arising in individual consciousness is always a product of refraction of external stimuli through the extremely complex prism of the forms of social consciousness the individual has appropriated. This 'prism' is a product of social human development. Alone, face to face with nature, the individual has no such prism, and it cannot be understood from an analysis of the relations of an isolated individual to nature.

The Robinson Crusoe epistemological model attempts to comprehend the mechanism of production of conscious notions and concepts precisely in the context of such a fairy-tale situation. The social nature of any, even the most elementary, act of production of conscious notions is here ignored from the outset, and it is assumed that the individual first experiences isolated sensual impressions, then inductively abstracts something general from them, designates it by a word, then assumes an attitude of 'reflection' towards this general, regarding his own mental actions and their products—'general ideas' (that is, general notions recorded in speech)—as a specific object of study. In short, the matter is presented in the manner outlined by John Locke, the classic representative and systematiser of this view, in his *Essay Concerning Human Understanding*.

But the social human nature of individual consciousness, which this theory drives out of the door, gets back through the window. 'Reflection', that is, consideration of the products of mental activity and operations upon them (syllogisms, reasoning based on concepts only), reveals at once that these products contain a certain result that is fundamentally inexplicable from the limited personal experience. Insofar as social human experience is here interpreted only as reiterated personal experience, as a mere sum of separate experiences (rather than as the history of entire human culture), all forms of consciousness that have matured in the long and contradictory development of culture, appear to be in general inexplicable from experience, given a priori. There is no way in which they could necessarily be deduced from individual experience, and yet they most actively determine this experience, shaping the form in which it proceeds.

This conception is ultimately embodied in Kant's doctrine of 'the unity of transcendental apperception', in connection with which Kant gives his definition of the concept as a general notion, or notion of those general elements that are inherent in many objects of contemplation. Kant's doctrine of the concept is not reduced to this simple definition, of course; but it underlies all his constructions and has integral ties with them. At first sight, this definition coincides with one-sided empirical interpretation of the concept by Locke. And that is indeed so. But narrow empiricism is inevitably complemented by its counterpart, the idea of extra-experiential, non-empirical origin of a number of most important concepts of reason, the categories. The categories of reason, constituting a most complicated product of thousands of years of development of the culture of human thought, cannot be interpreted as general notions, as notions about the general element in many objects given in individual contemplation.

The universal concepts, the categories (cause, quality, property, quantity, possibility, necessity, and so on) refer to all objects of contemplation without exception, rather than to 'many'. Consequently they must contain a guarantee of universality and necessity, a guarantee that a contradictory case will never come up in human experience in the future (a phenomenon without a cause, or a thing devoid of qualities or unamenable to quantitative measurement, etc.). Empirical inductive abstraction naturally cannot contain such a guarantee—it is always threatened by the same kind of unpleasantness that happened to the proposition 'all swans are white'.

For this reason Kant in fact adopts a fundamentally different definition for these concepts as a priori forms of transcendental apperception and not at all as 'general notions'. The very concept of concept is thus rent by dualism. In actual fact there are two mutually excluding definitions.

On the one hand, the concept is simply identified with the general notion, and on the other, concept and notion are separated by a gap. The 'pure' ('transcendental') form of concept, a category of reason, proves to be entirely a priori, whereas the ordinary concept is simply reduced to a general notion. That is the inevitable retribution for the sin of narrow-minded empiricism, which no school of logic can escape which identifies the concept with the meaning of any term, with the sense of a word.

The materialist dialectics of Marx, Engels, and Lenin gave a fine solution to the difficulties of defining the concept and its relation to the notion expressed in speech, as it fully took into account the socio-human, socio-historical nature of all forms and categories of cognition, including the forms of the empirical stage in cognition.

Owing to speech, the individual 'sees' the world not only and not so much through his own eyes as through millions of eyes. Marx and Engels therefore always interpret notions as something other than sensual images of things retained in individual memory. From the standpoint of epistemology centred on the social individual, a notion is a social reality, too. The content of a notion comprehends that which is retained in social memory, in the forms of this social memory as represented, first of all, by speech, by language. If an individual has acquired a notion of a thing from other individuals who observed it directly, the acquired form of consciousness of it is precisely that which he would have received had he contemplated this thing with his own eyes. Having a notion means having a socially comprehended (that is, expressed in speech or capable of being expressed in speech) contemplation. Neither I nor some other individual form a concept of some thing if I, through speech, observe this thing through the eyes of another individual or this other individual contemplates it through my eyes. We engage in mutual exchange of notions. A notion is precisely that—verbally expressed contemplation.

Contemplation and notion thereby appear as categories expressing the socio-historical nature of sensuality, of the empirical form of knowledge, rather than an individual's psychological states. The notion always contains only that which I in my individual contemplation perceive in a social manner, that is, am capable of making the property of another individual through speech, and thereby my own property as a socially contemplating individual. Being capable of expressing the sensually contemplated facts in speech means being capable of transposing the individually contemplated onto the plane of notion as social consciousness.

But this in no way coincides yet with the ability and capability of working out *concepts,* the ability for logical processing of contemplation and notion into concept. It does not yet mean an ability for proceeding from the first, sensual stage of knowledge to the stage of logical assimilation.

In referring to theoretical processing of sensual data, Marx takes these data mostly to be something different from what the individual carrying out this logical processing directly *saw* with his own eyes or *touched* with his fingers. Marx always has in mind the entire *totality* of the factual *empirical data, the socially implemented contemplation.* The material of logical activity available to the theoretician, his sensual data, are not only and not so much what he as an individual contemplated directly but rather everything that he knows about the object from *all other* men. And he can know all this from other men only through speech, only due to millions of facts having been already recorded in social notions.

This determines an approach to comprehending the process of cognition quite different from the one that may be established from the standpoint of nominalist interpretation of thinking and its relation to sensuality: contemplation and notion are for Marx only the first, *sensual* stage in cognition. And that is sharply different from the interpretation of the sensual stage of cognition characteristic of the followers of Locke and Helvétius. The latter two, inevitably, refer that form of consciousness that Marx calls notion (*Vorstellung*), to the rational, logical stage in reflection, owing to their abstract anthropological conception of the subject of cognition.

The difference between concept and general notion expressed in word was originally clearly established by the dialectician Hegel, and he did it in the framework of logic (something no one had done before him). The reason that he could do so was that his starting point in logic was mankind as a whole in its development rather than an isolated individual.

Hegel pointed out on numerous occasions that if the process of cognition is considered from the psychological standpoint, that is, in the form in which it goes on in the head of an isolated individual, 'one can stick to the tale that we begin with sensations and contemplations and that intellect extracts something general or abstract from the diversity of the latter'.[32]

This phase of the development Hegel calls the transition from contemplation to notion, that is, a certain stable form of consciousness, an abstract general image that is given a name, an expression in speech, in a term.

However, thought striving for truth does not take this form of consciousness to be either its goal or result but merely a premise, material for its specific activity. Old logic, notes Hegel, constantly confuses psychological premises of a concept with the concept itself, taking any abstract general notion to be a concept once it has been expressed in a term, a word, in speech.

For old logic, any abstract general notion recorded in a word is already a concept, a form of rational cognition of things. For Hegel it is merely a prerequisite of an actual concept, that is, of such a form of consciousness which expresses the real (dialectical) nature of things.

'In the new times, *no other* concept fared worse than the concept itself, the concept by and for itself, for concept is usually taken to mean abstract definiteness and one-sidedness of conception or of intellectual thinking, with which, of course, one cannot cognitively bring into consciousness either the entirety of the truth or beauty concrete by itself.'[33]

Hegel further explains that the concept is interpreted in this logic extremely one-sidedly or lopsidedly, namely, it is considered only from the side which is equally inherent both in the concept and in the general notion.

In this framework, the concept is essentially equated with the simple general notion, and all those specific features of the concept owing to which it proves to be capable of expressing the concrete nature of the object are left outside the sphere of interest of old logic.

'What one usually calls concepts, and moreover definite concepts, e.g. man, house, animal, etc., are least of all con-

---

[32] G. W. F. Hegel, Wissenschaft der Logik, 2. Teil, *Sämtliche Werke*, Bd. 5, F. Frommann, Stuttgart, 1928, S. 21.

[33] G. W. F. Hegel, Vorlesungen über die Ästhetik, *Sämtliche Werke,* Bd. 12, 1927, S. 136.

cepts, they are simple definitions and abstract notions—abstractions which borrow from the concept only the element of generality and leave out the particular and the individual, thereby being abstractions precisely from the concept.'[34]

It is easy to see that this distinction is closely linked with Hegel's critique of the metaphysical approach in logic and epistemology. In no way rejecting the quite obvious fact that the concept is always something abstract in comparison with the sensually concrete image of a thing, Hegel shows at the same time the superficiality of the view reducing the concept to mere expression of the abstractly identical, abstractly general property, feature or relation inherent in a whole series of phenomena. This reduction explains absolutely nothing about its ability to reflect the nature of the object more profoundly, correctly, and completely than do contemplation and notion.

'However, if what is taken over into the concept from the concrete event must serve merely as a *marker* or *sign*, it may, indeed, be some merely sensual individual definition of the object.'[35]

The difference between the image of living contemplation and the concept is thus reduced to a purely quantitative one. The concept expresses or, to be more precise, designates only one of the sensual properties of the phenomenon, whereas the sensual image contains a whole series of them. As a result, the concept is considered only as something more meagre than the image of living contemplation—only as an abstract one-sided expression of this image.

The transition from the image of contemplation to the concept is thus regarded merely as destruction of the sensually given concreteness, as elimination of a great number of sensually perceived properties for the sake of one of them.

'The abstract [says Hegel in this connection] is counted of less worth than the concrete, because from the former so much of that kind of material has been omitted. To those who hold this view, the process of abstraction means

[34] G. W. F. Hegel, Enzyklcpädie der philosophischen Wissenschaften im Grundrisse, *Sämtliche Werke*, Bd. 6, 1927, S. 99.

[35] G. W. F. Hegel, *Wissenschaft der Logik*, *Sämtliche Werke*, Bd. 5, S. 21.

that *for our subjective needs* one or another characteristic is taken out of the concrete ... and it is only the *incapacity* of understanding to absorb such riches that forces it to rest content with meagre abstraction.' [36]

The transition from concrete contemplation to abstractions of thought appears, as a result, only as departure from reality given in direct contemplation, only as manifestation of the 'incapacity', weakness of thought. Not surprisingly, Kant, starting out from this premise, comes to the conclusion that thought is incapable of attaining objective truth.

Lenin took very copious notes of this passage in Hegel, making this remark *à propos* of it:

'*Essentially*, Hegel is completely right as opposed to Kant. Thought proceeding from the concrete to the abstract—provided it is *correct* (NB) (and Kant, like all philosophers, speaks of correct thought)—does not get away *from* the truth but comes closer to it.' [37]

In other words, the concept may be something abstract as compared to the sensually perceived concreteness, but its strength and advantages over contemplation do not lie therein. The ascent from the sensually contemplated concreteness to the abstract expression of it is merely the form in which a more meaningful process is realised—the process of attaining the truth which contemplation is incapable of grasping. In commenting on Hegel, Lenin points out that scientific (that is, correct, serious, not absurd) abstractions reflect nature not only more deeply and correctly than living contemplation or notion but also *more fully*. And 'more fully' in the language of dialectical logic means nothing else but 'more concretely'.

'Consequently [continues Hegel in the passage quoted by Lenin] abstracting thought must not be considered as a mere setting aside of the sensuous material, whose reality is said not to be lowered thereby; but it is its transcendence, and the reduction of it (as mere appearance) to the essential, which manifests itself in the Notion only.' [38]

---

[36] Quoted from: V. I. Lenin, Conspectus of Hegel's Book *The Science of Logic*, *Collected Works*, Vol. 38, 1961, p. 170 (here and elsewhere Progress Publishers, Moscow).

[37] Ibid., p. 171.

[38] Ibid., pp. 170-71.

In the process, the concrete is by no means lost, as Kant believes, along with the empiricists; on the contrary, its real meaning and content are brought out by thinking. That is precisely why Hegel regards the transition from the sensually contemplated concreteness to the concept as a form of movement from appearance to essence, from consequence to its antecedent.

A concept, according to Hegel, expresses the essence of contemplated phenomena. And that essence is by no means reducible to the abstractly identical in different phenomena, to the identical elements observed in each of the phenomena taken in isolation. The essence of an object is almost always contained in the unity of distinct and opposed elements, in their concatenation and mutual determination. That is why Hegel says of the concept: 'As far as the nature of *concept as such* is concerned, taken by itself it is not an *abstract unity* opposed to the *distinctions of reality,* but, as a concept, it is already a unity of different definitenesses, and thereby concrete reality. So notions like "man", "blue", etc., should not be called concepts but abstract general notions, which only become concepts when it is shown that they contain distinct aspects in unity, whereby this unity determined within itself constitutes the concept.' [39]

If man's thinking merely reduces the sensually concrete image of an object to an abstract one-sided definition, it produces only a general notion and not a concept. This is quite a natural process if it is interpreted as transition from contemplation to notion. But if it is taken to be what it is not, namely, transition to the concept, the most important feature of this transition is left unexplained.

Lenin stressed, on more than one occasion, Hegel's idea that transition from notion to concept should be considered in logic first of all as transition from superficial knowledge to deeper, fuller, and more correct knowledge.

' "The object in its existence without thought and Notion is an image or a name: it *is* what it *is* in the determinations of thought and Notion," says Hegel, and Lenin makes a marginal note:

---

[39] G. W. F. Hegel, Vorlesungen über die Ästhetik, *Sämtliche Werke*, Bd. 12, S. 156.

'That is correct! *Image* and *thought*, the development of both, nil aliud.' [40]

In analysing Hegel's arguments about the relation of notion to thought, Lenin deemed it necessary to point out that Hegel's idealism was not in evidence in regard to this point:

'Here, in the concept of time (and not in the relation of sensuous representation to thought) is the idealism of Hegel.' [41]

Hegel's main idea is that intellectual abstractions do not take consciousness beyond the empirical stage of cognition, that they are forms of sensual empirical consciousness rather than thought in the strict sense of the term, are notions and not concepts. Confusing the two, identifying notion with concept on the grounds that both are abstractions, is a most characteristic mark of metaphysics in logic, of the logic of metaphysical thinking.

Therefore the first task of logic as a science studying logical processing of empirical data into concepts (transition from contemplation and notion to concept) is strict objective delimitation of concept and verbally expressed notion.

This delimitation is by no means a theoretical nicety. It is of enormous significance for epistemology as well as pedagogics. Formation of abstract general notions is in itself a sufficiently complicated and contradictory process. As such, it forms the subject-matter of special investigation, although not in logic.

The task of logic as a science grows out of the real needs of the developing cognition of the phenomena of the surrounding world. The question with which a thinking man turns to logic as a science is not at all the question of how abstractions should be made in general, how one can learn to abstract the general from the sensually given facts. To do that, one need not at all ask the logicians' advice, one merely has to have a command of one's native language and the ability to concentrate one's attention on the sensually given similarities and differences.

The question with which one turns to logic and which can only be answered by logic involves a much more complicated cognitive task: how is one to work out an abstraction which would express the objective essence of facts

[40] V. I. Lenin, Conspectus of Hegel's Book *The Science of Logic*, *Collected Works*, Vol. 38, p. 225.

[41] Ibid., p. 228.

given in contemplation and notions? The manner in which processing a mass of empirically obvious facts yields a generalisation expressing the real nature of the object under study—that is the actual problem, whose solution is identical with that of the problem of the nature of concepts as distinct from abstract general notions.

Concepts being defined as reflection of the essentially general, materialism in logic compels one to distinguish most strictly between what is essential for the subject (his desires, aspirations, goals, etc.) and that which is essential for the objective definition of the nature of the object entirely independent of the subjective aspirations.

Neo-Kantian logic consciously blurs this distinction, purporting to prove that the criterion for distinguishing between the subjectively essential and that which is essential as far as the object itself is concerned can neither be found nor given. This view is most consistently developed in pragmatist and instrumentalist conceptions. Any concept is construed as a projection of subjective desires, aspirations and impulses on the chaos of sensually given phenomena. Clearly, it is not only the boundary between the subjective and the objective that is obliterated here but also the boundary between the spontaneously formed notion and concept, between empirical and rational logical cognition.

As an illustration, let us cite a characteristic example of present-day philosophising on the subject of the abstract and the concrete—an article by Rudolf Schottlaender, a West-German theoretician, which reflects, as in a mirror, the level of bourgeois thought in the field of dialectical categories.[42]

The Alpha and Omega of his approach is the opposition of the abstract and the concrete as categories belonging to two fundamentally different spheres. For Schottlaender, the abstract is only a mode of action of the subject of cognition. The concrete is identified with the sensually perceived image of living contemplation in its entirety, while the object outside consciousness is not distinguished at all from its sensual experience. The subject 'takes out', 'extracts', 'takes away' from the concrete certain general abstract fea-

[42] Rudolf Schottlaender, Recht und Unrecht der Abstraktion, *Zeitschrift für philosophische Forschung*, Bd. VII, Heft 2, Meisenheim/Wien, 1953, S. 220.

tures, apparently motivated by a purely subjective purpose, constructing a concept out of these features. Whether the features abstracted are essential or inessential is determined, according to Schottlaender, entirely by the goals of the subject of cognition, his 'practical' attitude to the thing. One cannot consider the essential *from the standpoint of the object itself*, Schottlaender believes, without going back to the positions of the 'scholastic quintessence', of the 'real essence'.

The abstract and the concrete are thereby metaphysically distributed between two different worlds—the world of 'the subject of cognition' and the world of 'the object of cognition'. On these grounds Schottlaender believes it expedient to drop the problem of the relation of the abstract to the concrete *as a question of logic*, which studies the world of the subject.

And, since he is dealing with logic, it is not the concrete that he opposes to the abstract but the 'Subtrahendum' invented for the purpose, that is, everything that the subject making an abstraction consciously or unconsciously leaves aside, the unused remainder of the richness of the sensually perceived image of the thing. And further he believes it expedient, in the spirit of the modern semantic tradition, also to rename the abstract 'Extrahendum' (that is, what is extracted and incorporated in the concept).

Inasmuch as a complete synthesis of abstractions corresponding to the infinite fulness of the sensual image is unattainable, philosophical justification of any abstraction (the 'Extrahendum') may be reduced to an indication of the goal or value for the sake of which the subject of cognition has made the extraction. The sensually, intuitively grasped fulness of the thing minus the 'Extrahendum' is called the 'Subtrahendum'. The latter is stored away by the subject of cognition as reserve for the occasion when 'the essential' will turn out to be precisely there, in the light of other objectives, values, or aspirations.

* * *

In approaching the question of the relation of concept to notion one must apparently fully take into account the fact that the notion, as a form and a stage in reflecting objective reality in man's mind is also an abstraction, whose formation is affected by a great number of factors, and first of all the direct practical interest, man's need and the purpose reflecting the need ideally.

The links between the concept—a theoretical abstraction expressing the objective essence of the thing—and practice is much broader, deeper, and more complicated. In the concept, the object is comprehended from the standpoint of mankind's practice in its entire volume throughout the history of world development, rather than from the standpoint of the particular, narrow pragmatic objective and need. Only this viewpoint coincides in the long run with consideration of the object from the object's own point of view. Only from this standpoint can one distinguish the objectively essential definitions of the thing—'that in which the object is what it is'; in other words, the abstraction of a concept is formed.

To define a concept does not at all mean to find out the sense imparted by men to the corresponding term. To define a concept means to define the object. From the standpoint of materialism, it is one and the same thing. The only correct definition is therefore to arrive at the essence of the matter.

One can always establish a convention or agreement on the meaning or sense of a term; the content of a concept is quite a different thing. Although the content of a concept is always directly brought out as the 'meaning of a term', that is by no means one and the same thing.

That is an extremely important point closely linked with the problem of concreteness of the concept as interpreted in materialist dialectics (dialectical logic).

Neopositivists reduce the problem of defining the concept to establishing the meaning of a term in a system of terms built according to formal rules, and the question of correspondence between definitions of the concept and its object existing outside and independently from consciousness, that is, from definition, is thus eliminated in general. As a result, they arrive at the absolutely insoluble problem of the so-called abstract object. This designation refers to the meaning of such a term that cannot be applied as a name to an individual thing given in the individual's immediate sensual experience. Let us note that the sensual image of the single object in the individual's consciousness is here again named the concrete object, which is in complete agreement with the age-long traditions of extreme empiricism.

Insofar as the whole of actual science consists of definitions that have no immediate equivalent in the individual's sensual experience (that is, have some 'abstract object' for their meaning), the question of the relation of the abstract to the concrete is transformed into the problem of the relation of a general term to an individual image in the consciousness. As a question of logic, it is also ignored, being replaced by a partly psychological, partly formal linguistic question. But on this plane it is indeed impossible to solve the problem of the objective truth of any general concept, for the formulation of the question itself precludes any possibility of answering it. Neopositivist 'logic' focused on the study of links and transitions between one concept and another (in actual fact, between one term and another), assuming beforehand that there is no transition from the concept to an object outside consciousness (that is, outside the definition and sensual experience), and there can be no such transition. Passing from term to term, this logic can at no point discover a bridge from a term to an object rather than to another term, a bridge to 'concreteness' in its genuine sense rather than to a thing given to an individual in his direct experience.

The only bridge leading from term to object, from the abstract to the concrete and back, a bridge that permits to establish a firm unambiguous connection between the two, is, as Marx and Engels showed already in *The German Ideology*, practical activity involving objects, the objective being of things and men. The purely theoretical act is not enough here.

'One of the most difficult tasks confronting philosophers is to descend from the world of thought to the actual world. *Language* is the immediate actuality of thought. Just as philosophers have given thought an independent existence, so they were bound to make language into an independent realm. This is the secret of philosophical language, in which thoughts in the form of words have their own content,' [43] wrote Marx as early as 1845, almost a hundred years before the latest positivist discoveries in the field of logic were made. As a result of this operation, 'the problem of descending from the world of thoughts to the actual world is turned

---

[43] K. Marx and F. Engels, The German Ideology, *Collected Works*, Vol. 5, Progress Publishers, Moscow, 1976, p.446.

into the problem of descending from language to life',[44] and it is perceived by philosophers of this trend as a task to be solved verbally, too, as a task in inventing special magic words which, while remaining words, would nevertheless be something more than mere words.

In *The German Ideology,* Marx and Engels demonstrated brilliantly that that task was an imaginary one, arising merely from the view that language and thought are separate spheres organised according to their own immanent rules and laws rather than forms of expression of real life, of objective being of men and things.

'We have seen that the whole problem of transition from thought to reality, hence from language to life, exists only in philosophical illusion.... This great problem ... was bound, of course, to result finally in one of these knights-errant setting out in search of a word which, as a *word,* formed the transition in question, which, as a word, ceases to be simply a word, and which, as a word, in a mysterious superlinguistic manner, points from within language to the actual object it denotes.'[45]

In these days too, many bourgeois philosophers attempt to solve this pseudoproblem rooted in the conception that the whole gigantic system of 'abstract concepts' is based on such a shaky and elusive foundation as the individual image in an individual's perception, as 'the only individual' that is, apart from everything else, termed the 'concrete' object. All this is but the old search for the absolute. While Hegel looked for the absolute in the concept, neopositivists are searching for it in the sphere of words or signs combined according to absolute rules.

Marx and Engels, resolutely discarding idealism in philosophy, viewed thought and language as 'only *manifestations* of actual life',[46] and definitions of concepts, as verbally recorded definitions of reality. But reality was here construed not as simply a sea of individual things in which separate individuals catch abstract general definitions in the net of abstraction, but rather a concreteness organised in itself, that is, an articulate system of men's relations to nature. Language and thought are precisely a direct expression (form of manifestation) of this system of men and things.

[44] K. Marx and F. Engels, op. cit., p. 446.
[45] Ibid., p. 449.
[46] Ibid., p. 447.

On this basis Marx and Engels solved the problem of the objective meaning of all those 'abstractions' which to this day appear in idealist philosophy (including neopositivist philosophy) as specific 'abstract objects' independently existing in language.

Marx and Engels gave a materialist interpretation to all those mysterious abstractions which, according to idealist philosophy, exist only in consciousness, in thought and language, finding their objective factual equivalents in concrete reality. The problem of the relation of the abstract to the concrete thereby ceased to be one of relation of a verbally expressed abstraction to an individual, sensually given thing. It emerged as the problem of internal division of concrete reality within itself, as the problem of the relationship between the discrete elements of this reality.

The solution of the problem found by Marx and Engels is apparently very simple: definitions of concepts are nothing but definitions of different elements of the actual concreteness, that is, of the law-governed organisation of a system of relations of man to man and of man to things. Scientific study of this concrete reality must yield 'abstract' definitions of concepts expressing its structure, its organisation. Each abstract definition of the concept must express a discrete element that is actually (objectively) singled out in the concrete reality. The solution is very simple at first sight, yet it cuts at a stroke the Gordian knot of problems that idealist philosophy has so far been unable to unravel.

The abstract is not, from this point of view, just a synonym of the purely ideal, existing only in the consciousness, in man's brain in the shape of sense or meaning of a word-sign. This term is also applied by Marx, with every justification, to reality outside consciousness, e.g.: 'human labour in the abstract',[47] or the abstract—*isolated*—human individual,[48] or 'Gold as *the material aspect of abstract wealth*',[49] and so on.

All these expressions will seem absurd and incomprehensible to logicians and philosophers for whom the abstract is

---

[47] Karl Marx, *Capital*, Vol. I, p. 46.

[48] See K. Marx, Theses on Feuerbach, K. Marx and F. Engels, *Collected Works*, Vol. 5, p. 5.

[49] Karl Marx, *A Contribution to the Critique of Political Economy*, p. 124.

a synonym of the purely ideal, mental, intellectual, while the concrete is a synonym of the individual, sensually perceived. That is solely due to the fact that their kind of logic would never be able to solve the dialectical task that the concrete reality of capitalist relations poses before thought. From the standpoint of school logic, this reality will appear wholely mystical. Here, for instance, it is not 'the abstract' that has the meaning of an aspect or property of 'the concrete', but on the contrary, the sensually concrete has the meaning of mere form of manifestation of the abstractly universal. In this inversion, the essence of which was not revealed before Marx, lies the whole difficulty of the understanding of value form.

'This *inversion,* through which the sensually concrete emerges only as a form of the abstractly general, and not, conversely, the abstractly general as a property of the concrete, characterises the expression of value. That is what makes its comprehension difficult. If I say that Roman law and German law are both laws, that is self-obvious. If I say, on the contrary, *the* law, this abstraction, *realises itself* in Roman law and in German law, in these concrete laws, then the relationship becomes mystical.' [50]

And that is not simply a mystifying form of expressing facts in speech, in language, neither is it a speculative Hegelian turn of speech, but rather a completely accurate verbal expression of the actual 'inversion' of elements of reality connected with one another. That is an expression of nothing but the actual fact of universal dependence of the separate isolated links of social production upon each other, a fact completely independent of either men's consciousness or their will. To man, this fact inevitably appears as the mystic power of 'the abstract' over 'the concrete', that is, the power of a universal law guiding the movements of separate (individual) things and persons over each individual person and each individual thing.

This 'mystical' turn of speech, so reminiscent of the Hegelian mode of expression, reflects the real dialectics of 'things' and 'relations' within which the thing exists. The most interesting point is, however, that the mystical nature of this expression results precisely from the fact that 'the

---

[50] Karl Marx, *Das Kapital,* Bd. 1, Meissner, Hamburg, 1867, S. 771.

abstract' and 'the concrete' are used in the sense attributed to them by school logic.

Indeed, if 'concrete' is applied to the definition of a thing, and 'abstract', to the definition of a relation between them, regarded as a special and independent object of thought and definition, a fact like money instantly begins to appear quite mystical. For objectively, apart from the illusions that one may have on this score, 'money, though a physical *object* with distinct properties, represents a social *relation* of production'[51] (italics mine—*E.I.*). For this reason bourgeois economists, as Marx remarks, are continually amazed 'when the phenomenon that they have just ponderously described as a thing reappears as a social relation and, a moment later, having been defined as a social relation, teases them once more as a thing'.[52]

Let us point out that this 'mystique' is not a feature specific for capitalist production only. The dialectics of the relation between an individual 'thing' (that is, the object of a 'concrete concept') and that 'relation' within which the thing is this particular thing (that is, the object of the 'abstract concept') is a universal relation. This is a manifestation of the objectively universal fact that there are in general no things in the world that would exist in isolation from the universal links—things always exist in a system of relations to one another. This system of interacting things (what Marx calls concreteness) is always something determining and therefore *logically primary* with regard to each separate sensually perceived thing. The extraordinary situation when 'relation' is taken for a 'thing', and a 'thing' for a 'relation', arises precisely due to this dialectics.

A system of interacting things, a certain law-governed system of their relations (that is, 'the concrete') always appears in contemplation as a separate sensually perceived thing, but it appears only in some fragmentary, particular manifestation, that is, abstractly. The whole difficulty of theoretical analysis is that neither the 'relation' between things should be regarded abstractly, as a specific independent object, nor conversely the 'thing' should be viewed as an isolated object existing outside a system of relations to

---

[51] Karl Marx, *A Contribution to the Critique of Political Economy*, p. 35.

[52] Ibid.

other things, but rather each thing should be interpreted as an element or moment of a certain concrete system of interacting things, as a concrete individual manifestation of a certain system of 'relations'.

The turn of speech presenting 'the concrete' as something subordinated to 'the abstract' and even as its product (and that is the root of the entire Hegelian mystification of the problem of the universal, the particular, and the individual) expresses in actual fact the absolutely real circumstance that each individual phenomenon (thing, event, etc.) is always born and exists in its definiteness and later dies within a certain concrete whole, within a system of individual things developing in a law-governed way. The 'power' or the determining action of the law (and law is the reality of the universal in nature and society) with regard to each individual thing, the determining significance of the whole in relation to its parts, is exactly what is perceived as the power of 'the abstract' over 'the concrete'. The result is the mystifying expression.

Marx uncovered this mystification by showing the reality of 'the concrete' as a whole system of interacting things, developing and resulting from development, as a whole divided in accordance with some law, rather than as an individual isolated thing. Given this interpretation, any shade of mystification disappears.

The concrete (and not the abstract)—as reality taken as a whole in its development, in its law-governed division—is always something primary with respect to the abstract (whether this abstract should be construed as a separate relatively isolated moment of reality or its mental verbally recorded reflection). At the same time any concreteness exists only through its own discrete elements (things, relations) as their specific combination, synthesis, unity.

That is exactly why the concrete is reflected in thought only as a unity of diverse definitions, each of which records precisely one of the moments actually distinguished in its structure. Consistent mental reproduction of the concrete is therefore realised as 'ascent from the abstract to the concrete', that is, as logical combination (synthesis) of particular definitions into an aggregate overall theoretical picture of reality, as movement of thought from the particular to the general.

The order of singling out the separate (particular) definitions and linking them up is by no means arbitrary. This sequence is generally determined, as the classics of Marxism-Leninism showed, by the historical process of the birth, formation, and growing complexity of the concrete sphere of reality which in this given case is reproduced in thought. The fundamental, primary, universal abstract definitions of the whole, with which a theoretical construction should always begin, are not formed here, by any means, through simple formal abstraction from all the 'particulars' without exception which form part of the whole.

Thus value, the primary universal category of *Capital,* is not defined through abstractions that would retain the general features equally inherent in commodity, money, capital, profit, and rent, but through the finest theoretical definitions of one 'particular', namely, commodity, all the other particulars, however, being strictly left out of account.

Analysis of commodity, this elementary economic concreteness, yields universal (and in this sense abstract) definitions pertaining to any other 'particular' form of economic relations. The whole point is, however, that commodity is the kind of particular which simultaneously is a universal condition of the existence of the other particulars recorded in other categories. That is a particular entity whose whole specificity lies in being the universal and the abstract, that is, undeveloped, elementary, "cellular" formation, developing through contradictions immanently inherent in it into other, more complex and well-developed formations.

The dialectics of the abstract and the concrete in the concept reflects quite precisely the objective dialectics of the development of one kind of actual (historically defined) relations between men into other kinds of relations, just as actual, mediated by things. The entire movement of thought from the abstract to the concrete is therefore at the same time absolutely strict movement of thought from fact to fact, transition from considering one fact to considering another fact, rather than movement 'from concept to concept'.

This specific feature of Marx's method had to be continually stressed by the classics of Marxism in their arguments against Kantian interpretations of the logic of *Capital.* This specific feature consists in that in applying this method 'we are dealing here not only with a purely logical process, but with a historical process and its explanatory reflection in thought, the logical pursuance of its inner connection'.[53]

The problem of the relation of the abstract to the concrete in the concept is correctly solved only on the basis of this approach. Every concept is abstract in the sense that it records only one of the particular moments of concrete reality rather than concrete reality in its entirety. Each concept is concrete, too, for it does not record the formal general 'features' of heterogeneous facts but rather expresses in a more precise manner the concrete definiteness of the fact to which it pertains, its specific feature due to which it plays this and not some other role in the aggregate whole that is reality, having this particular function and 'meaning' and not some other.

Every concept (if it is really a well-developed concept and not merely a verbally fixed general notion) is therefore a concrete abstraction, however contradictory that may sound from the standpoint of old logic. It is always a thing that is expressed in it (that is, a sensually, empirically stated fact), but a thing considered with regard to its property which it has specifically as an element of a given concrete system of interacting things (facts) rather than simply as an abstract thing belonging to an indeterminate sphere of reality. A thing regarded outside any concrete system of relations with other things is also an abstraction—no better than relation or property regarded as a specific object unconnected with things, the material carriers of relations and properties.

The Marxist conception of the categories of the abstract and the concrete as logical (universal) categories was further elaborated in Lenin's numerous philosophical works and fragments as well as in his excursions into logic which he undertook in considering social, politico-economic, and political problems. Whenever he touched on these problems, Lenin unswervingly defended the views developed by Marx and Engels, emphasising the objective significance of theoretical abstractions and sharply rejecting empty formal abstractions which record in verbal form arbitrarily chosen formal affinities, 'similar features' of heterogeneous actual-

[53] Karl Marx, *Capital*, Vol. III, Progress Publishers, Moscow, 1974, p. 895.

ly unconnected phenomena. For Lenin, 'the abstract' was always a synonym of verbiage divorced from life, a synonym of formal wordcreation, of an empty and untrue definition to which no definite fact corresponds in reality. And on the contrary, Lenin always insisted on the concrete nature of the truth and of concepts expressing reality, on the indissoluble links between word and deed, for it is only these links that ensure actual reasonable synthesis of the abstract with the concrete, of the universal with the particular and the individual. Lenin's views on this score are of enormous importance for logic, requiring further careful study, generalisation, and systematisation. It is easy to see that these views have nothing in common with the metaphysical division of concepts, given once and for all, into 'abstract' (concepts of individual things or facts) and 'concrete' (referring to relations and properties considered 'in isolation from things', as 'specific objects'). Lenin assessed concepts of both type as equally abstract, he did not value them highly at all, always insisting that facts and things should be comprehended in their overall cohesion and concrete interaction (that is, in their 'relations'), while any consideration of social relations should always be based on a most careful and thoughtful treatment of 'things', of strictly attested facts, the social relations never to be taken as 'a specific object' considered separately from things and facts. In other words, Lenin insisted on all occasions on concrete thinking, for concreteness was to him, just as to Marx, a synonym of the objective meaning and truth of concepts, while abstractness, a synonym of their emptiness.

What we have said here warrants the following conclusion: both in dialectical and formal logic, it is inadmissible to divide concepts, once and for all, into two classes—abstract and concrete. This division is connected with traditions in philosophy that are far from the best, precisely those traditions against which not only Marx and Lenin fought but also Hegel, Spinoza, and generally all those thinkers who understood that concept (as a form of thought) and term (a verbal symbol) were essentially different things. There are certain grounds for dividing terms into names of separate things sensually perceived by the individual and names of their 'general' properties and relations, while in regard to concepts this division has no sense. It is not a logical division. There are no grounds for it in logic.

THE CONCEPT OF MAN AND SOME CONCLUSIONS FROM ITS ANALYSIS

Let us now consider the concept of man in the light of the above. What is man? At first sight, the question appears to be ridiculously simple. Each of us links up quite a definite notion with this word, easily distinguishing man from any other being or object on the basis of this notion. From the standpoint of pre-Marxian logic that means that every individual of common sense possesses the concept of man. However, no other concept, it seems, has occasioned more acrimonious debate among philosophers than this one.

According to the metaphysical (antidialectical) view it is not difficult to define this concept, just as any other. For this purpose one should abstract that general element that is equally inherent in every individual representative of the human race but not in any other beings.

An attempt to carry out this recommendation, however, immediately runs into a number of difficulties of fundamental philosophical significance. It turns out that before making such an abstraction, one has to decide first of all what living beings could be included in the human race and what could not. Considerations that are by no means of formal nature immediately come into play here. For instance, Aristotle did not take slaves into account in working out his famous definition of man as a 'political being'. Slaves were included into a different 'genus', namely that of 'instruments', albeit 'speaking' ones. For Aristotle as an ideologue of his own class, only the activity of a free citizen was 'genuinely human'.

Elementary analysis of the concept of man discloses at once that it is bound by a thousand ties to the existence and struggle of classes and their worldviews and to a definite interpretation of humanism that has never been nonpartisan or purely academic.

The bourgeois system, asserting itself in the struggle against feudal law, proved its advantages by insisting that it was the only structure to conform to the genuine nature of man, while feudalism was based on distorted and false preconceptions of his nature. The ideologists of contemporary imperialism endeavour to prove that socialism is incompatible with 'the demands of human nature' only to be satisfied under the 'free enterprise' system.

Let us analyse in this connection the situation depicted in a novel by Vercors, a progressive French author.[54] In a generalised, acute, and witty form, the novel outlines the typical views of man conflicting in the modern world. The plot is as follows. A community of strange creatures is discovered in a remote part of tropical forest. According to some criteria current in modern science these are anthropoid apes, according to others, they are men. One thing is clear: it is an extraordinary previously unknown *transitional* form between the animal, biological world and the human, social world. The whole question is whether they have made the step across that hardly perceptible boundary that separates man from animal, or not.

That is seemingly a purely academic question with which only a specialist in biology or anthropology may be concerned. In these days, however, there are no purely academic questions, and neither can there be. The *tropi* (as the creatures invented by the author are called) very soon become the centre of conflicts of diverse interests and therefore of different viewpoints. An abstract theoretical question, 'Are these men or animals?' demands a definite and quite concrete answer. The main protagonist of the novel consciously kills one of these beings. If *tropi* are men, then he is a murderer who will have to be executed. If they are animals, there is no *corpus delicti*. The same question torments the old clergyman. If *tropi* are men, he is obliged to save their souls, to perform the rite of baptism. But supposing these are merely animals? In that case he risks a repetition of the sacrilege of St Maël who, being purblind, baptised penguins. Another powerful interest is that of an industrial company that sees the *tropi* as ideal labour force. Trained animals that know neither trade unions nor class struggle nor needs above the physiological ones—what can be better from the point of view of a capitalist?

The company on whose territory the *tropi* are discovered tries to prove that these are animals constituting the company's private property. The debate about the nature of the *tropi* involves hundreds of men, dozens of theories and doctrines, its scope gets wider and the problem itself more and more entangled, the whole thing growing into a debate about quite different objects and values. The characters of

[54] See: Vercors, *Les animaux dénaturés,* Michel, Paris, 1952.

the novel are compelled to ponder the criterion for solving the question in a rigorous and unambiguous manner. This proves to be a more difficult task than might seem at first sight.

If preference is given to a certain 'property of man', the *tropi* are included in the category of men, and if another one is preferred, they are not. Working out a series of such features does not help either, for in this case the question arises as to the number of such features, and the difficulty remains the same. By increasing the number of men's properties, including in this number those which the *tropi* do not have, one automatically leaves the *tropi* outside the human race. By paring down the number of features, leaving only those that both the previously known men and the *tropi* have, one obtains a definition which includes the *tropi* in the family of men. The thinking gets into the rut of a vicious circle: to define the nature of the *tropi,* one has to have a previous definition of man. But one cannot define man unless one has decided beforehand whether one will include the *tropi* as a species of the *homo sapiens* or not.

Besides, interpretation of each of the features immediately leads to explosive debate. What is one to understand by thinking? How is one to interpret speech? How is one to define labour? And so on and so forth. In one sense of these concepts, the *tropi* possess both thinking and speech, while in a different sense they do not. In other words, on each attribute of man the same kind of debate flares up as regards the concept of man itself. There is no visible end to the debate, it reaches the sphere of the most general philosophical concepts only to flare up with greater force and fury.

The debate becomes particularly acute when it touches on the subject of which of the modes of life activity should be regarded as 'genuinely human', what organisation of life 'conforms with man's nature', and wherein lies this 'nature'?

All attempts to establish that 'general and essential feature' that would permit to distinguish strictly between man and non-man, again and again run into an ancient difficulty. Such a feature may only be defined if a boundary between man and his nearest animal forebears is previously drawn; but how is one to draw this boundary line unless one has in one's head that very 'general feature' which has to be determined? It is not difficult to tell very cold water from very hot; but what about warm water? One stone does not make a heap, and neither do two stones. How many stones does one need to make a heap? Where is the point at which a balding man becomes bald? Does such a clear-cut boundary exist at all? Isn't it simply an arbitrary imaginary line drawn for the sake of convenience of classification only? In that case, where should it lie? It will be drawn where the powers that be will want to draw it—that is the conviction to which the hero of the novel comes. Indeed, the subjective idealist doctrines (pragmatism, instrumentalism, etc.) hand over the solution of this question to the powers that be. Their voice becomes the criterion of truth; everything is made dependent on their will and caprice. All the misfortunes of this world stem from the fact that men have not grasped yet what man is, and they have not agreed about what they would like him to be—that is the way the protagonist of the novel philosophises.

Having found from practical experience that the general and essential feature of man is not so easy to discover as might appear at first sight, the heroes of the novel are compelled to look for a solution in philosophical and sociological conceptions. But where is one to find the criterion of the truth of the latter? Here it all begins from the beginning. Vercors and his heroes are familiar with Marxist answer to this question. Yet it appears 'one-sided' to them. Vercors believes that a conception proceeding from 'the real relations of men in material production' ignores 'other forms of human solidarity', first of all 'ritual philosophy': 'there are many tribes in the world whose human solidarity is built on hunting, wars, or fetishist rituals rather than on material production'; 'the strongest tie now binding 300 million Hindoos is their ritual philosophy rather than their backward agriculture'. The heroes of the novel vacillate, at the author's will, between the Marxist and the idealist Christian definition of the general and essential criterion of the human being, daring to accept neither. They are looking for a third one, that would reconcile dialectical materialism and Christianity.

'Each man is a man first and foremost, and only then is he a follower of Plato, Christ, or Marx,' wrote Vercors in the afterword to the Russian edition of the book. 'In my view it is much more important to show the way in which points of contact may be found between Marxism and Christianity proceeding from such a criterion, than to emphasise their differences.' The essence of man as such regardless of the ideological differences, does not lie in adherence to some doctrine or other. But wherein does it lie? In the fact that 'man is first and foremost . . . man'. That is the only answer that Vercors was able to oppose to the 'one-sided' view of dialectical materialism. But this kind of 'answer' takes us back to the starting point—to a simple name unendowed with any definite content. To move away from the tautology, one will have to take up the line of reasoning from the very beginning.

The position so vividly and wittily outlined by Vercors expresses very well the attitudes of those sections of Western intellectuals who struggle agonisingly with the burning issues of our times yet have not solved so far the problem for themselves—where lie the ways of redeeming the noble ideals of humanism? They see clearly that capitalism is innately hostile to these ideals. Yet they do not dare to take up communism for fear of losing in it 'independence of thinking', the sham 'privileges of the thinking part of mankind'. While this part of mankind agonises over the choice between these two real poles of the modern world, any uncomplicated theoretical question grows out of any proportion into a most intricate and completely insoluble problem, while attempts to solve it with the aid of the most sophisticated instruments of formal logic ultimately lead to a tautology: A=A, man is man. Nothing else can result from a search for a definition of man through establishing the abstractly identical property which each individual representative of present-day mankind possesses. Logic based on this kind of axiom is absolutely powerless to do anything here. The essence of man to be expressed in the universal definition is by no means an abstraction inherent in each individual, it is not the identical feature which each individual representative of the human race taken separately possesses. A universal definition of man cannot be obtained on this path. Here one needs a different kind of logic, a logic based on the dialectical materialist conception of the relationship between the universal and the individual.

This essence is impossible to discover in a series of abstract features inherent in every individual. The universal cannot be found here however hard one might look for it. The search along this path is fruitless also in the case when it is assisted by most sophisticated logic. An excellent illustration of this point is to be found in *Dialectic*, by Gustav E. Mueller,[55] an American philosopher. Judging from the book, the author has learnt something from Hegel. He even assimilated the Hegelian propositions on the interpenetration of opposites, on the role of contradictions in the development of scientific theses, on the relation of consciousness to self-consciousness, and many other things. However, all this formal dialectical erudition runs idle, resulting in vacuity.

'Man could not know what man is, could he not *identify* man with himself; yet equally man could have no experience of man, if he could not differentiate himself from what he experiences of himself.'[56] A series of 'identifications' and 'differentiations' which Mueller's man carries out within himself according to the rules of formal dialectical schemes bring him to constructions so unintelligible and involved that their creator cannot untangle them himself. The end result of this pseudodialectical logic is as follows: man is so complicated and contradictory a being that the more you study him, the less you can hope to understand him. The only 'general feature' that Mueller manages to isolate in the intricate complexity of interacting individuals ultimately proves to be the 'power of reflection' and 'love for reflection'. 'His true humanity lies in this power of reflection... And the better the self thus knows itself, the more questionable and uncertain it appears. To embrace in the questionable individual the absolute, is what Plato calls *Eros*, love. Man's true self is *Love*.'[57]

One would be hard put to it to discern here the 'power of reflection'. Powerlessness is much more in evidence. Man's essence certainly has nothing to do with this. What is expressed here is merely the essence of a philosopher and his love for contemplating the way he contemplates. Reproaching Mueller himself for all this is both unkind

---

[55] Gustav E. Mueller, *Dialectic*, Bookman, New York, 1953.
[56] Ibid., p. 214.
[57] Ibid., p. 230.

and useless. The impotence of his thought is first of all to be blamed on the conditions that create such a one-sided and abstract psychology—the psychology of an intellectual completely divorced from the real life and struggle of the masses, the psychology of the man who contemplates only the manner in which he contemplates. If Mueller sees this contemplation of contemplation as 'true humanity', it is easy to appreciate his position: after all, one must have some consolation. However, real humanity, the working and fighting humanity, will hardly agree to its essence being identified with the individuality of a personalist philosopher nurturing in solitude his love for impotent contemplation and contemplation about this impotent love.

The essence of modern humanity, and thereby a universal definition of man, is of course a subject-matter worthy of the closest attention of a philosopher. A clear view of the world is the first and necessary premise for approaching this problem correctly. But one also needs a more developed logic than that which suggests that the solution lies in searching for the 'general and essential property' inherent in all the individual representatives of modern mankind taken separately and reducing the universal to the merely identical. Such logic cannot yield anything but empty tautologies. Besides, the abstract motto, 'Look for the general, and thou shalt find the knowledge of the essence', gives a free hand to arbitrariness and subjectivism in delimiting the range of facts from which the general is abstracted.

All of this is evidence of the fact that the links between logic and worldview are integral ones, just as those between the operations of generalisation and a definite party position in life and philosophy. A most sophisticated system of formal rules for generalisation will not ensure true generalisation unless it is combined with a clear and progressive worldview principle.

And another thing is no less true. A progressive worldview cannot be mechanically combined with a logic that posits its neutrality with regard to any worldview as a virtue, restricting itself to working out such abstract rules as may be employed this way and that, depending on the irrationally emotional bias for some worldview or other.

The Marxist-Leninist worldview is based on a scientifically worked out conception of facts rather than on ethical postulates. It is logical through and through. However, the logic with the aid of which this worldview has been worked out also contains within itself, in its own propositions, rather than somewhere outside, a certain worldview principle. The warmest emotional attachment to the working class and communist ideals will not redeem a theoretician if he employs the ancient purely formal logic with its claim to 'nonpartisanship'. Such a theoretician will never arrive at correct conclusions and generalisations.

In his theses on Feuerbach Marx opposed his dialectical materialist conception of the essence of man to all previous attempts to define this much talked-of essence, saying that 'the essence of man is no abstraction inherent in each single individual. In its reality it is the ensemble of the social relations.'[58] This expresses not only a worldview, sociological truth but also a profound logical tenet or principle, one of the most important propositions of dialectical logic. It is easy to see that this proposition assumes a conception of the categories of the abstract, the concrete, the universal, and the individual quite different from the one on which old, nondialectical logic was based. Translated into the language of logic, this proposition means: it is useless to look for universal definitions of the essence of a genus through abstraction of the identical property possessed by each individual representative of this genus.

An expression of the essence of a genus is not to be found in a series of 'abstractions', hard as one might try, for it is not contained in this series.

The essence of human nature in general, and thereby the genuine human nature of each man, can only be revealed through quite a concrete study of the 'ensemble of the social relations', through a concrete analysis of those laws which govern the birth and development of human society as a whole and of each human individual.

Human society is a most typical case of concrete community, and the relation of a human individual to society is a characteristic instance of the relation of the individual to the universal. The dialectical nature of this relation appears here in sharp relief, while the question of

---

[58] Karl Marx, Theses on Feuerbach, K. Marx and F. Engels, *Collected Works,* Vol. 5, p. 4.

the relation of the abstract to the concrete is closely interwoven with the problem of the relation of the universal to the particular and the individual.

THE CONCRETE AND THE DIALECTICS OF THE UNIVERSAL AND THE INDIVIDUAL

The search for the essence of man through ideally equating men in the concept of the genus assumes a metaphysical conception of the relation of the universal to the individual.

For the metaphysician only the individual is concrete—an individual sensually perceived thing, object, phenomenon, event, a separate human individual, etc. For him, the abstract is the product of mental separation whose counterpart in reality is similarity of many (or all) individual things, phenomena, men.

According to this position, the universal exists in reality only as similarity between many individual things, only as one of the aspects of a concrete individual thing, while its being separately from the individual thing, its being as such, is only realised in man's head, only as a word, as the sense and meaning of a term.

At first sight, this view of the relation between the universal and the individual appears to be the only materialist and common-sensical one. But that is only at first sight. The thing is that this position completely ignores, in the very approach to the problem, the dialectics of the universal and the individual in the things themselves, in the reality outside the head.

This can be shown most graphically by considering the way in which the Feuerbachian and Marxist-Leninist conception of the essence of man diverge. While criticising Hegel quite sharply for his idealism, for taking 'pure thought' to be the essence of man, Feuerbach proved to be incapable of opposing to Hegel a conception of dialectics contained in the relations of man to man and of man to nature, in the material production of the life of society.

That was why he remained centred on the *abstract* individual both in sociology and epistemology, despite his own insistence that he was concerned with the 'concrete', 'real', 'actual' man. This man proved to be 'concrete' only in Feuerbach's imagination. He failed to see wherein lay the actual concreteness of man. Apart from everything else, that means that the terms 'the concrete' and 'the abstract' were used by Feuerbach in a sense directly opposite to their true philosophical sense: what he calls concrete is in fact, as brilliantly proved by Marx and Engels, extremely *abstract*, and vice versa.

The term 'concrete' is applied by Feuerbach to an aggregate of sensually perceived qualities inherent in each individual and common to all individuals. His conception of man is based on these qualities. From the point of view of Marx and Engels, from the dialectical standpoint, that is a typically abstract portrayal of man.

Marx and Engels were the first to show, from the materialist viewpoint, wherein lies the genuine concreteness of human existence and what is the objective reality to which a philosopher is entitled to apply the term 'concrete' in its full meaning.

They discovered man's concrete essence in the overall process of social life and laws of its development rather than in a series of qualities inherent in each individual. The question of man's concrete nature is here formulated and solved as the problem of development of a system of social relations of man to man and of man to nature. The universal (socially concrete) system of interaction between men and things appears, with regard to a separate individual, as his own human reality that was formed outside of and independently from him.

Nature as such creates absolutely nothing 'human'. Man with all his specifically human features is from beginning to end the result and product of his own labour. Even walking straight, which appears at first sight man's natural, anatomically innate trait, is in actual fact a result of educating the child within an established society: a child isolated from society à la Mowgli (and such cases are numerous) prefers to run on all fours, and it takes a lot of effort to break him of the habit.

In other words, only those features, properties, and peculiarities of the individual that are ultimately products of social labour, are specifically human. Of course, it is mother nature that provides the anatomic and physiological prerequisites. However, the specifically human form which they ultimately assume is the product of labour, and it can only be comprehended or deduced from labour. Conversely, all those properties of man that are not a product of labour, do not belong to the features expressing man's essence (e.g., soft lobes of the ear, although they are a 'specific feature' of man and not of any other living being).

An individual awaking to human life activity, that is, a natural biological being becoming a social one, is compelled to assimilate all forms of this activity through education. None of them are inherited biologically. What is inherited is the physiological potential for assimilating them. At first they confront him as something existing outside and independently from him, as something entirely objective, as an object for assimilation and imitation. Through education, these forms of social human activity are transformed into a personal, individual, subjective possession and are even consolidated physiologically: an adult person is no longer able to walk on all fours, even if he wants to do so, and that is not at all because he would be ridiculed; raw meat makes him sick.

In other words, all those features the sum of which makes up the much talked-of essence of man, are results and products (ultimate ones, of course) of socio-human labour activity. Man does not owe them to nature as such, still less to a supernatural force, whether it be called God or by some other name (e.g., idea). He owes them only to himself and the labour of previous generations. This is even more true of the more complex forms of human activity, both sensual and objective (material) and spiritual, than of straight walking.

Mankind's culture accumulated throughout history appears to a modern individual as something primary, determining his individual human activity. From the scientific (materialist) point of view the individual, the human personality should therefore be regarded as a unitary embodiment of universal human culture, both material and spiritual. This culture is naturally realised in the individual in a more or less one-sided and incomplete manner. The extent to which an individual can make the riches of culture into his property does not depend on him alone; to a much greater degree it depends on society and on the mode of division of labour characteristic of society.

Actual assimilation of some area of culture or other, some form of human activity or other, means assimilating it to such an extent as to be able to develop it further in an independent, individual, and creative manner. Nothing can be assimilated through passive contemplation—that is like building castles in the air. Assimilation without active practice yields no results. That is why the form of assimilating universal human culture by the individual is determined by the form of the division of labour. Of course, there is one-sidedness and one-sidedness. The principal achievement of Marx and Engels in the solution of this problem was their careful and concrete study of the contradictions of the bourgeois division of labour.

The antagonistic class division of labour makes each individual into an extremely one-sided man, a 'partial' man. It develops some of his abilities through eliminating the possibility of developing others. Certain abilities are developed in some individuals, while others, in other individuals, and it is this *one-sidedness* of development that links individuals with one another as men, acting as the form in which universal development is realised.

The concrete fulness of human development is here due to the fulness of personal, individual development, to the fact that each individual taken separately proves to be a defective, one-sided, that is, abstract, man.

If Feuerbach regarded such an *objectively abstract* individual as a 'concrete' man, that was a manifestation not only of the limitations of a bourgeois theoretician, of an ideological illusion veiling the actual state of things, but also of the logical weakness of his position. To construct a concrete conception of the essence of man, of man as such, Feuerbach made an abstraction from all the actual differences developed by history, looking for that general property that would be equally characteristic of tailor and painter, locksmith and clerk, peasant and clergyman, wage worker and entrepreneur. He endeavoured to find the essence of man, the genuine concrete nature of the human being, amongst properties common to individuals of any class and any occupation. He made an abstraction precisely from all the elements that constituted the *real essence* of mankind, developing through opposites as a totality of mutually conditioning modes of human activity.

According to the logic of Marx and Engels, a concrete theoretical conception of man, a concrete expression of the essence of man could only be formed in the diametrically opposite way, through considering exactly those differences and oppositions (class, professional, and individual) which Feuerbach ignores. The essence of man is real only as a well-developed and articulated system of abilities, as a complex system of the division of labour which, in accordance with its needs, moulds the individuals—mathematicians, carpenters, weavers, philosophers, entrepreneurs, bankers, servants, etc.

In other words, a theoretical definition of the essence of man can only consist in revealing the necessity which gives rise to and develops all the multiform manifestations and modes of socio-human activity.

In regard of the most general characteristic of this system, of the 'universal definition' of human nature, one must point out that that characteristic should express the real, objectively universal foundation on which the entire wealth of human culture necessarily grows. Man, as is well known, becomes separated from the animal world when he begins to work using implements of labour which he himself created. Production of labour implements is exactly the first (in essence and in time, logically and historically) form of human life activity, of human existence.

Thus the real universal basis of everything that is human in man is production of instruments of production. It is from this basis that other diverse qualities of the human being developed, including consciousness and will, speech and thinking, erect walk and all the rest of it.

If one were to attempt a universal definition of man in general, a short definition of the concept, it would sound like this: 'man is a being producing implements of labour'. That will be a characteristic example of a concrete universal definition of a concept.

This definition, from the standpoint of old logic, is inadmissibly 'concrete' to be universal. Such undoubted representatives of the human race as Mozart or Raphael, Pushkin or Aristotle, can hardly be included in this definition by means of simple formal abstraction, through a syllogistic figure.

On the other hand, the definition of man as 'a being producing implements of labour' will be assessed by old logic as a purely particular definition of man rather than a universal one, it will be recognised to be a definition of quite a specific type, class, or occupation of men—workers of machine-building plants or shopworks and nothing but,

What is the cause of this divergence? The fact of the matter is that the logic of Marx, on the basis of which this concrete universal definition was worked out, is founded on a different conception of the correlation between the universal, the particular, and the individual (separate) from that of nondialectical logic.

Production of implements of labour, of instruments of production is indeed a real and therefore quite *specific* form of human existence. At the same time that does not make it less real as a *universal* basis of the rest of human development, a universal genetic basis of all that is human in man.

Production of labour implements as the first universal form of human activity, as the objective basis for all other human traits without exception, as the simplest, elementary form of man's human being—that is what is expressed in the universal concept of the essence of man in the system of Marx and Engels. But, being an objectively universal basis of man's entire most complex social reality, production of labour implements was a thousand years ago, is now, and will be in the future quite a particular form of man's activity actually realised in individual acts performed by individual men. Analysis of the social act of the production of labour implements should reveal the internal contradictions of this act and the nature of their development giving rise to such abilities of man as speech, will, thought, artistic feeling, and further, class division of the collective, emergence of law, politics, art, philosophy, state, etc.

In this conception, *the universal* is not metaphysically opposed to *the particular* and *the individual* as a mental abstraction to a sensually given fulness of phenomena, but is rather opposed, as a real *unity* of the universal, the particular, and the individual, as an objective fact, to other just as objective facts within one and the same concrete historically developed system, in this case, to man's social and historical reality.

The problem of the relation of the universal to the individual arises in this case not only and not so much as the problem of the relation of mental abstraction to the sensually given objective reality but as the problem of the relation of sensually given facts to other sensually given facts, as *the object's internal relation to the object itself*, the relation of its different aspects to one another, as the problem of internal differentiation of objective concreteness within itself. On this basis and as a consequence of it, it arises as the problem of the relation between the concepts expressing in this connection the objective articulated concreteness.

To determine whether the *abstract* universal is extracted correctly or incorrectly, one should see whether it comprehends directly, through simple formal abstraction, each particular and individual fact without exception. If it does not, then we are wrong in considering a given notion as universal.

The situation is different in the case of the relation of the *concrete* universal concept to the sensually given diversity of particular and individual facts. To find out whether a given concept has revealed a universal definition of the object or a nonuniversal one, one should undertake a much more complex and meaningful analysis. In this case one should ask oneself the question whether the particular phenomenon directly expressed in it is at the same time the universal genetic basis from the development of which all other, just as particular, phenomena of the given concrete system may be understood in their necessity.

Is the act of production of labour implements that kind of social reality from which all other human traits may be *deduced in their necessity*, or is it not? The answer to this question determines the logical characterisation of the concept as a universal or nonuniversal one. Concrete analysis of the *content* of the concept yields in this case an affirmative answer.

Analysis of the same concept from the standpoint of the abstract logic of the intellect yields a negative answer. The overwhelming majority of beings that are undoubtedly individual representatives of the human race do not directly conform to this definition. From the standpoint of old nondialectical logic this concept is too concrete to be justified as a universal one. In the logic of Marx, however, this concept is genuinely universal exactly because it directly reflects the factual objective basis of all the other traits of man which have developed out of this basis factually, historically, the concrete universal basis of anything that is human.

In other words, the question of the universal character of a concept is transferred to another sphere, that of the study of the real *process of development.* The developmental approach becomes thereby the approach of *logic.* This approach also determines the proposition of materialist dialectics to the effect that the concept should not express the abstractly universal but rather that universal which, according to Lenin's apt formula, embodies in itself the richness of the particular, the individual, the single, being the *concrete universal.*

This richness of the particular and the individual is naturally embodied not in the *concept* as such but rather in the objective reality which is reflected in the concept, that particular (and even individual) sensually given reality whose characteristics are abstracted as definitions of a universal concept.

Thus, it is not the concept of man as a being producing labour implements that contains in itself the concepts of all the other human traits but rather the actual fact of producing labour implements contains in itself the necessity of their origin and development. It is not the commodity concept or value concept that contains in itself the entire diversity of other theoretical definitions of capitalism but rather the real commodity form of links between producers is the embryo from which all the 'riches', including the poverty of the wage workers, develop. That was why Marx was able to reveal *all* the contradictions of modern society in his analysis of simple commodity exchange as an actual, directly observable relation between men.

Nothing of this sort, naturally, is to be observed in the concept of commodity. In his polemics with bourgeois critics of *Capital*, Marx had to emphasise the fact that the first sections of his book do not contain an analysis of the concept of commodity at all but an elementary economic concreteness called commodity relation—a real sensually contemplated fact, and not an abstraction existing in the head.

The *universality* of the category of value is therefore a characteristic not only and not so much of the concept, of mental abstraction, as, first of all, of *the objective role* played by the commodity form in the emergence of capitalism. Only as a result of this does universality prove to be also a logical characteristic of the concept expressing this reality and its role in the structure of the whole under study.

The word 'value' and the corresponding, rather definite, notion, were not created by Petty or Smith or Ricardo. Anything that could be bought, sold, or exchanged, everything that *cost* something, was referred to as value by any merchant of those times. Had theoreticians of political economy attempted an elaboration of the concept through abstracting the general element possessed by all the objects referred to as 'value' in the traditional usage, they would never construct a *concept*, of course. They would have merely brought out the meaning of the word 'value', precisely the same meaning that was implied by any merchant. They would have enumerated the properties of those phenomena to which the word 'value' was applicable. The whole thing would not have gone beyond finding out the limits of the applicability of the word, the name, beyond an analysis of the sense implied in the name.

The whole point is, however, that they formulated this question in quite a different way, so that the resultant answer to it proved to be a *concept*. Marx clearly showed the real essence of such an approach. The classics of political economy, beginning with Petty, did not at all engage in making abstraction from all those individual cases that were observed on the surface of capitalist commodity circulation and that the current usage referred to as cases of the movement of values. They raised the question, quite explicitly and directly, of the *real source* of the value properties of things, of the *substance* of value.

Their main achievement lay precisely in that they attempted to strictly define the substance of value through considering elementary commodity exchange. Owing to this, they discovered that the substance of value was contained in social labour. In working out the concept of value, they actually closely studied the exchange of one commodity for another in an attempt to understand why, on what objective basis, within what concrete substance, one thing was actually equated with another. In other words, without realising clearly the logical essence of their operations, they actually considered one specific case of the movement of values, namely the *fact of simple commodity exchange.* Analysis of this specific case yielded the concept of value.

William Petty, the first English economist, obtained the concept of value by reasoning thus: 'If a man can bring to London an ounce of Silver out of the Earth in Peru, *in the same time* that he can produce a Bushel of Corn, then one is the natural price of the other....'[59]

Let us note that this argument does not contain the word 'value' at all—Petty speaks of 'natural price'. Yet what emerges here is exactly the *concept of value* as the embodiment of socially necessary quantity of labour time in a commodity.

A concept, inasmuch as it is a real concept rather than merely a general notion expressed in a term, always expresses the *concretely universal*, not the abstractly universal, that is, it expresses a reality which, while being quite a particular phenomenon among other particular phenomena, is at the same time a genuinely universal, concretely universal element, a 'cell' in all the other particular phenomena.

The classic representatives of bourgeois political economy spontaneously, by trial and error, discovered this correct path of defining value. But they did not quite realise the genuine significance of this mode of thought. The philosophy of Locke, at which their thinking was consciously oriented, offered them no key to the problem of defining universal concepts. This led them to a number of paradoxes, quite instructive from the logical viewpoint, and a number of fundamental difficulties, the genuine meaning of which was only elucidated in Marx' analysis.

The cardinal difference between Marxian analysis of value as the universal basis for all the other categories of capitalist economy, and that kind of analysis which was attained in bourgeois political economy, lay precisely in the fact that Marx formed scientific definitions of 'value in general', 'value as such', on the basis of concrete consideration of direct exchange of one commodity for another involving no money. In doing so, Marx made a strict abstraction from all the other kinds of value developed on this basis (surplus-value, profit, rent, interest, and so on). Ricardo's main error, according to Marx, lay in his inability 'to forget profit' in considering 'value as such', so that his abstraction turns out to be incomplete, insufficient, 'formal'.

Marx includes in the definitions of 'value in general' only those definitions that were revealed through analysis of

---

[59] Quoted from: Karl Marx, *Theories of Surplus-Value* (Vol. IV of *Capital*), Part I, Progress Publishers, Moscow, 1975, p. 356.

one kind of value, precisely that kind of value which proves to be elementary, primordial both logically and historically (that is, both in essence and in time). The product of his analysis are genuinely universal definitions of value in general, definitions that have the meaning of concretely universal definitions in regard of money and profit alike. In other words, these are the concretely universal definitions of all the other specific kinds of manifestation of value.

That is a most splendid example of a concretely universal concept. Its definitions express that real (rather than formal) general moment which constitutes the elementary, 'generic' essence of all the other particular categories. These genuinely universal definitions are further reproduced in money, in profit, in rent, constituting definitions common to all these categories. But, as Marx shows, one would never have been able to reveal these definitions through simple formal abstraction from the specific features of commodity, money, profit, and rent.

Universal definitions of value directly coincide in *Capital* with the theoretical expression of the specific features of simple commodity exchange, of the laws which reveal these specific features. The reason for that is that the specific feature of simple commodity form lies exactly in that it constitutes the genuinely universal foundation of the whole system, its 'elementary cell', the first real form of manifestation of 'value in general'.

In considering this specific instance, Marx reveals in it, through his analysis, by 'the power of abstraction', the universal definitions of value. Analysis of exchange of linen for a coat, an individual instance at first sight, yields universal rather than individual definitions as its conclusion. One sees at a glance that this raising of the individual to the universal is radically different from the simple act of formal abstraction. The specific properties of the elementary commodity form distinguishing it from profit, rent, and other kinds of value are not ignored here as something inessential. On the contrary, theoretical analysis of these properties leads to the formation of a universal concept. That is the dialectical way of raising the individual to the universal.

Old non-dialectical logic would here recommend a different approach. In accordance with its principles, a definition of 'value in general' would have to be formed through abstraction from the specific features of *all* kinds of value, *including simple commodity exchange*, through identifying the common features of commodity, profit, rent, interest, etc. The specific features of the commodity form of value would have been ignored as 'inessential'. The universal would have been taken in isolation from the particular.

Marx practises quite a different approach. Insofar as the universal exists in reality only through the particular and the individual, it can only be revealed by a thorough analysis of the particular rather than an act of abstraction from the particular. The universal is the theoretical expression of the particular and the individual, an expression of the law of their existence. The reality of the universal in nature is the law of the existence of the particular and the individual rather than mere formal affinity of phenomena in some respect, serving as a basis for including them in one class.

It is Marxian dialectics that permits to bring out the actual, real general content of the commodity form, of money, of profit, and of all the other categories. This general content cannot be revealed through an act of simple formal abstraction. It is only useful in the initial classification of phenomena. It proves inadequate where a more serious task arises—that of working out universal objective theoretical definitions, concepts; moreover, it is here applied beyond its sphere and cannot solve the task. A more profound method is needed here.

It is indicative that Hegel, who came very close to the correct dialectical conception of the problem of the concretely universal, betrayed dialectics on the most significant point, and that owing to the idealist nature of his conception.

In explaining his conception of the dialectics of the universal and the particular, Hegel comments on the well-known argument of Aristotle on geometric figures. According to Aristotle, ' "amongst figures, only the triangle and the other definite figures", the rectangle, the parallelogram etc. "are really something. For the common is the figure; but this general figure, that is the common, does not exist", it is nothing real, it is nothing, an empty thing of the mind, it is only an abstraction. "On the contrary, the triangle is the first figure, the real, general, which also appears in the rectangle, etc."—the figure reduced to the simplest definition. On the one hand the triangle stands side by side with the rectangle, the pentagon, etc., as a particular thing, but on the other hand—and here lies the greatness of Aristotle's intellect—it is a real figure, a really general figure.'[60]

At first sight, Hegel sees the principal difference between the concrete universal concept and the empty abstraction in that it has an immediately objective meaning and expresses a certain empirically given concreteness. Hegel himself often warned, however, that the relationship between the universal, the particular, and the individual should by no means be likened to mathematical (including geometric) images and their relations. The latter, according to his explanation, are merely a certain allegory of a concept: they are too much 'burdened with sensuality'. The genuinely universal, which he interprets as a concept and nothing but a concept, should be conceived fully freed from the 'sensual matter', 'from the matter of sensuality'. He attacked materialists on this point, for their interpretation of the universal essentially eliminates the universal, transforming it into 'the particular side by side with other instances of the particular [*Besonderen*]'.

The universal as such, the universal which includes the richness of the particular and the individual, exists according to Hegel only as a concept, only in the ether of pure thought, by no means in the sphere of 'external reality'. That was, properly speaking, the reason why Hegel believed materialism to be impossible as philosophy (for philosophy is a science of the universal, and the universal is thought and nothing but thought).

For the same reason, the definition of man as a creature producing labour implements is just as unacceptable to Hegelian logic as a universal definition, as it is to the logic that preceded it. In Hegel's view, that is also merely a particular definition of man, a particular form of the revelation of his universal 'thinking' nature.

An idealist conception of the universal, its interpretation only as a concept, directly leads Hegel to the same result as its metaphysical interpretation. If Hegel's logic in its original dogmatic form were to be applied to the analysis of Marx's *Capital*, Marx's entire line of reasoning would

---

[60] G. W. F. Hegel, Vorlesungen über die Geschichte der Philosophie, *Sämtliche Werke,* Bd. 18, 1928, S. 374.

appear to be incorrect. According to Hegel, definitions of value cannot be obtained in the way Marx obtained them. A Hegelian adept would say about the first sections of *Capital* that definitions of one particular form of value are there taken to be universal definitions of value, while they are not universal definitions at all. He would recommend to deduce universal definitions of value from definitions of reasonable will (the way they are deduced by Hegel in *The Philosophy of Law*).

All of this proves that Hegelian logic, despite all its advantages over the old metaphysical logic, cannot be adopted by materialism without a radical critique, without radical elimination of all traces of idealism. The category of value in Marx is fundamentally different from mere formal abstraction as well as from Hegel's 'pure concept'. It is obviously 'burdened with sensuality', appearing as theoretical expression of the particular. Value, says Marx, has a 'sensual-supersensual' character, something that, from the Hegelian viewpoint, just cannot be. Moreover, the simple (universal) form of value, as Marx emphasises, by no means was the universal form of economic relations at all times, not at the beginning. Only capitalist development turned it into such a form.

Direct commodity exchange, as a phenomenon in considering which one may obtain a universal definition of value, as a phenomenon in which value is represented in pure form, is realised before the appearance of money, surplus-value and other particular well-developed forms of value. That means, apart from other things, that the form of economic relations which becomes genuinely general under capitalism, was realised before that as quite a particular phenomenon or even as an accidental individual phenomenon.

In reality it always happens that a phenomenon which later becomes universal originally emerges as an individual, particular, specific phenomenon, as an exception from the rule. It cannot actually emerge in any other way. Otherwise history would have a rather mysterious form.

Thus, any new improvement of labour, every new mode of man's action in production, before becoming generally accepted and recognised, first emerge as a certain deviation from previously accepted and codified norms. Having emerged as an *individual exception* from the rule in the labour of one or several men, the new form is then taken over by others, becoming in time a new *universal norm.* If the new norm did not originally appear in this exact manner, it would never become a really universal form, but would exist merely in fantasy, in wishful thinking.

In the same way, a concept expressing the really universal, directly includes in it a conception of the dialectics of the transformation of the individual and the particular into the universal, directly expressing *the individual and the particular* which in reality, outside man's head, *constitutes the universal* form of development.

In his conspectuses and notes on Hegel's logic, Lenin continually refers to one of the pivotal points of dialectics—to the conception of the universal as the concretely universal as opposed to abstractly universal distillations of the intellect. The relation of the universal to the particular and the individual is expressed in dialectics by 'a beautiful formula', as Lenin puts it: ' "Not merely an abstract universal, but a universal which comprises in itself the wealth of the particular." '

'Cf. *Capital,*' Lenin makes a note in the margin, and then continues:

'A beautiful formula: "Not merely an abstract universal, but a universal which comprises in itself the wealth of the particular, the individual, the single" (all the wealth of the particular and the single!)!! Très bien!.'[61]

The concrete universal expressed in the concept does not, of course, comprise in itself all this wealth in the sense that it comprehends all the specific instances and is applicable to them as their general name. That is exactly the metaphysical conception which Hegel opposes, and that is what Lenin approves about his position. A concrete universal concept comprises in itself 'the wealth of the particulars' in its concrete definitions—in two senses.

First, a concrete universal concept expresses in its definitions the specific concrete content (the internal law-governed structure) of a single, quite definite form of the development of an object under study. It comprises in itself 'the whole wealth' of the definitions of this form, its structure and its specificity. Second, it does not express in its

[61] V. I. Lenin, Conspectus of Hegel's Book *The Science of Logic, Collected Works,* Vol. 38, p. 99.

definitions some arbitrarily chosen form of development of the object as a whole but that, and only that, form which constitutes the really universal basis or foundation on which 'the whole wealth' of other formations grows.

A most striking example of such a concept is the value category in *Capital.* This concept is the result of an exhaustive analysis of one 'most elementary economic concreteness' of the capitalist world—direct exchange of one commodity for another involving no money. The specificity of this form consists in that it contains, like a 'cell' or embryo, the wealth of more complex, more developed forms of capitalist relations. That is why 'in this very simple phenomenon (in this "cell" of bourgeois society) analysis reveals *all* the contradictions (or the germs of *all* the contradictions) of modern society'.[62] That is why the result and product of this analysis, expressed in definitions of the category of value, offers a key to a theoretical conception of the whole of the capitalist world.

The difference of this category from mere abstractions (like 'furniture', 'courage', or 'sweetness') is of fundamental nature. The latter, of course, do not contain any 'wealth of the particular and the individual'—this 'wealth' is merely externally correlated with them as with general names. The concrete definitions of such concepts do not in any way express this wealth. The concept of furniture in general records merely the general element which a table has in common with a chair, a cupboard, etc. It does not contain specific characteristics of chair, table, or cupboard. Definitions of this kind do not express a single species. On the contrary, the category of value comprises in itself an exhaustive expression of such a *species* whose specificity lies in being simultaneously the genus.

That does not, of course, belittle the significance and cognitive role of elementary, 'intellectual' general abstractions. Their role is great: no concrete universal concept would be possible without them. They constitute the prerequisite and condition of the emergence of complex scientific concepts. A concrete universal concept is also an abstraction—in the sense that it does not record in its definitions the absolutely individual, the unique. It expresses the essense of the typical and in this sense of the general, mil-

[62] Ibid., pp. 360-61.

lion-fold repeated phenomenon, of an individual instance that is an expression of the universal law. In analysing the simple form of value, Marx is not interested, of course, in the individual features of a coat or linen. Nevertheless the relation of coat and linen is taken for the immediate object of analysis, and precisely for the reason that it is a typical (and in this sense general) case of simple commodity exchange, a case corresponding to the typical peculiarities of exchange without money. 'In a general analysis of this kind it is usually always assumed that the actual conditions correspond to their conception, or, what is the same, that actual conditions are represented only to the extent that they are typically of their own general case.'[63]

Of course, concrete universal concepts are for this reason similar to simple intellectual abstractions in that they always express a certain general nature of individual cases, things, phenomena, also being products of 'raising the individual to the universal'. This moment or aspect pointing to an affinity between a scientific concept and any elementary abstraction is certainly always present in the concept and is easy to discover in it. The point is, however, that this moment in no way gives a specific characterisation of the scientific concept, it does not express its specificity. That is precisely the reason why logical theories that simply equate such abstractions as value and whiteness, matter and furniture, on the grounds that both kinds equally refer to many individual phenomena rather than to a single individual one and are in this sense equally abstract and general, do not assert something absurd at all. Yet this conception, sufficient for simple abstractions, is quite inadequate for complex scientific ones. And if this is taken to be the essence of scientific concepts, this view becomes false, just as, for instance, the proposition 'value is the product of labour' is false. A concrete phenomenon is here characterised in a much too general and abstract way and therefore quite incorrectly. Of course, man is an animal, and a scientific concept is an abstraction. The inadequacy of such a definition, however, lies in its extreme abstractness.

Dialectical logic does not at all reject the truth of the proposition that a universal concept is an abstraction expressing the 'general nature', the 'mean type' of the sepa-

---

[63] Karl Marx, *Capital*, Vol. III, p. 143.

rate cases, individual things, phenomena, events, yet it goes further and deeper, and therein lies the difference between its conceptions and those of old logic. A dialectical conception of the universal assumes the transformation of the individual into the universal and of the universal into the individual, a transformation continually going on in any actual development.

It is easy to see, however, that this position presupposes a *historical view* of things, of the *objective reality* expressed in concepts. That is why neither Locke and Helvétius nor even Hegel could give a rational solution to the problem of the relation of the abstract to the concrete. Hegel was unable to offer such a solution, because the idea of development, the historical approach were only put fully into practice in his system with regard to thought but not to the objective reality itself constituting the subject-matter of thought. Objective reality develops in Hegel's view only inasmuch as it becomes the external form of the development of thought, of spirit, inasmuch as the spirit, imbuing it, quickens it from within, making it move and even develop. Objective sensual reality does not possess its own immanent spontaneous movement. Therefore in his eyes it is not genuinely concrete, for the living dialectical interconnection and interdependence of its different aspects belongs in fact to the spirit permeating it rather than to reality itself as such. Therefore in Hegel only the concept and nothing but the concept is concrete as the ideal principle of ideal interconnection of individual phenomena. Taken in themselves, individual things and phenomena are abstract and abstract only.

However, this conception contains not only idealism but also a dialectical view of cognition, of the process of apprehension of sensual data. Hegel calls an individual thing, phenomenon or fact abstract, and this usage is well founded: if consciousness has perceived an individual things as such, without grasping the whole *concrete chain of interconnections* within which the thing actually exists, that means it has perceived the thing in an extremely abstract way despite the fact that it has perceived it in direct concrete sensual observation, in all the fulness of its sensually tangible image.

On the contrary, when consciousness has perceived a thing in its *interconnections* with all the other, just as individual things, facts, phenomena, if it has grasped the individual through its universal interconnections, then it has for the first time perceived it concretely, even if a notion of it was formed not through direct contemplation, touching or smelling but rather through speech from other individuals and is consequently devoid of immediately sensual features.

In other words, already in Hegel abstractness and concreteness lose the meaning of immediate psychological characteristics of the form in which knowledge exists in an individual head, becoming logical (meaningful) characteristics of knowledge, of the content of consciousness.

If an individual thing is not understood through the universal concrete interconnection within which it actually emerged, exists, and develops, through the concrete system of interconnections that constitutes its genuine nature, that means that only abstract knowledge and consciousness have been obtained. If, on the other hand, an individual thing (phenomenon, fact, object, event) is understood in its objective links with other things forming an integral coherent system, that means that it has been understood, realised, cognised, conceived *concretely* in the strictest and fullest meaning of this word.

In the eyes of a materialist metaphysician, only the sensually perceived individual is concrete, while the universal is a synonym of the abstract. For a dialectical materialist things are quite different. From his viewpoint, concreteness is, first of all, precisely *the universal objective interconnection and interdependence of a mass of individual phenomena, 'unity in diversity', the unity of the distinct and the mutually opposed* rather than an abstract identity, the abstract dead unity. At best, the latter only indicates or hints at the possibility of the presence in things of internal links, of latent unity of phenomena, yet that is not always the case and by no means obligatory: a billiard ball and the Sirius are identical in their geometric form, but it would not do at all to look for any real interaction here, of course.

CONCRETE UNITY AS UNITY OF OPPOSITES

We have thus established that thinking in concepts is directed at revealing the living real unity of things, their *concrete connection of interaction* rather than at defining their abstract unity, dead identity.

The analysis of the category of interaction shows directly, however, that mere sameness, simple identity of two individual things is by no means an expression of the principle of their mutual connection.

In general, interaction proves to be strong if an object finds in another object a complement of itself, something that it is lacking as such.

'Sameness' is always assumed, of course, as the premise or condition under which the link of interconnection is established. But the very essence of interconnection is not realised through sameness. Two gears are locked exactly because the tooth of the pinion is placed opposite a space between two teeth of the drive gear rather than opposite the same kind of tooth.

When two chemical particles, previously apparently identical, are 'locked' into a molecule, the structure of each of them undergoes a certain change. Each of the two particles actually bound in the molecule has its own complement in the other one: at each moment they exchange the electrons of their outermost shell, this mutual exchange binding them into a single whole. Each of them gravitates towards the other, because at each given moment its electron (or electrons) is within the other particle, the very same electron which it lacks for this precise reason. Where such a continually arising and continually disappearing difference does not exist, no cohesion or interaction exists either; what we have is more or less accidental external contact.

If one were to take a hypothetical case, quite impossible in reality—two phenomena absolutely identical in all their characteristics—one would be hard put to it to imagine or conceive a strong bond or cohesion or interaction between them.

It is even more important to take this point into account when we are dealing with links between two (or more) developing phenomena involved in this process. Of course, two completely identical phenomena may very well coexist side by side and even come into certain contact. This contact, however, will not yield anything new at all until it elicits in each of them internal changes which will transform them into different and mutually opposed moments within a certain coherent whole.

Patriarchal subsistence households, each of which produces within itself everything that it needs, the same things that a neighbouring household produces, do not need one another. There are no strong links between them, for there is no division of labour, an organisation of labour under which one does something that someone else does not. Where differences arise between subsistence households, the possibility for mutual exchange of labour products also arises for the first time. The bond emerging here consolidates and further develops the difference and, along with it, the mutual connection. The development of differences between once identical (and precisely for this reason indifferently coexisting) households is the development of *mutual links* between them, it is the process of their transformation into distinct and opposed elements of a single economic whole, an integral producing organism.

In general, the development of forms of labour division is at the same time the development of forms of interaction between men in the production of material life. Where there is no division of labour, not in elementary form even, there is no society—there is only a herd bound by biological rather than social ties. Division of labour may take antagonistic class form and it may, on the other hand, take the form of comradely collaboration. Yet it always remains *division* of labour and can never be 'identification' of all forms of labour: communism assumes maximal development of each individual's capabilities both in spiritual and material production, rather than levelling of these abilities. Each individual here becomes a personality in the full and noble meaning of this concept exactly because every other individual interacting with him is also a unique creative individuality rather than a being performing the same stereotype, standardised, abstractly identical actions or operations. Such operations are in general moved outside the scope of human activity and handed over to machines. And exactly for this reason each individual here is needed by and of interest to others much more than in the world of capitalist division of labour. The social links binding personality to personality are here much more direct, comprehensive and strong than the links in commodity production.

That is why concreteness understood as an expression of living, factual, objective bond and interaction between real individual things, cannot be expressed as an abstract identity, bare equality, or pure similarity of things under consideration. Any instance of real interaction in nature, society, or consciousness, be it ever so elementary, necessarily contains identity of the distinct, a *unity of opposites*, rather than mere identity. Interaction assumes that one object realises its given specific nature only through its interrelation with another object and cannot exist outside this relation as such, as 'this one', as a specifically definite object.

To express the individual in thought, to *understand* the individual in its organic links with other instances of the individual and the concrete essence of their connection, one must not look for a naked abstraction, for an identical feature abstractly common to all of them taken separately.

Let us now take a more complex and at the same time more striking example. Wherein lies, for instance, the actual, living, concrete and objective bond between the capitalist and the wage workers, that 'general element' which each of these individual economic characters has in comparison with others? The fact that both of them are men, both of them need food, clothing, etc., both of them are capable of reasoning, talking, working? Undoubtedly they have all of these features. Moreover, all of this even constitutes the necessary *premise* of their bond as capitalist and wage worker, yet it in no wise constitutes the very essence of their relation *as capitalist and wage worker*. Their actual bond is founded on the fact that each of them has an economic trait that the other lacks, that their economic definitions are diametrically opposed. The point is that one of them possesses a feature that the other lacks, and he possesses it exactly because the other does not have it. Each mutually needs the other because of the diametrical opposition of their economic definitions. And that is exactly what makes them the necessary poles of an identical relation binding them stronger than anything they might have in common ('their sameness').

One individual thing is as it is, and not the other thing, exactly because the other is diametrically opposed to it in all characteristics. That is exactly why it cannot exist as such without the other, outside its connection with its own opposite. As long as a capitalist remains a capitalist and a wage worker, a wage worker, each of them necessarily reproduces in the other a diametrically opposed economic definiteness. One of them appears as a wage worker because the other is a capitalist vis-à-vis the former, the two economic figures having diametrically opposed traits.

That means that the essence of their bond *within the given concrete relationship* is based precisely on complete absence of a definition abstractly common to both.

A capitalist cannot, within this bond, have any traits that a wage worker possesses, and vice versa. And that means that none of them possesses an economic definition that would be simultaneously inherent in the other, that would be common to both. It is precisely this community that is lacking in their concrete economic bond.

It is a well-known fact that the banal apologists castigated by Marx insisted on looking for the basis of the mutual links between capitalist and worker in the community of their economic characteristics. From Marx's viewpoint, the really concrete unity of two or more interacting individual, particular things (phenomena, processes, men, etc.) always appears as the *unity of mutually exclusive* opposites. Between them, between aspects of this concrete interaction there is nothing abstractly identical or abstractly general and neither can there be.

In this case, the common as concretely general is exactly that very mutual bond between the elements of interaction as polar, mutually complementary, and mutually presupposing opposites. Each of the concretely interacting sides is what it is, that is, what it is in the context of a given concrete link, only through its relation to its own opposite.

The term 'common' does not coincide here in its meaning with 'identical' or 'the same'. Yet this usage, characteristic of dialectical logic, is by no means alien to the common usage and is based on a shade of meaning present in the word 'common'. Thus, in all languages an object in joint or collective possession is called 'common': e.g., one speaks of a 'common field', a 'common ancestor', and so on. The dialectical approach has always been based on this etymological shade of meaning. Here 'common' has the meaning of bond which by no means coincides in its content with the identical features of different correlated objects, men, and so on. The essence of the concrete bond between men jointly possessing a field is by no means contained in those identical traits they may have in common. What is common to them here is that particular object which each of them has outside them, confronting them, that object through relation to which the relation between them is established. The essence of their mutual bond is thereby given by a more general system of conditions, a system of interaction, within which they can play most diverse roles.

What does a reader have in common with the book which he reads, what is the essence of their mutual relation? Certainly the community does not lie in that both reader and book are three-dimensional, that both of them belong to spatially defined objects, that both consist of identical atoms, molecules, chemical elements, etc. That which is common to them does not consist in the identical properties of both. Quite the contrary: the reader is the reader exactly because he is confronted, as a condition without which he is not a reader, by that which is read, the reader's concrete opposite.

One exists as such, as a given concretely defined object, exactly because and only because it is confronted by something different as *concretely different from it*—an object whose definitions are all diametrically opposed to those of the former object. Definitions of one are inverted definitions of the other. That is the only way in which concrete unity of opposites, concrete community, is expressed in a concept.

The essence of concrete links (concrete community, concrete unity) is therefore determined not by looking for the identical traits abstractly inherent in each of the elements of such a community but by other means.

Analysis is in this case directed at the concrete system of conditions within which two elements, objects, phenomena, etc., emerge which simultaneously both mutually exclude one another and mutually assume one another. To establish the opposites whose mutual relations give existence to the interaction system in question, a given, concrete community, means to solve the task. Analysis of dialectical community therefore proves to be the study of the process that creates the two elements of interaction (e.g., capitalist and wage worker or reader and book) each of which cannot exist without the other because it has a characteristic which the other does not possess, and vice versa.

In this case, in each of the two interacting objects a definition will be discovered which is inherent in it as a member of the given, uniquely specific, concrete mode of interaction. Only in this case in each of the two related objects that aspect will be discovered (and singled out through abstraction) which makes this object into an element of the given concrete whole.

Concrete identity, identity of opposites—these are the dialectical formulas: identity of the different, the concrete unity of mutually excluding and therefore mutually assuming definitions. A thing has to be conceived as an element, as an individual expression of a universal (concrete universal) substance. That is the task of cognition.

This point of view explains, for instance, the difficulties which prevented Aristotle from discovering the essence, the substance of the exchange relation, the mystery of the equality of one house and five beds. The great dialectician of antiquity here, too, tried to find an *internal unity* of the two things rather than their *abstract identity*. Nothing could be easier than to find the latter, while discovering the former is quite hard.

In considering the exchange relation between a house and a bed, Aristotle came up against a task that was insoluble at the time, though not because he could not see anything that the two had in common. A brain much less sophisticated in logic will find abstract features common to both house and bed; Aristotle had plenty of words at his disposal to express something that a house and a bed had in common. Both house and bed are equally objects of everyday life, part of man's household environment, both are sensually perceived things existing in time and space, both have weight, form, hardness, etc., *ad infinitum*. It should be assumed that Aristotle would not have been too much surprised if someone drew his attention to the fact that both house and bed were equally made by the hands of man (or slave), that both were products of human labour.

So Aristotle's difficulty did not at all lie in finding an abstract general property common to both house and bed or in including both in a 'common genus' but rather in revealing the real substance in which they are equated irrespective of the will of the subject, of the abstraction-making head and of the purely artificial devices man invented for purposes of practical convenience. Aristotle gives up further analysis not because he cannot find anything that a house and a bed will have in common but rather because he cannot find an entity which necessarily *requires* the *fact of mutual exchange*, of mutual substitution of two different objects for its realisation or manifestation. Aristotle's inability to find something in common between two so different things reveals the *dialectical* strength and profundity of his thinking rather than a weakness of his logical abilities or lack of observation. Not satisfied by the abstract general, he attempts to discover the deeper roots of the fact. He is not interested merely in the proximate genus in which both may be included, if one so desires, but in the *real genus,* of which he has a much more meaningful conception than that for which the school tradition in logic has made him responsible.

Aristotle wants to find a reality that is only implemented as a property of a bed and a house due to the exchange relation between them, something general that requires *exchange* for its manifestation. However, all those common properties that he observes in them also exist when they have no reference to exchange and consequently do not form the specific essence of exchange. Aristotle thus towers head and shoulders above those theoreticians who, two thousands years after, saw the essence and substance of the value qualities of a thing in its utility. The utility of a thing is not at all necessarily connected with exchange, it does not obligatorily require exchange to be revealed.

In other words, Aristotle wants to find an essence which manifests itself only through exchange and is in no way manifested outside exchange though it constitutes the 'latent nature' of the thing. Marx showed clearly what precluded Aristotle's comprehending the essence of the exchange relation: the *absence of the value concept.* Aristotle could not understand or reveal the real essence, the real substance of the exchange properties of things as this substance is in fact social labour. The whole point is that the *concepts* of value and labour did not exist. Let us point out at the same time that a general abstract *notion* of both did exist at his time. 'Labour seems to be a very simple category. The notion of labour in this universal form, as labour in general, is also extremely old',[64] and Aristotle was certainly aware of it. Including both house and bed in the abstract notion of 'products of labour in general' would not have been an overly complicated and still less insoluble logical task for Aristotle.

[64] Karl Marx, *A Contribution to the Critique of Political Economy,* p. 209.

What Aristotle lacked was the *concept* of value. The word, the name that contained the simple abstraction of value did exist in his time, of course,* as in his time, too, there existed merchants who regarded all things from the abstract viewpoint of buying and selling.

But the *concept* of labour did not exist in that epoch. That merely shows, once again, that in Marx's terminology a concept is something different from an abstract general notion fixed in a term. What is it, then?

The concept of labour (as distinct from and opposed to an abstract general notion of it) assumes a realisation of the role of labour in the overall process of human life. In Aristotle's epoch, labour was not seen as a universal substance of all phenomena of social life, as the 'real essence' of all that was human, as the real source of all human qualities without exception.

The *concept* of a phenomenon exists, in general, only where this phenomenon is understood not abstractly (that is, not as a recurring phenomenon) but concretely, that is, in regard to its position and role in a definite system of interacting phenomena, in a system forming a certain coherent whole. A concept exists where the particular and the individual are realised as more than merely the individual and the particular (though recurrent)—they are realised through their mutual links, through the *universal* construed as an expression of the *principle* of these links.

Aristotle did not have such a conception of labour, for mankind had not yet worked out at that epoch any clear realisation of the role and place of labour in the system of social life. Moreover, Aristotle's contemporaries did not believe labour to be a form of life activity that might be included in the sphere of human life proper. He did not conceive labour as the real substance of all forms and modes of human life. Not surprisingly, he failed to understand it as the substance of the exchange properties of a thing. In Marx's terminology, that means precisely this, that he did not have a concept of labour and value but only an abstract notion of them. This abstract notion could not serve as the key to understanding the essence of commodity exchange.

The classic representatives of bourgeois economy were the first to perceive labour as the real substance of all forms

* The old Greek word αεια is a precise counterpart of the German *Wert*—'price, value, virtue'.

of economic life including, first and foremost, such a form as commodity exchange. That means that they were the first to form a concept of that reality of which Aristotle had only an abstract notion. The reason for that is not, of course, that English economists proved to be greater logicians than the Stagirite. The reason is that the economists studied this reality within a better developed social environment.

Marx showed clearly what was involved here: the object of study itself, in this case human society, matured to the degree that it was necessary and possible to study it in terms of concepts expressing the concrete substance of all its manifestations.

Labour as the universal substance, as an 'active form' appeared here, not only in consciousness but also in reality, as that 'proximate real genus' which Aristotle failed to see. The reduction of all phenomena to 'labour in general', to labour devoid of all qualitative differences, for the first time took place here in the reality of economic relations itself rather than in the abstract-making heads of theoreticians. Value became that *goal* for the sake of which each thing was realised in labour; it became an 'active form', a concrete universal law governing the destinies of each separate thing and each separate individual.

The point is that reduction to labour devoid of all differences appears here as an abstraction, but as a *real* abstraction 'which is made every day in the social process of production'.[65] As Marx puts it, this reduction is no more and no less of an abstraction than resolution of organic bodies into air. 'Labour, thus measured by time, does not seem, indeed, to be the labour of different persons, but on the contrary the different working individuals seem to be mere organs of this labour.'[66]

Here labour in general, labour as such appears as a concrete universal substance, and a single individual and the single product of his labour, as *manifestations of this universal essence.*

The concept of labour expresses something greater than merely the identical elements that can be abstracted from the labour activities of individual persons. It is a real uni-

---

[65] Karl Marx, *A Contribution to the Critique of Political Economy*, p. 30.
[66] Ibid.

versal law which dominates the individual and the particular, determines their destinies, controls them, makes them into its organs, forcing them to perform the given functions and not some others.

The particular and individual itself is formed in accordance with the requirements contained in this real universal, and the impression is that the individual in its particularity appears as the individual embodiment of the really universal. Distinctions between individuals themselves prove to be a form of manifestation of the universal rather than something standing side by side with the universal and having no relation to it.

A concept is a theoretical expression of this universal. Through the concept, every particular and individual element is apprehended precisely in those aspects which belong to the given whole, is an expression of the given concrete substance and is comprehended as an emerging and disappearing element of the movement of the concrete specific system of interaction. The substance itself, the concrete system of interacting phenomena is understood as a system that was historically formed.

A concept (as distinct from a general notion expressed in a word) does not merely equate one thing (object, phenomenon, event, fact, etc.) to another in the proximate genus, extinguishing in it all its specific differences, abstracting from them. Something quite different takes place in the concept: the individual object is reflected in its particular features which make it a necessary element of some whole, an individual (one-sided) expression of a concrete whole. Each separate element of any dialectically divided whole expresses, one-sidedly, the universal nature of this whole precisely in its difference from other elements rather than through abstract affinity to them.

The concept (in its strict and precise sense) is not therefore a monopoly of scientific theoretical thought. Every man has a concept, rather than a general notion expressed in a term, about such things as table or chair, knife or matches. Everybody understands quite well both the role of these things in our lives and the specific features owing to which they play a given role rather than some other one and occupy a given position, rather than some other one, in the system of conditions of social life in which they were made, in which they emerged. In this case the concept is present in the fulness of its definition, and every man consciously handles things in accordance with their concept, proving thereby that he has this concept.

Things like the atom or art are quite a different matter. Not every artist has a well-developed concept of art, by any means, although he may create magnificent works of art. The present author is not ashamed to admit that he has a rather vague notion of the atom, as compared to a physicist. But it is not every physicist that has a concept of the concept. A physicist who shuns philosophy is not likely to acquire it.

To avoid misunderstandings, we shall have to make the following qualification. In the present work thought is taken to mean first of all scientific theoretical thought, that is, thought operating in scientific theoretical study of the world. This restriction on the scope of the work does not at all mean that the so-called everyday thinking is not worthy of logic as science or that it develops according to different laws. The whole point is that scientific theoretical thought is the best developed form of thought. Its analysis therefore permits to establish, with greater facility, the laws which operate in thought in general. On the other hand, thought as it is practised everyday does not so easily lend itself to the discovery of these universal laws and forms of thought: they are always hidden from view by a mass of complications, of various factors and circumstances. The process of thinking is here often interrupted by interferences due to pure association or purely individual emotional motives; very often a number of links in the chain of reasoning is simply omitted, the gap being filled with an argument based on purely individual experiences crossing one's mind; no less frequently man orients himself in a situation, in his relation to another man or event with the aid of well-developed esthetic taste and perception, while reasoning in the strict sense plays an accessory or auxiliary role, etc., etc. For all these reasons everyday thinking is a very inconvenient object of logical analysis, a study aimed at establishing universal laws of thought in general. These laws operate here permanently, but it is much more difficult to study them in isolation from the effect of complicating circumstances than in the analysis of the scientific theoretical process. In the latter, the universal forms and laws of thought generally appear in much 'purer' aspect; here as everywhere the more developed form enables us to understand the less developed one in its genuine essence, the more so that the possibilities and prospects of development towards a higher and more advanced form can be taken into account.

Scientific theoretical thought is exactly in this kind of relation to everyday thinking: anatomy of man offers a key to the anatomy of ape, not vice versa, and 'rudiments of more advanced forms' may only be correctly understood when these more advanced forms are known by themselves. Proceeding from this general methodological assumption, we consider the laws and forms of thought in general mostly in regard to the way they appear in scientific theoretical thought. We thereby obtain the key to comprehending all other forms and applications of thought that are in a certain sense more complicated than scientific thought, than application of the ability to think to the solution of scientific theoretical problems, of clearly and strictly delineated problems. It stands to reason that the universal laws of thought are the same both in the scientific and so-called everyday thinking. But they are easier to discern in scientific thought for the same reason for which the universal laws of the development of the capitalist formation could be easier established, in mid-19th century, by the analysis of English capitalism rather than Russian or Italian.

Chapter 2

THE UNITY OF THE ABSTRACT AND THE CONCRETE AS A LAW OF THOUGHT

THE ABSTRACT AS AN EXPRESSION OF THE CONCRETE

We have thus established that knowledge reflecting an individual fact, though it may be a frequently recurring one, but failing to grasp its internal structure and internally necessary links with other such facts, is extremely abstract knowledge even if it is direct and sensually perceived. That is exactly why 'the general law of the change of form of motion is much more concrete than any single "concrete" example of it',[1] and even the most graphic examples cannot make a meagre thought poor in definitions into a concrete one.

Graphic examples illustrating a meagre abstraction can only camouflage its abstractness, creating merely an appearance or illusion of concrete consideration. Regrettably this procedure is often resorted to by persons who restrict theoretical consideration to amassing examples. The interpretation of concreteness as sensual tangibility of knowledge is naturally more convenient for them than Marx's definition, for the latter requires further analysis of facts.

Actually this position has nothing in common with that of Marx. To be more precise, there is something 'in common', of course—the words 'abstract' and 'concrete'. Yet these identical words cover up completely opposed concepts of the abstract and the concrete, an opposition of a genuine and imaginary comprehension of the role and place of both in thinking, in processing contemplation and notion.

Wherein lies, according to Marx, the really abstract consideration of the object? Abstractness as such is, in his

[1] Frederick Engels, *Dialectics of Nature,* Progress Publishers, Moscow, 1974, p. 222.

view, one-sidedness of cognition, the kind of knowledge of a thing which reflects only that aspect of it which is similar or identical in many other things of the same kind. An abstraction expressing the concrete specific nature of a thing is quite a different matter. In its logical characteristics, such an abstraction is something diametrically opposed to a simple abstraction, to the abstract as such.

What does it mean, to make a genuine generalisation, to create an objective concrete abstraction of a phenomenon?

It means considering a quite particular recurring fact with respect to its own immanent content, it means considering it 'in itself', as the familiar phrase has it, ignoring everything that this fact owes to the entire totality of the external influences of the broader sphere of reality in which it exists.

That is the path Marx follows in *Capital* in studying the phenomena of simple commodity exchange. He obtains the real objective characteristics of value 'abstractly considered, that is, apart from circumstances not immediately flowing from the laws of the simple circulation of commodities. . .'.[2]

Of paramount importance here is the fact that Marx from the very outset has in view *reproduction of the concrete in thought* as the overall objective in the light of which each separate logical procedure, each separate act of forming abstraction is measured. Each particular phenomenon is regarded in *Capital* directly with respect to its place and role in the whole, in the concrete system within which and through which it acquires its specific definiteness. Each concrete abstraction registers this definiteness, which is not characteristic of each separate phenomenon if it exists outside the given concrete system and is acquired by it as soon as it forms part of the system. In actual fact Marx considers the universal interconnection of the whole, that is, of the entire totality of the interacting particular phenomena, through abstract analysis of a particular phenomenon, consciously ignoring everything that the given phenomenon owes to other phenomena interacting with it.

At first sight, this appears to be paradoxical: the universal connectedness of phenomena is established through its opposite—a rigorous abstraction from everything that one

[2] Karl Marx, *Capital,* Vol. I, p. 156.

phenomenon possesses due to its universal interconnections with others, from everything that does not flow from the immanent laws of the given particular phenomenon.

The point is, however, that the very right to consider the given particular phenomenon *abstractly* presupposes comprehending its specific role and place in the whole, within the universal interconnection, within an ensemble of mutually conditioning particular phenomena; exactly the fact that simple commodity exchange, commodity and form of commodity are considered abstractly is the logical expression of the quite specific role played by commodity in the given and no other whole.

The fact that commodity is considered abstractly, independently from all the other phenomena of capitalist production, expresses logically (theoretically) its concrete historically unique form of dependence on the system of production relations as a whole.

The point is that the commodity form of connection proves to be the universal, elementary form of interconnections between men only within the developed system of capitalist production and in no other system of production relations. In no other concrete historical system of production relations, commodity and exchange of commodities have played, are playing or can play such a role.

This specific role and significance of the simple commodity form within developed capitalism is also theoretically expressed in the circumstance that the purely abstract consideration of commodity and its immanent laws reveals at the same time the *universal* theoretical definition of *the system as a whole*, an expression of its concrete universal regularity. Had any system of social production relations other than the capitalist one (socialism or feudalism, the primitive communal system or the slave-owning formation) been theoretically studied as the subject-matter, nothing would have been more erroneous, in Marxian logic, than to consider the commodity form abstractly, as it is considered in the economic theory of capitalism.

Abstract consideration of the commodity form would be useless for a theoretical understanding of the universal connection of a system if this system had developed from some other basis. In that case, in considering commodity in the abstract, thought will not make a single step forward in the concrete consideration of the economic system under study, will not abstract a single concrete theoretical definition of the object.

While the theoretician has not merely a right but even an obligation to consider the commodity form in abstraction within the capitalist system, he has no logical right to consider just as abstractly any other form of economic connection in the same capitalist organism, e.g., profit or rent.

Such an attempt will not result in working out a concrete theoretical understanding of the role and place of profit within the overall interconnection. This is in general impossible to do unless surplus-value, money and commodity have been first analysed. If we single out the phenomenon of profit at the outset, without previously analysing commodity, money, surplus-value, etc., and begin to consider it in the abstract, that is, leaving aside all the circumstances that do not flow from its immanent laws, we shall understand nothing in its motion. At best we shall obtain a description of the phenomena of profit motion, an abstract notion of them rather than a concrete theoretical concept.

Thus the right to abstract consideration of a phenomenon is determined by the concrete role of this phenomenon in the whole under study, in a concrete system of interacting phenomena. If the starting point of the development of a theory is taken correctly, its abstract consideration happens *to coincide directly* with a concrete consideration of the system as a whole. If abstract analysis deals with some phenomenon other than that which objectively constitutes the universal, simplest, elementary form of the being of the object as a whole, its real 'cell', then abstract consideration remains abstract in the bad sense of the word and does not coincide with the path of concrete cognition.

Taking the phenomena of profit, one may form an abstract generalised notion of them. But one cannot obtain a concrete concept of profit on this path, for a concrete conception of the place and role of profit in the motion of the system of capitalist relations assumes an understanding of their real proximate substance, surplus-value, that is, of a different economic phenomenon, and the latter in its turn presupposes cognition of the immanent laws of motion of the commodity-money sphere, an understanding of value as such, irrespective of profit or surplus-value. In other words, abstract consideration of profit is itself possible only when phenomena independent from it are previously analysed. Profit may be understood through surplus-value only, through 'something different', whereas surplus-value may and must be understood 'by itself', and in analysing it one should strictly leave aside all circumstances that do not directly follow from its immanent laws; first and foremost, one must leave alone profit. One cannot do anything of the kind in analysing profit, however, one cannot leave alone circumstances following from the immanent laws of a different phenomenon, one cannot consider profit abstractly.

Thus abstract consideration of a phenomenon comprises in itself a *concrete* approach to this phenomenon and directly expresses its role in the given concrete historical system of phenomena as a whole.

An abstract consideration of the subject, leaving aside all circumstances that do not follow directly from the immanent laws of the given phenomenon, concentrates on the immanent laws, on the analysis of the phenomenon 'in and for itself', to use a Hegelian phrase. Analysis of the laws of motion of the commodity-money sphere in Marx's *Capital* is a model of such study. The phenomenon is here considered 'by itself', in strict abstraction from all the influences of other, more complicated and developed phenomena connected, first of all, with the production of surplus-value. That also means that the phenomenon is considered abstractly.

This conception and application of abstract consideration is not metaphysically opposed to concrete consideration but rather a real coincidence of the abstract and the concrete, *their dialectical unity*. Concrete consideration appears as one where the circumstances that do not follow from the immanent laws of the given phenomenon are taken into account rather than left aside. Concrete understanding of the phenomena of the commodity-money sphere coincides with taking into account all those influences exerted upon it by all the developed and increasingly complicated forms of economic relations within capitalism.

In other words, a concrete conception of commodity that was originally considered only in the abstract, coincides with the theoretical understanding of the entire totality of the interacting forms of economic life, of the entire economic structure of capitalism. This conception is attained only in the overall system of the science, in the theory as a whole.

THE DIALECTICAL AND THE ECLECTIC-EMPIRICAL CONCEPTION OF COMPREHENSIVE CONSIDERATION

If we insist that the demand for comprehensive consideration of all facts, of all the elements of interaction alone can ensure genuinely concrete knowledge, that is only true on condition that the requirement of 'allround consideration' itself is interpreted dialectically. This point is important, because this requirement is most frequently and willingly exploited in the speculations within one of the antiscientific forms of thought—creeping empiricism posing as theoretical thought.

Lenin, a genius at applying revolutionary dialectics, many times warned, following Marx, against confusing the dialectical conception of concreteness with its eclectic parody, the more so that this confusion often acquired direct political meaning.

'In falsifying Marxism in opportunist fashion, the substitution of eclecticism for dialectics is the easiest way of deceiving the people. It gives an illusory satisfaction; it seems to take into account all sides of the process, all trends of development, all the conflicting influences, and so forth, whereas in reality it provides no integral and revolutionary conception of the process of social development at all.' [3]

These words clearly refer not only to social development but to any field of knowledge or activity, thereby containing a universal logical requirement.

One of the most widely used arguments of the enemies of scientific communism fighting against the theory of Marx, Engels, and Lenin, is accusation of this theory and the political line following from it, of 'stubborn one-sidedness', 'abstractedness', 'lack of flexibility', etc.

A characteristic example of eclectic falsification of dialectics is Bukharin's opportunist position in the discussion on the trade unions at the Tenth Congress of the Russian Communist Party (Bolsheviks). Assuming the posture of an arbiter in the controversy between the Party and the Trotsky group, Bukharin made an attempt at a philosophical sub-

---

[3] V. I. Lenin, The State and Revolution, *Collected Works,* Vol. 25, 1974, p. 405.

stantiation of his position. In his arguments against Bukharin's position, Lenin showed brilliantly the deep essence of the dialectical interpretation of the concreteness of the truth. This episode is very instructive for logic as a science.

Let us briefly recall the circumstances of this philosophical controversy. The debate concerned the principles of Party policy on trade unions. The Party's position on this point, recorded in a number of documents, was as follows: Soviet trade unions are a 'school of communism'. This short formula assumed that trade unions by their place and role in the system of the proletarian dictatorship, are a mass organisation whose goal is the education and enlightenment of the masses in the spirit of communism, and preparation of the masses for conscious participation in the management of the national economy. This conception was opposed by Trotsky, who formulated his own platform, regarding trade unions, first and foremost, as an 'administrative technical apparatus for production control'. That was a conflict of two clearcut positions, two political lines—the Leninist policy of the Party and the leftist policy of Trotskyism, the notorious policy of 'tightening the nuts'.

In this situation Bukharin made an excursion into the field of philosophy trying to find in it a substantiation of his political position, a position that allegedly reconciled the opposing extremes.

The formula of the Leninist Party defined trade unions as 'the school of communism', Trotsky's formula, as 'administrative technical apparatus of control', while Bukharin reasoned thus:

'I see no logical grounds for proof that either proposition is wrong; both, and a combination of both, are right.'

Lenin sharply condemned this 'logical' argument: 'When Comrade Bukharin speaks of "logical" grounds, his whole reasoning shows that he takes—unconsciously, perhaps—the standpoint of formal or scholastic logic, and not of dialectical or Marxist logic.'[4]

Taking up the elementary example used by Bukharin during the polemics, Lenin gave a brilliant demonstration

---

[4] V. I. Lenin, Once Again on the Trade Unions, the Current Situation and the Mistakes of Trotsky and Bukharin, *Collected Works*, Vol. 32, 1965, pp. 92-93.

of the difference between the dialectical interpretation of 'comprehensive consideration' and its eclectic variant.

A 'logical argument' of the 'on-the-one-hand, on-the-other-hand' type, an argument more or less accidentally isolating various aspects of the objects and placing them in more or less accidental connection, was rightly ridiculed by Lenin as argument in the spirit of scholastic formal logic.

'A tumbler is assuredly both a glass cylinder and a drinking vessel. But there are more than these two properties, qualities or facets to it; there are an infinite number of them, an infinite number of "mediacies" and inter-relationships with the rest of the world. A tumbler is a heavy object which can be used as a missile; it can serve as a paper-weight, a receptacle for a captive butterfly, or a valuable object with an artistic engraving or design, and this has nothing at all to do with whether or not it can be used for drinking, is made of glass, is cylindrical or not quite, and so on and so forth.'[5]

Reasoning gliding from one abstract one-sided definition of the object to another, just as abstract and one-sided, is endless and does not lead to anything definite. If the Party reasoned about trade unions according to this principle, there could be no hope for any principled, scientifically worked-out political line. It would have been tantamount to a complete rejection of a theoretical attitude to things in general.

The position of the Party, clearly expressed by Lenin, in no way rejects the fact that under different social conditions and at different stages in the development of society, trade unions can play different roles and be used for different purposes, and that the forms of their organisation and methods of work may vary accordingly.

But a concrete formulation of the problem proceeding from a realisation of the role which trade unions play or may play objectively, irrespective of someone's desires or aspirations, in the system of the organs of proletarian dictatorship during the transition from capitalism to socialism, leads to the conclusion that trade unions are not one thing, on the one hand, and another thing, on the other, but, *looked at from all sides, are a school of communism and a school of communism only*, a school of unity, a school of so-

[5] V. I. Lenin, op. cit., p. 93.

lidarity, a school of the defence of the proletariat's interests by the proletariat itself, a school of management and administration.[6]

Lenin stresses this point particularly, pointing out that in the polemics against the erroneous platform propounded by Trotsky, trade unions have to be regarded as a school and in no other way. For that is their only objective role, their goal prompted by their position in the system of proletarian dictatorship.

If anyone should use a tumbler not the way it ought to be used—say, as a missile rather than a drinking vessel, there is no great harm in that. But when such an 'object' as trade unions is involved, the whole thing may end in a disaster. That was why the RCP(B) reacted so strongly to Trotsky's platform according to which trade unions are an 'administrative technical apparatus for production control', and to Bukharin's attempt to justify this interpretation as a 'one-sided' one.

Lenin stands by the view that this platform cannot be accepted either as an exhaustive definition or as an abstract one-sided definition of the essence of trade unions.

The concrete historical role, purpose, and place of trade unions in the system of organs of proletarian dictatorship are only expressed in the Party position: Soviet trade unions, any way you look at them, are a *school*. All other definitions are derivative from this basic, principal, and determining one. This definition expresses the specific nature of trade unions, the reason why they can play their role as an organ of proletarian dictatorship side by side with the Party and state and in close cooperation with them.

That was why Lenin, continuing the ironic analogy with the tumbler, defines Trotsky's position as that of a man who wants to use the tumbler for its real purpose, as an instrument for drinking, but wishes that it should have no bottom. While regarding Soviet trade unions as an instrument of proletarian dictatorship, Trotsky rejects precisely that which enables them to play their specific and necessary role distinct from the role of the state. 'His (Trotsky's) platform says that a tumbler is a drinking vessel, but this particular tumbler happens to have no bottom.'[7]

---

[6] Ibid., p. 96.
[7] Ibid., p. 100.

As for Bukharin's position, Lenin describes it as dead and meaningless eclecticism, that is, senseless enumeration of one abstract definition of the object after another, an enumeration that does not stop at anything concrete and does not lead anywhere, merely disconcerting the Party.

To both these platforms Lenin opposes a clear, principled, and concrete position of the Party: Soviet trade unions are an instrument of communist education of the broad working masses, a school of communist unity, solidarity, defence of the interests of the proletariat from the bureaucratic elements in the state organs, a school of management and administration, it is an instrument for transforming the working people into conscious builders of communism.

This concrete definition expresses an objective role of trade unions in the system of organisations implementing the socialist transformation of society, that is, their essence and nature independent of someone's caprice or subjective goals.

Eclecticism, which has always served as the methodology of opportunism and revisionism, prides itself on its love for all-sided approaches. An eclectic will willingly hold forth on the 'harm of any one-sidedness' and on the need to take into account a thousand and one things. In his hands, however, the requirement for all-sided consideration becomes an instrument of fighting dialectics and the principle of concreteness in its real meaning.

The way to a concrete theoretical conception is here replaced by endless wandering from one abstraction to another in no way different from the first. Instead of ascending from the abstract to the concrete, an eclectic will move from the abstract to something just as abstract. And his occupation is just as easy as it is fruitless.

It is easy because even the smallest and most insignificant object indeed possesses an actually infinite number of aspects and links with the surrounding world. Each drop of water reflects the entire richness of the universe. Even apparently unconnected phenomena worlds apart will, through a billion intermediate links, prove to have something in common; even Napoleon's cold in the head was a factor in the Battle of Borodino. If one interprets the requirement of concrete analysis as a demand for taking into account absolutely all, without exception, empirical details, facts and circumstances connected in some way or other with the object under study, the concreteness (just as any metaphysically interpreted category) will prove to be a mere naked abstraction, a kind of unattainable ideal existing merely in imagination but never realised in actual knowledge. The theoretician professing this conception of concreteness finds himself in the position of the Maeterlinck's hero pursuing the Blue Bird, which ceases to be blue the moment he touches it.

Here, in the problem of the relation of the abstract to the concrete, metaphysics proves to be that bridge by which thought inevitably arrives at agnosticism and in the final analysis at liquidation of theory as such, at the view that theory is forever doomed to move in the sphere of more or less subjective abstractions, never grasping objective concreteness.

The metaphysical interpretation of concreteness as taking into account absolutely all available circumstances, inevitably makes the person professing it extremely susceptible to the arguments of subjective idealists and agnostics.

The argument 'from the infinite complexity and confusion' of the world is probably worked harder than any other argument by contemporary bourgeois philosophers in their struggle against the Marxist-Leninist theory of social development. Karl Jaspers, the existentialist, frankly begins his attack on Marxism with the statement that Marx's whole theory is based on the belief in the one and only and is in nature of a total outlook. This belief in the ability of thought to grasp the object in the entirety of all its necessary aspects and to perceive it as 'unity in diversity' is, according to Jaspers, an obsolete philosophical prejudice given up by 'modern science'. 'The real modern science ... as opposed to the Marxist science of the integral, is particularist,'[8] says Jaspers; it has long given up its pride, being modestly content with 'particulars'. 'Unity of knowledge' is an unattainable ideal or myth, according to Jaspers.

Jaspers expresses rather openly the cause of his dislike for 'Marx's total view'. He resents 'the unity of theory' and 'the unity of theory and practice', namely the practice of communist transformation of the world: 'And this policy be-

---

[8] Karl Jaspers, *Vernunft und Widervernunft in unserer Zeit,* Piper, München, 1950, S. 13, 14.

lieves in its ability, based on this understanding, to do what no previous policy was able to do. Having a total view of the past, it can make total plans and realise them.'[9]

Henri Niel, a French supporter of Jaspers, echoes the latter's views. He rejects the dialectical materialist conception of concreteness for the same reasons, writing that whether in Hegelian or Marxist form, dialectics is based on man's ability to grasp mentally the totality of existence and therefore inevitably becomes a religion of the plan.[10]

Existentialists believe that the form of knowledge was borrowed from Hegel and applied, by a *tour de force,* to the specificially modern content.

In actual fact, Marx's and Lenin's conception of concreteness of theory is hostile and alien to any 'superimposition of the form of knowledge' upon its material, upon the real diversity of phenomena.

To think concretely means 'to build a reliable foundation of precise and indisputable facts that can be confronted to any of the "general" or "example-based" arguments now so grossly misused in certain countries'.[11]

Precisely established and indisputable facts in their proper total interconnection, facts taken as a whole, as concretely and historically conditioned—that is what Lenin insists on, first of all, in expounding the Marxist principle of 'concreteness of thought'. The whole point of the principle is that 'we must take not individual facts, but the *sum total* of facts, without *a single* exception, relating to the question under discussion'.[12]

That is the principle attacked by Jaspers as he makes a virtue of the 'particularism' allegedly inherent in modern science, that is, of that very trick of arbitrarily isolating facts from their objective interconnection to be further interpreted outside their connection, outside a whole, outside their interdependence, which is extremely characteristic of bourgeois thinking in these days.

Here is another tirade of the same sort. 'Reality is very confused. But neither thought nor experience are in a posi-

---

[9] Karl Jaspers, op. cit., S. 15.

[10] See Henri Niel, *La dialectique de Hegel et la dialectique marxiste,* Paris, 1956, p. 235.

[11] V. I. Lenin, Statistics and Sociology, *Collected Works,* Vol. 23, 1964, p. 272.

[12] Ibid.

tion to present reality in its unity and entirety. We cannot conceive reality or grasp it empirically; we can only experience it in its entirety.'[13]

As for cognition, the reasoning is as follows: 'Any mental cognition of infinite reality by the finite human spirit is founded on the silent assumption that each time only a finite part of the same can be the subject of scientific perception and that this is the only "essential" part in the sense that is worth knowing.'[14] The question of what we should be interested in and what we may neglect, what is 'worth knowing' and what is not, 'is a question of value and can only be solved on the basis of subjective assessments'.[15]

In other words, and objectively (i.e. on an objective basis) circumscribed whole can never form the subject-matter of science—only a particular area of facts whose boundaries any scientist is free to draw anywhere he likes.

'Choice is always of necessity subjective. Making choices is the business of each individual man of science. No one can prescribe or even advise him, for choice is always linked with value. But one cannot prove values.'[16]

When it is a question of the subject-matter of political economy, this view comes to mean the following: the subject-matter of political economy is 'the field of interest of all those who designate themselves as economists or of those who are called so by others'.[17] The subject-matter of political economy thus comprises everything that is so referred to by 'all educated persons'. 'The unity of the object ... is not the logical structure of problems...; it is the conceptual connections of the problems that constitute the working area of a science.'[18]

These arguments are taken from the works of most diverse authors—contemporary bourgeois economists, existen-

---

[13] Francesco Vito, Bemerkungen über grundlegende Fragen der Wirtschaftstheorie, *Jahrbücher für Nationalökonomie und Statistik,* Bd. 153, Heft 3/4, Verlag von Gustav Fischer, Jena, 1941, S. 332.

[14] Max Weber, *Gesammelte Aufsätze zur Wissenschaftslehre,* Mohr, Tübingen, 1951, S. 171.

[15] Max Weber, *Gesammelte Aufsätze zur Soziologie und Sozialpolitik,* Mohr, Tübingen, 1924, S. 420.

[16] Helmut Tagwerker, *Beiträge zur Methode und Erkenntnis in der theoretischen Nationalökonomie,* Notring der wissenschaftlichen Verbände Österreich, Wien, 1957, S. 43.

[17] Ibid., S. 26.

[18] Ibid., S. 28.

tialist philosophers, neopositivists, and representatives of the 'sociology of knowledge'. They differ in many respects, yet they form a united front against the materialist conception of 'concreteness of knowledge'. The line of reasoning is everywhere the same: since no single whole can be grasped by thought because of its infinite complexity, one must be satisfied with 'particularist knowledge', with more or less arbitrarily selected groups of facts.

'The most widely used, and most fallacious, method in the realm of social phenomena is to tear out *individual* minor facts and juggle with examples,'[19] wrote Lenin. Contemporary bourgeois philosophy makes a virtue of this sharp practice. It is of course much easier to select examples and minor facts to suit a previously chosen and completely unproven proposition concerning 'values' than to study facts with the same thoroughness as Marx did in collecting materials for *Capital* in the space of more than 25 years. But science cannot be guided by the principle of 'ease' or 'economy of mental effort'. Science is hard work. And its highest principle is the principle of concreteness of knowledge and truth.

SPIRAL-LIKE CHARACTER OF DEVELOPMENT OF REALITY AND ITS THEORETICAL REFLECTION

Thus materialist dialectics interprets concreteness of theory as a reflection of *all the necessary aspects* of the object in their mutual conditionality and *internal interaction.*

The mutual nature of conditioning typical of any dialectically divided whole imposes stringent demands on theory and at the same time gives theoreticians a clear criterion for singling out only internally necessary definitions from the sensually given multiformity.

In a more immediate sense that signifies that each of the concrete abstractions (whose totality constitutes a theory) reflects only that form of the existence of an object which is at the same time a universal necessary *condition* of all the others and just as universal and necessary *consequence* of their interaction.

---

[19] V. I. Lenin, Statistics and Sociology, *Collected Works*, Vol. 23, p. 272.

This condition is satisfied, for example, by the earlier analysed definition of man as a being producing implements of labour. Production of labour implements, production of means of production, is not only a universal (both logically and historically) *prerequisite* of all the other forms of human life activity but also a continually reproduced *result* or *consequence* of the social development as a whole.

At each moment in its development mankind is necessarily compelled to reproduce, that is, posit as its product, its own universal basis, the universal condition of the existence of the social human organism as a whole.

Today, the production of labour implements, that have developed into fantastically complex machines and assemblies of machines remains, on the one hand, a universal objective basis of the rest of human development, just as at the dawn of mankind. But, on the other hand, it essentially depends on the level of development of science, its own remote offspring, on its own consequence, and the dependence is so strong that machines may be regarded (within a materialist framework) as *'organs of the human brain created by man's hand'*.[20] In like manner, commodities, money, 'free' labour force—all of these are no less products of capital, consequences of its specific movement, than they are its historical premises, the conditions of its emergence. And these are the kind of products which capital reproduces on an ever increasing scale inconceivable before its emergence.

This dialectics of all real development, in which the universal necessary condition of the emergence of an object becomes its own universal and necessary consequence, this dialectical inversion in which the condition becomes the conditioned, the cause becomes the effect, the universal becomes the particular, is a characteristic feature of internal interaction through which actual development assumes the form of a circle or, to be more precise, of a spiral which extends the scope of its motion all the time, with each new turn.

At the same time there is a kind of 'locking in itself' here which transforms an aggregate of individual phenomena into a relatively closed system, a concrete integral organ-

---

[20] K. Marx, *Grundrisse der Kritik der politischen Ökonomie (Rohentwurf). 1857-1858,* Verlag für fremdsprachige Literatur, Moskau, 1939, S. 594.

ism historically developing according to its immanent laws.

Marx resolutely emphasised this nature of interaction within the system of capitalist production: 'If in a developed bourgeois system ... anything that is *posited* is at the same time a *premise, the same thing takes place in any organic system.*'[21] The words italicised in the above directly express the fact that the 'circular' nature of interaction is by no means a specific law of the existence and development of capitalism but rather a *universal law* of dialectical development, a law of dialectics. That is exactly the law that underlies the logical law of coincidence of the abstract and the concrete and the dialectical materialist conception of theoretical concreteness.

However, the same law of spiral-like development of a system of interacting phenomena poses some specific difficulties for thought—difficulties that are not to be overcome without the dialectical method in general and without a clear conception of the dialectics of the abstract and the concrete in particular.

Bourgeois economists, as they came up in their studies against this circumstance, the spiral-like nature of the mutual conditioning of the diverse forms of bourgeois wealth, inevitably lapsed into circularity in defining the most important categories. Marx discovered this hopeless circularity already in his first attempt at an analysis of English economic theories in 1844. In analysing Say's argumentation he discovers that the latter, just as other economists, everywhere substitutes the concept of value for an explanation of phenomena which are themselves silently assumed in explaining value, e.g., the concepts of 'wealth', 'division of labour', 'capital', etc.

'Wealth. Here the concept of *value*, which has not yet been developed, is already assumed; for wealth is defined as "the sum total of values", "sum total of valuable things" that one possesses.'[22]

Fifteen years later, returning to this point, Marx reveals the mystery of this hopeless logical circle: 'In theory, the value concept precedes the concept of capital but, on the

---

[21] K. Marx, op. cit., S. 189 (italics ours—*E. I.*).

[22] K. Marx, F. Engels, *Historisch-kritische Gesamtausgabe (MEGA)*, 1. Abt., Bd. 3, Marx-Engels-Verlag GMBH, Berlin, 1932, S. 449.

other hand, assumes a mode of production based on capital as a condition of its pure development, and the same thing happens in practice. Therefore, inevitably, economists now regard capital as creator of values, their source, and now assume values as premises for the formation of capital, representing capital itself as a sum total of values in a certain function.'[23]

This logical circularity in definitions inevitably happens for the reason that any object is in fact a product of dialectical development, owing to which the reality studied by science always appears as a system of *mutually conditioning* aspects, as a historically emerging and developing concreteness.

Assuming indeed both money and value as *premises* for its emergence, capital at its birth immediately transforms them into universal forms of its own movement, into abstract moments of its specific being. As a result, it emerges before the observer contemplating a historically established relation as the creator of value. The difficulty here lies in that it is only the emergence of capital that transforms value into a *real universal* economic form of all production, of the entire system of economic relations. Before that, before the emergence of capital, value is anything but the *universal* economic relation if only because it does not comprise such a significant 'particular' factor of production as labour force.

It is impossible to break up the logical circularity in the definition of value and capital by any sophisticated logical procedures or semantic manipulations with concepts and their definitions, for the circularity arises not from a fault in the definitions of concepts but from a failure to understand the dialectical nature of interaction between them, from a failure to implement a genuinely historical approach to the study of this interaction. It is only a historical approach that enables one to find a way out of the vicious circle, or rather a way into it. Insofar as bourgeois economists are alien to such an approach, the circularity is hopeless for them.

The failure of such attempts is determined by the inability to grasp concreteness as a historically developed system of internally interacting phenomena which undergoes fur-

[23] K. Marx, *Grundrisse der Kritik der politischen Ökonomie, (Rohentwurf). 1857-1858*, S. 163.

ther development, as a historically evolving 'unity in diversity'. But it was exactly this dialectical conception of concreteness that gave Marx a methodological key to the solution of the basic theoretical problems of political economy; in particular, it explains the fact that it was Marx who revealed the mystery of the fetishism of commodities. The concreteness of the capitalist world comprises only those objective forms of motion which this world assumes as its prerequisites and, moreover, reproduces as its specific *product*, positing them as *its consequence*.

The sun, commodities, natural resources, money, free labour force, availability of machines—all of these are equally objective premises and conditions in the absence of which capital can neither emerge nor exist. But neither the natural circumstances of its origin, nor the technical parameters of machines, nor man's anthropological features, and his ability to work, form the universal and necessary immanent forms of the existence of capital.

Marx's analysis singles out, as the concrete theoretical characteristics, only those universal and necessary conditions of the being of capital which are reproduced by the movement of capital itself. Capitalism does not reproduce labour force as such or natural resources and other material components but rather labour force as *commodity*, that is, as that social form in which labour force functions within the developed system of capitalist relations.

Labour force as such, as a sum total of psychological or physiological abilities, is produced and reproduced by other process or processes. Capitalism does not produce it, just as it does not produce sunlight or natural resources or air, etc., but it does produce those social forms within which and through which all these things are involved in its specific movement and move within its organism as its forms.

The criterion Marx applied here for distinguishing immanent forms of the object's motion is essentially a universal, logical criterion. That means that any individual object, thing, phenomenon, or fact is given a certain concrete form of its existence by the concrete process in the movement of which it happens to be involved; any individual object owes any concrete form of its existence to the concrete historically established system of things within which it emerged and of which it forms a part, rather than to itself, its own self-contained individual nature.

Gold taken by itself is not money. It becomes money in the circulation of money and commodities in which it is involved. 'A chair with four legs and a velvet canopy is, under certain circumstances, a *throne*; therefore this chair, a thing that serves as a seat, is not a throne through the nature of its use-value',[24] that is to say, by its immanent nature, 'in and for itself', taken in abstraction from those specific conditions which alone make it a throne, it is not a throne at all.

It thus becomes apparent what enormous significance the dialectical conception of the concreteness of theoretical abstractions had for the overcoming of naturalist fetishist illusions veiling the nature of value as well as of all its derivative forms including interest, rent, etc.

In its nature, gold is no more money than coal is fuel for a locomotive, the moon a protectress of lovers, and man is slave or patrician, proletarian or bourgeois, philosopher or mathematician.

There is a fine point here, however, that dialectics has to take into account. Gold, coal, and man in themselves have to possess certain features and qualities owing to which the process wherein they are involved can transform them into forms of its own movement, of its existence.

It is gold rather than clay or bits of granite that proves to be the natural material in which the universal form of value is realised. Here the natural physical-chemical qualities do play a role. But these natural properties are of no consequence when we are dealing with the *essence*, the *nature* of the money form of value as such. This form develops in commodity circulation irrespective of the natural properties of gold. It is the sphere of circulation that develops the 'pure economic form' which later 'finds' the most flexible material for its implementation appropriate for its aims. As soon as gold proves to be an insufficiently flexible and plastic means or substance for expressing newly developing traits of the money form, it is replaced by paper, bank-notes, written-order clearing, etc.

This discussion shows what objective reality was mystified by the Aristotelian (and later Hegelian) dialectics in the shape of the teaching of entelechy, of the 'pure form' exist-

---

[24] *Arkhiv Marksa i Engelsa* (Marx and Engels' Archives), Vol. II (VII), Moscow, 1933, p. 46.

ing outside and independent of 'matter' in which it is subsequently embodied, and which it moulds after its own fashion, in accordance with the requirements contained in it. That is the *real objective concreteness as a system of interacting things* where the individual thing, once it gets into the system, conforms to its requirements and acquires a form of existence previously unknown to it.

The dialectical materialist conception of concreteness thereby destroyed the last refuge of intelligent, dialectical idealism, as it gave a rational solution to the mystery of entelechy, the mystery of the universal as the 'goal cause', as 'pure form' developing outside and independently of the world of individual things and subordinating these things to its specific motion.

Reality which is expressed in an idealist and mystified manner in the notion of concept as a goal cause, as an active form, is nothing but real objective concreteness, that is a historically emerging and developing system of mutually conditioning phenomena, a complex dialectically divided whole which includes each individual thing and conditions the concrete nature and form of the things.

The materialistically interpreted category of reciprocal action reveals the mystery of the 'goal cause': 'reciprocal action is the true *causa finalis* of things',[25] is the way Engels formulates this proposition.

The above requires an essential qualification. Each science obviously reflects in its categories only specific forms and laws of a concrete system of interacting phenomena constituting its special subject-matter, making abstraction from everything else, despite the fact that without this 'everything else' its subject-matter is impossible and inconceivable.

For example, political economy reveals in a systematic form the concrete totality of social production relations between men, leaving aside the technological aspects of communication and the biological relations between individuals, despite the fact that men do not and cannot exist without either.

It is quite apparent that all those changes which take place within the system of production relations, the entire evolution of the system of production relations and forms

[25] Frederick Engels, *Dialectics of Nature*, p. 231.

of economic connection depend in actual fact on the development of man's productive force and, moreover, are determined by this development.

Nevertheless Marx considers in *Capital* the system of capitalist relations as a 'self-developing system', as a concreteness closed in itself, of which the motive forces of development lie within itself, in its internal contradictions, in the immanent contradictions of the economic form. But, strictly speaking, the actual motive forces of the evolution of a system of production relations are not contained within the system itself but rather in the development of productive forces. Unless the productive forces develop, no 'internal' dialectics of the system of economic relations will produce an evolution. However, Marx studies the mode of production as a whole and therefore registers a dialectical mutual conditioning of the productive forces and production relations. The development of productive forces is here taken not by itself, not only as a cause, but also as a consequence, result, and product of the reverse action of the system of production relations on the productive forces.

For instance, *Capital* shows the mechanism owing to which the emergence of the economic form of relative surplus-value causes a growth in labour productivity inducing the capitalist to replace manual labour by machine labour and to develop the technical basis of the production of surplus-value.

It is clear, however (and it is shown by Marx himself), that in actual fact it is the appearance of machines that is the real cause of the absolute form of surplus-value being ousted out by its relative form.

Relative surplus-value clearly becomes the dominant form of surplus-value exactly for the reason that it is in better conformity with machine labour than absolute surplus-value, which is increased by a simple lengthening of the working day, labour productivity remaining unaltered.

The whole point is, however, that the correspondence itself between the economic form of a stage in the development of a productive force is, in its turn, a dialectical correspondence. Relative surplus-value conforms to machine production exactly because it does not remain a passive form within which machines work but rather becomes an *active form* exerting a very strong reverse effect on machine production, that is, on its own basis that gave rise to it, developing this basis and thereby creating a new incentive for its own movement.

Here, the transformation of cause into effect takes place that is characteristic of any real development. This circumstance is extremely important for understanding the paths chosen by Marx in his research.

Marx considered the evolution of the system of production relations based on wage labour. He was mostly concerned with those changes that take place within the system of production relations, within the economic structure of society. As for the development of productive forces as such, independent from any form of production relations, it is not considered in *Capital*. That is the subject-matter of another science, the science of technology.

Marx takes as given the fact that the productive forces as such develop independently from a certain concrete historical form of relations between men, assuming it to be a fact that is not to be studied specially within political economy.

Does that mean that the development of production relations is in general considered by him as unrelated to the development of productive forces? On the contrary. Actually, exactly those changes are considered within the system of economic relations that are caused by the development of productive forces. Moreover, precisely because political economy does not consider the development of productive forces *in itself* (*'an und für sich'*, *'an sich'*, *'für sich'*), the effect of this development on the system of economic forms, its interaction with the latter is conceived in a concrete historical manner, that is, exactly in that form in which this effect works in the world of private capitalist ownership.

The nature of a change introduced by a new accretion of the productive forces to the system of production relations entirely depends on the specific features of the system in which this change is introduced.

Any new accretion of the productive forces does not automatically create an economic relation or socio-economic form directly conforming to it, but rather determines the *direction* in which the already existing historically formed system of economic relations evolves. The situation is not affected by the fact that the earlier formed system of economic relations is in its turn, from beginning to end, a product of the entire preceding development of the productive forces.

A concrete historically formed system of economy is always a relatively independent organism producing a reverse effect on its own basis—the sum total of productive forces, and refracting any effect of the latter through its own specific nature. The totality of economic forms woven into a single system developing out of an identical basis, constitutes the specific nature of an economic organism which thereby acquires a relative independence with regard to the productive forces themselves.

Political economy as a special science has for its subject-matter exactly those forms which express the relative independence of the system of production relations. The determining effect of productive forces on production relations is revealed in a concrete historical manner precisely because the development of productive forces as such is not considered; what is considered is only the internal logic of the evolution of the system of production relations, the internal logic of the formation and development of this system. Thereby the process in which productive forces create appropriate production relations is traced quite *concretely*. Otherwise the study would remain abstract verbiage.

All of this has a bearing not only on political economy but on any theoretical science. Every science is required to develop a systematic conception of precisely those forms of the existence of an object which express its relative independence, rather than of those abstract features it has in common with others.

The productive forces do not create anything each time anew from scratch (this is an actual possibility only at the dawn of human development); they determine the type and character of changes taking place within an already established system of production relations. The situation is the same in the development of all forms of spiritual culture, law, political institutions, philosophy, and art.

'Here economy creates nothing anew, but it determines the way in which the body of thought found in existence is altered and further developed, and that too for the most part indirectly,' [26] stressed Engels, considering this point to

[26] Frederick Engels to Conrad Schmidt in Berlin, London, October 27, 1890, K. Marx, F. Engels, *Selected Correspondence,* Progress Publishers, Moscow, 1975, p. 401.

be a most important trait distinguishing the theory of historical materialism from the abstract deliberation of vulgar economists who reduced the entire concrete complexity of the actual process of spiritual development to the abstract insistence on the primacy of economy and the derived nature of everything else.

Thus historical materialism fully takes into account the fact that economy always prevails 'within the terms laid down by the particular sphere itself', [27] that is, one and the same economic shift produces a certain effect in the sphere of art and quite a different one, unlike the former, in the sphere of law, and so on.

The difficulty is never in reducing a certain phenomenon in the sphere of law or art to its economic cause. That is not so difficult to do. But that is not historical materialism. In general, Marxist philosophy takes the standpoint of deduction rather than reduction, requiring that in each concrete case it should be understood why the given shift in the economy was reflected in politics or art in the given rather than some other way.

This task assumes, however, a theoretical understanding of the specific nature in which the economic shift is reflected and transformed. Each of the superstructural spheres of the activity of social man must be understood and explained as a system of historically established concrete forms, specific for this sphere, of reflecting economy, man's social being.

All the philosophical and logical principles applied by Marx to the study of the system of capitalist relations as a historically established system of interaction, are applicable to any natural or social science.

Let us consider only one example—the origin of legal norms. A necessary and universal condition for the emergence of any legal norm is the 'factual relation', a term applied by jurists to a non-legal, purely economic fact. This fact, taken by itself, is outside the competence of a law scholar, referring to the sphere of political economy.

The point is, however, that it is not any economic relation, any 'factual relation' that engenders an appropriate legal norm, but only one which objectively needs legal protection, that is, requires a forcible subjugation of the

---

[27] Ibid.

will of individuals. In other words, only that economic relation needs protection which, with the aid of a legal norm, is later asserted as the *result of the action of law.* Under communism, for instance, the need for law and for a system of legal norms itself will wither away exactly because the form itself of economic relations, the communist form of ownership (as a 'factual relation') will assume a character that will no longer need a legal form for its assertion.

It follows that only such an economic relation, a non-legal fact, which requires a legal form for its assertion, constitutes a real premise and condition of emergence of a legal norm. In other words, only that non-legal fact will become a real condition of a legal norm which is *actively* (that is, in consequence of applying law) asserted and protected by the entire system of functioning law. If a certain 'factual relation' does not need legal protection and assertion, if it is not a *consequence* of applying law, then neither is it the *cause* of law. In this case a legal norm does not emerge at all: a moral or some other norm does.

Accordingly, only that economic relation between men constitutes a real premise and condition of the emergence of a legal norm, which is asserted by the legal norm as a *product*, a *consequence* of its application, and appears on the surface as a *consequence* of law, and not as its cause. In this case we deal again with a dialectical transformation of cause into effect, which stems from the spiral-like character of any real development of mutually conditioning phenomena. It is this real fact, being comprehended and elucidated in a one-sided manner, only from the standpoint of active reverse effect of social consciousness in all its forms on social being, on the sphere of economic relations between men and of men to nature, which gives rise to diverse idealist conceptions.

Abstract absolutisation of this aspect, of the active reverse effect of thought on all other spheres of activity, including economy and the field of relations between man and nature, formed the basis for the Hegelian conception, which ultimately declared man's entire social life and even nature itself to be a consequence or product of thinking in terms of concepts, an outcome of the logical activity of universal reason. It is this fact of relative independence of thought, of man's logical development, owing to which thought has an active reverse effect on all spheres of man's activity (including economy), that Hegel stresses one-sidedly. This one-sidedness coincides with the objective-idealist view of the relation of thought to being.

Rejecting the thesis concerning *absolute* independence of the logical process, of the system of logical categories, Marxist-Leninist logic takes into account *relative* independence of the sphere of social man's logical activity, activity of logical categories in the perception and analysis of sensual data. Thought is not a simple passive replica of the 'general forms' of sensually given facts, it is rather a specific mode of spiritual activity of a socially developed subject. The universal forms in which this activity is realised (logical categories) is not merely an accidental aggregate of the most general abstractions but a system within which each category is concretely defined through all the others.

The system of logical categories implements the same subordination that the system of concepts of any science does which reflects a dialectically divided whole. This subordination is not of the genus-to-species nature: the category of quantity, for instance, is neither a species of quality nor a genus with regard to causality or essence. A logical category cannot therefore be in principle defined by inclusion in a higher genus and indication of its own specific feature. This confirms once again the fact that a real concept exists only in a *system* of concepts and through it, becoming outside a system an empty abstraction without any clear definition—a mere term or designation.

SCIENTIFIC ABSTRACTION (CONCEPT) AND PRACTICE

Practice, social man's sensual objective activity, has always been and still is a universal prerequisite and condition on the basis of which the entire complex mechanism of man's cognitive abilities, actively transforming sensual impressions, emerges and develops. Having emerged and, still more so, having developed to a high level, a system of forms of logical activity (categories) has a very considerable reverse effect on practice itself. On this basis Marxist-Leninist philosophy solves the problem of the relation of empirical abstractions to the abstractions of theoretical thought.

In the phenomenon open to direct contemplation things mostly look quite different from what they are in essence expressed in a concept. If both coincided directly, science as special theoretical analysis of phenomena would not be needed at all.

And that is exactly why the mere reference to the fact that such and such 'general traits' may be recorded in a phenomenon open to direct contemplation, cannot as yet serve as a weighty argument either for or against the abstraction of concept. At the time when Jean-Jacque Rousseau formulated his historical thesis, 'Man is born free, and everywhere he is in chains', most men indeed spent their lives virtually 'in chains', from the cradle to the grave. The thesis that all men from birth are essentially equal could not at that time be proved by referring to the empirical general state of affairs. And yet, historically and theoretically, the philosophical conceptions of the Enlightenment were true, and not those of their opponents.

Direct contemplation and the abstractions arising from it always and everywhere reflect phenomena of the world in the light of practical relations among men and of men to nature existing at the moment. Nature is contemplated by a living concrete historically definite individual woven into a network of social relations, that is, a being standing in an active practical objective relation to the world, rather than the imaginary, allegedly 'passively contemplative', subject. And that is exactly why socio-historical properties of things very often merge in the eyes of the individual with their natural properties, while transitory properties of things and of man himself begin to seem eternal properties bound with the very essence of things. These fetishist naturalist illusions (commodity fetishism is only an example) and the abstractions expressing them cannot therefore be refuted by mere indication of things given in contemplation. The things given in contemplation to an individual of bourgeois ('civic') society are superficially exactly the way they seem to him. These illusions and abstractions are formed not only in the consciousness of an individual of bourgeois society but in the reality itself of the economic social relations which he contemplates. That was why Marx pointed out that the contemplative viewpoint of the individual moulded by 'civic', that is, bourgeois, society, does not permit to see reality in its genuine light. From this standpoint (and that was, as Marx pointed out, the standpoint of the entire old materialism, including that of Feuerbach), things appear in contemplation, too, shrouded in a mist of fetishist illusions. In living contemplation the individual is always active; 'passive contemplation' which allegedly permits to see things as they are in actual fact belongs in the realm of the phantasies of old philosophy. In real living contemplation things are always given in the light of existing practice.

That does not of course mean that things must appear in theoretical thought outside any connection with practice, being comprehended 'in a purely disinterested manner', as materialists before Marx believed. On the contrary. The difference here is that abstractions of theoretical thought are linked with practice in a less direct way than abstractions of living contemplation but, to make up for that, the links are deeper and more comprehensive.

Empirical abstractions born in the head of a practically active member of bourgeois society are criticised by Marx from the standpoint of practice itself. But practice is here taken in its entire real scope and, what is even more important, in a certain perspective.

Marx's principle of critically overcoming empirical abstractions of bourgeois consciousness is as follows: he proceeds from the fact that, if one takes the standpoint of a contemplative individual of bourgeois society, things will indeed look exactly the way they seem to him. Consequently, a critique of the abstractions of the individual's empirical consciousness must begin with the critique of the viewpoint, of the position from which he considers things, with showing up the narrowness of this viewpoint.

A wider view comprehending the phenomena in their entire actual content, coincides in Marx with the standpoint of practice taken in its necessary perspective mentally stretched into the future. Breaking through the narrow horizon of the existing (bourgeois) practice, a theoretical view of things breaks away not from practice (as it seemed to Feuerbach) but only with its given historically transient form. Thereby a theoretical view of things coincides with practice in its real meaning, in its revolutionary and revolutionising meaning, and thus with the standpoint of the class realising this practice.

Marx's epistemology is linked with this interpretation of the relation of abstractions to practice. The standpoint of practice, as Lenin indicates, is the starting point of epistenology. One should only bear in mind that what is meant here is the actual standpoint of revolutionary practice in its entire scope and perspective and by no means the narrow pragmatic viewpoint, as is slanderously asserted by some revisionists echoing the wishful talk of bourgeois ideologists.

This interpretation is also linked with the views of Marx and Lenin on concept, in particular their proposition that a mere correspondence to the directly observable 'general features' of the phenomenon is not yet a criterion of the truth of a concept. It may come about, as a result of practical change, that those features of a thing which were observed as constantly recurring or general will disappear entirely, and what appeared to be exceptional in the phenomenon open to contemplation will prove to be the expression of the essence of the thing.

To check whether our conception of the situation outside our consciousness is correct or incorrect (that is, whether our conception corresponds to the thing or not), it is enough to look at the thing carefully, comparing the notion with the actual situation, with the general in the facts. But to define whether or not these general elements are *necessarily* inherent in the thing, in its *concrete* nature, will require a different criterion. The criterion is practice which actively changes the thing, rather than passive contemplation, however thorough and attentive it may be.

The truth of a concept is not proved by comparing its definitions with empirical general features of facts but rather in a more complicated and mediated manner including a practical transformation of empirical reality. Practice is the highest instance of verifying a concept. The correspondence of a concept to an object is fully proved only when man succeeds in finding, reproducing or creating an object corresponding to the concept which he has formed.

Inasmuch as a concept expresses the essence of a thing rather than the abstract general features open to contemplation and expressible in notions, a concept can neither be confirmed nor refuted by reference to all individual facts available to contemplation possessing (or not possessing) given features at a given moment. Marx was never as contemptuous as in mocking the manner of theorising practised by vulgar economists, who believed that they could refute a theory by showing that things in phenomenal form looked different from what they appeared in essence expressed by concept. '...The vulgar economist thinks he has made a great discovery when, in face of the disclosure of intrinsic interconnection, he proudly states that on the surface things look different. In fact, he boasts that he sticks to appearance, and takes it for the ultimate. Why, then, have any science at all?'[28]

The essence of a thing expressed in a concept lies in the concrete system of its interaction with other things, in the system of objective conditions within which and through which it is what it is. Each individual separately taken thing comprises its own essence potentially, only as an element of some concrete system of interacting things, rather than in the form of an actually given general feature. This essence is not implemented in the thing in reality (and therefore not in contemplation either) as the directly observable general, and if it is, that does not happen all at once but only in the process of its motion, change, and development.

The significance of this point may be well illustrated by considering the history of the concept of the proletariat, a most important category of the Marxist-Leninist theory.

When Marx and Engels worked out the concept of the proletariat as the most revolutionary class of bourgeois society, as the gravedigger of capitalism, it was in principle impossible to obtain this concept by considering an abstractly general trait inherent in each separate proletarian and each particular stratum of the proletariat. A formal abstraction which could be made in the mid-19th century by comparing all individual representatives of the proletariat, by the kind of abstracting recommended by non-dialectical logic, would have characterised the proletariat as the most oppressed passively suffering poverty-ridden class capable, at best, only of a desperate hungry rebellion.

This concept of the proletariat was current in the innumerable studies of that time, in the philanthropic writings of the contemporaries of Marx and Engels, and in the works of utopian socialists. This abstraction was a precise reflection of the empirically general. But it was only Marx and Engels who obtained a *theoretical* expression of these em-

---

[28] Karl Marx to Ludwig Kugelmann in Hanover, London, July 11, 1868, K. Marx, F. Engels, *Selected Correspondence*, p. 197.

pirical facts, a conception of what the proletariat was as a 'class in itself' (*'an sich'*), in its internal nature expressed in the concept, what it was not yet 'for itself' (*'für sich'*), that is, in empirical reality directly reflected in a notion or simple empirical abstraction.

This conclusion, this concept expressing the real objective nature of the proletariat as a class was obtained through studying the entire totality of conditions in which the proletariat is inevitably formed as the most revolutionary class called upon to destroy to the very foundation the whole system of social conditions which gave rise to it. The concept of the proletariat, as distinct from the empirical general notion of it, was not a formal abstraction here but a theoretical expression of the objective conditions of its development containing a comprehension of its objective role and of the latter's tendency of development.

The truth of the concept of the proletariat worked out by Marx and Engels could not be proved by comparing it with the feature empirically common to all proletarians. This feature rather fit in with the abstraction current among philanthropists and utopians. The truth of this concept was shown, as is well known, by the real transformation of the proletariat from a 'class in itself' into a 'class for itself'. The proletariat developed, in the full sense of the term, towards a correspondence with 'its own concept', with the concept that was worked out by the classics of Marxism on the basis of analysing the objective conditions of its formation, the entire concrete totality of the social conditions of its being as the proletariat. Ceasing to be a mass of oppressed and downtrodden labourers scattered throughout the country and divided by competition, it becomes a monolithic class realising its world-historical mission—revolutionary abolition of private ownership and of the class form of the division of labour in general.

The same practice refuted the 'correct notion' which reflected quite precisely the trait that was common in direct empirical experience to each individual proletarian. It should be stressed in particular that taking into account this most fundamental requirement of materialist dialectics must form the basis of working out all the scientific concepts of the development of society.

It is ignoring (or conscious distortion) of the standpoint of practice as the starting point of theory that serves in the epoch of imperialism as the basis of revisionist and opportunist trends that do so much harm to the international working-class movement.

The policies of Right opportunists have always been marked by a failure to understand the course of the world-historical development of the revolutionary practice of the workers of the whole world.

Already before the October 1917 Revolution, which ushered in the practical transformation of the world on the principles of scientific communism, the opportunist Karl Kautsky forsook the path of revolutionary Marxism for the path of adaptation to the forces of world imperialism. He started with a little thing like assuming the abstract hypothesis of 'ultraimperialism'. The foresight of Lenin, who diagnosed quite precisely the danger of this disease in the international working-class movement, was here shown in full measure. Kautsky's abstract theoretical construction proceeded, at first sight, from entirely Marxist propositions. In the 20th century, Kautsky argued, capitalism develops towards uniting the barons of capital in one single supertrust. In Kautsky's view, the struggle and competition of isolated state capitals must be extinguished in this imperialist supertrust. The world system of imperialism would thus become an integral socialised economy which would merely have to be formally 'nationalised' to become socialism. Neither revolution nor proletarian dictatorship would be needed but merely a formal legal sanction to deprive the last owner of its private property in favour of the whole of society.

Hence the policy which Kautsky recommended to the international working-class movement already at that time: to wait until imperialism would socialise world economy by its own means, and to help it in this enterprise rather than hamper it. Lenin unerringly pointed to the deepest roots of this injurious theory and policy: divorcing theoretical thought from the actual development of revolutionary proletarian practice, and *abstract* reasoning.

Lenin pointed out that an ultraimperialist stage in the development of world capitalism could well be imagined in abstract reflection. 'Such a phase can be imagined. But in practice this means becoming an opportunist, turning away from the acute problems of the day to dream of the unacute problems of the future. In theory this means refusing to be guided by actual developments, *forsaking* them arbitrarily for such dreams.' [29]

If it was merely a matter of 'dreams', one could well ignore it. The thing is, however, that dreams in politics inevitably become a practical political platform.

Under no circumstances can theory, due to its nature and enormous role in social life, become divorced from practice in general. It can only keep aloof from certain forms of practice. But in this case, too, it is immediately employed by a different kind of practice. Theory is too valuable a thing to remain long without an owner.

In continuing his critical analysis of Kautsky's views, Lenin made a conclusion which was later borne out with literal accuracy by the course of events—precisely for the reason that Lenin always held the real revolutionary practice of millions of working people transforming the world to be the highest criterion of theoretical constructions.

'There is no doubt that the trend of development (of capitalism in the 20th century—*E. I.*) is *towards* a single world trust absorbing all enterprises without exception and all states without exception. But this development proceeds in such circumstances, at such a pace, through such contradictions, conflicts and upheavals—not only economic but political, national, etc.—that inevitably imperialism will burst and capitalism will be transformed into its opposite *long before* one world trust materialises, before the "ultra-imperialist", world-wide amalgamation of national finance capitals takes place.' [30]

What features distinguish Lenin's theoretical thought from Kautsky's abstract reasoning? First and foremost, its *concreteness*. And that means the following. Kautsky's theoretical constructions take into account the practice of imperialism, its forces and representatives, the ways this practice is going to take. But Kautsky completely ignores 'a little thing' like the practical activity and struggle of the oppressed masses. His constructions disregard them.

Lenin did not negate the fact that imperialism developed in the direction on which Kautsky discoursed, that the development of modern capitalism did indeed contain the abstract possibility of imperialist 'socialisation' of world

[29] V. I. Lenin, Preface to N. Bukharin's Pamphlet, *Imperialism and the World Economy, Collected Works,* Vol. 22, 1964, p. 107,

[30] Ibid.

economy, but he resolutely opposed to this abstract scheme the fundamental principle of revolutionary Marxism—the standpoint of revolutionary practice of the working classes. This example shows clearly that only this standpoint coincides with the concrete view of capitalist development under imperialism. And another thing becomes also apparent: Kautsky's abstract viewpoint inevitably leads to a rejection of dialectics. In the name of his abstract theoretical scheme he refuses to see the growing acuteness of class struggle. But the growing acuteness of class antagonism is precisely the form which capitalist 'socialisation' of world economy takes. In Kautsky, this 'socialisation' appears as a purely evolutionary process of reconciliation of class contradictions. Materialist dialectics of Marxism is discarded in favour of the typically Hegelian idea of reconciliation of opposites in the name of 'higher', above-class goals of mankind.

In the final analysis, Kautsky's abstract scheme leads to a conception that is entirely false in its theoretical content, to direct apology of imperialism, to a position hostile to existing socialism. The abstract scholastic non-revolutionary conception of the theory of Marxism proved to be the bridge by which Kautsky inevitably arrived at a complete betrayal of Marxism both in theory and in politics.

Lenin's concrete theoretical analysis of the same problem is quite different. Its starting point is the standpoint of the revolutionary practice of the working classes, of the masses. This principle throws light directly on the real, concrete dialectics of the actual process in its contradictions and tension. It also explains the fact that Lenin's theoretical forecast came true with literal accuracy two years after: in 1917 world imperialism burst at its weakest link, and the entire subsequent history took the form of more and more links in the world system of imperialism breaking down.

The dialectics of history is such that, replacing the weak links of the imperialist system, links of a new economic and political system emerge and gain strength from day to day, the links of the community of socialist countries. That is the way the modern world is transformed, in exact agreement with the concrete theoretical forecast of Lenin, that great master of dialectics.

Therein lies the lesson for Marxist theoreticians endeavouring to bring out in a scientific manner the laws of social development and to evolve theoretical concepts of it.

Chapter 3

ASCENT FROM THE ABSTRACT TO THE CONCRETE

ON THE FORMULATION OF THE QUESTION

In analysing the method of political economy, Marx advances a number of propositions of enormous philosophical import. These include the well-known thesis concerning ascent from the abstract to the concrete as the only possible and correct procedure for the solution by thought of the specific task of theoretical cognition of the world.

The concrete, in Marx's conception, is unity in diversity. 'It appears therefore in reasoning as a summing-up, a result, and not as the starting point, although it is the real point of origin, and thus also the point of origin of perception and imagination...

'The totality as a conceptual entity seen by the intellect is a product of the thinking intellect which assimilates the world in the only way open to it,* a way which differs from the artistic, religious and practical spiritual assimilation of the world.'[1]

The method of ascending from the abstract to the concrete, where 'abstract definitions lead to the reproduction of the concrete by way of thinking,[2] was defined by Marx as a correct method from the scientific standpoint. This method is, according to Marx, that specific 'mode in which thinking assimilates the concrete, reproducing it as the spiritually concrete'.[3]

---

* In the original literally 'in the only way possible for it' ('*ihm einzig möglichen Weise*'). See K. Marx, *Grundrisse der Kritik der politischen Ökonomie (Rohentwurf). 1857-1858*, S. 22.

[1] Karl Marx, *A Contribution to the Critique of Political Economy*, p. 207.

[2] K. Marx, *Grundrisse der Kritik der politischen Ökonomie (Rohentwurf). 1857-1858*, S. 22.

[3] Ibid.

It is only this method that permits the theoretician to solve his special task, the task of processing the data of contemplation and notion into concepts.

In view of particular significance of these propositions for comprehending the method of *Capital* one should dwell on them in greater detail, the more so that they have frequently become objects of falsification of Marx's economic and philosophical ideas by bourgeois philosophers and by revisionists.

Let us recall first of all that by the concrete Marx does not at all mean only the image of living contemplation, the sensual form of reflection of the object in consciousness, and neither does he interpret the abstract as 'mental distillation' only. If one reads Marx's above propositions from the standpoint of these notions of the abstract and the concrete, characteristic of narrow empiricism and neo-Kantianism, one would arrive at an absurdity incompatible with the theory of reflection. One would have the illusion that Marx recommends to ascend from a mental abstraction as something immediately given to the image of living contemplation as something secondary and derivative in regard of thought.

In reading Marx, one should therefore take care to free oneself from the notions uncritically borrowed from pre-Marxian and neo-Kantian treatises on epistemology.

From the standpoint of Marx's definitions of the abstract and the concrete, the above propositions characterise the dialectics of the transition from living contemplation to abstract thought, from contemplation and notion to concept, from the concrete as it is given in contemplation and notion to the concrete as it appears in theoretical thought.

Marx is first and foremost a materialist. In other words, he proceeds from the view that all those abstractions through which and by the synthesis of which a theoretician mentally reconstructs the world, are conceptual replicas of the separate moments of the objective reality itself revealed by analysis. In other words, it is assumed as something quite obvious that each abstract definition taken separately is a product of generalisation and analysis of the immediate data of contemplation. In this sense, and in this sense only, it is the product of the reduction of the concrete in reality to its abstract abridged expression in consciousness.

Marx says that all the definitions used in (pre-Marxian)

political economy were products of movement away from the concrete, given in the notion, to increasingly meagre abstractions. In describing the historical path traversed by political economy, Marx therefore characterises it as a path beginning with the real and concrete and leading first to 'meagre abstractions' and only after that, from the 'meagre abstractions' to a system, a synthesis, a combination of abstractions in theory.

The reduction of the concrete fulness of reality to its abridged (abstract) expression in consciousness is, self-obviously, a prerequisite and a condition without which no special theoretical research can either proceed or even begin. Moreover, this reduction is not only a prerequisite or historical condition of theoretical assimilation of the world but also an organic element of the process itself of constructing a system of scientific definitions, that is, of the mind's synthesising activity.

The definitions which the theoretician organises into a system are not, of course, borrowed ready-made from the previous phase (or stage) of cognition. His task is by no means restricted to a purely formal synthesis of ready-made 'meagre abstractions' according to the familiar rules for such synthesis. In constructing a system out of ready-made, earlier obtained abstractions, a theoretician always critically analyses them, checks them with facts and thus goes once again through the ascent from the concrete in reality to the abstract in thought. This ascent is thus not only and not so much a prerequisite of constructing a system of science as an organic element of the construction itself.

Separate abstract definitions, whose synthesis yields the 'concrete in thought', are formed in the course of ascent from the abstract to the concrete itself. Thus the theoretical process leading to the attainment of concrete knowledge is always, in each separate link as well as in the whole, also a process of reduction of the concrete to the abstract.

In other words, one can say that the ascent from the concrete to the abstract and the ascent from the abstract to the concrete, are two mutually assuming forms of theoretical assimilation of the world, of abstract thinking. Each of them is realised only through its opposite and in unity with it. The ascent from the abstract to the concrete without its opposite, without the ascent from the concrete to the abstract would become a purely scholastic linking up of ready-made meagre abstractions borrowed uncritically. Contrariwise, a reduction of the concrete to the abstract performed at random, without a clearly realised general idea of research, without a hypothesis, cannot and will not yield a theory either. It will only yield a disjoint heap of meagre abstractions.

And still why did Marx, taking all this into account, define the ascent from the abstract to the concrete as the only possible and scientifically correct mode of theoretical assimilation (reflection) of the world? The reason is that dialectics, as distinct from eclecticism, does not reason on the 'on-the-one-hand, on-the-other-hand' principle but always points out the determining aspect, that element in the unity of opposites which is in the given instance the leading or determining one. That is an axiom of dialectics.

The specific and characteristic feature of theoretical assimilation (as distinct from mere empirical familiarity with facts) is that each separate abstraction is formed within the general movement of research towards a fuller and more comprehensive, that is, concrete, conception of the object. Each separate generalisation (according to the formula 'from the concrete to the abstract') has a meaning only on condition that it is a step on the way to concrete comprehension of reality, along the way of ascending from an abstract reflection of the object in thought to its increasingly concrete expression in the concept.

If a separate act of generalisation is not simultaneously a step forward in the development of theory, a step along the way from the already available knowledge to new and fuller knowledge, if it does not push ahead theory as a whole enriching it with a new general definition but merely repeats what was known already, it proves to be simply meaningless in respect of the development of theory.

In other words, the concrete (that is, the continual movement to increasingly more concrete theoretical comprehension) emerges here as a specific goal of theoretical thought. As such goal, the concrete determines, as a law, the theoretician's mode of action (mental action are meant here, of course) in each particular case, in each separate generalisation.

The abstract from this standpoint proves to be merely a *means* of the theoretical process rather than its goal, while each separate act of generalisation (that is, of the reduction of the concrete to the abstract) emerges as a subordinate, disappearing moment of the overall movement. In the language of dialectics 'a disappearing moment' is one that has no significance by itself, divorced from the other moments—it is only significant in connection with these, in living interaction with them, in transition.

That is the whole point. Precisely because Marx was a dialectician, he did not restrict himself to a mere statement of the fact that in theoretical thought both movement from the concrete to the abstract and from the abstract to the concrete take place, but singled out first of all that form of the movement of thought which in the given instance proves to be the principal and dominant one, determining the weight and significance of the other, the opposite one. Such is the form of ascent from the abstract to the concrete in special theoretical studies. It is therefore a specific form of theoretical thought.

Of course, that does not mean at all that the other, opposite form has no place in thinking. It merely means that the reduction of the concrete fulness of facts to abstract expression in consciousness is neither a specific nor, still less, determining form of theoretical reflection of the world.

Man eats to live—he does not live to eat. But only a madman will conclude that man must do without food at all; it would be just as stupid to insist that this aphorism depriciates the role of food.

The same is true of the present instance. It is only a person quite ignorant in scientific matters that can take the absorption of the sensually concrete fulness of facts in abstraction for the principal and determining form of the theoretician's mental activity. In science this is only a means necessary for carrying out a more serious task, the task which is specific for the theoretical assimilation of the world, constituting the genuine goal of the theoretician's activity. *Reproduction of the concrete in thought* is the goal which determines the weight and significance of each separate act of generalisation.

The concrete in thinking is not, of course, the ultimate goal, an end in itself. Theory as a whole is also only 'a disappearing moment' in the real, practical objective exchange of matter between man and nature. From theory, transition is made to practice, and this transition can also be described as a transition from the abstract to the concrete. Practice no longer has a higher goal outside itself, it posits its own goals and appears as an end in itself. That is why each separate step and each generalisation in the course of working out a theory is constantly commensurated with the data of practice, tested by them, correlated with practice as the highest goal of theoretical activity. That is why Lenin, in speaking of the method of *Capital,* points out one of its most characteristic features: 'Testing by facts or by practice respectively, is to be found here in *each* step of the analysis.'[4]

Constant correlation of 'each step' in the analysis with the direction of the path of scientific research as a whole and ultimately with practice is linked with the very essence of Marx's conception of the specificity of the theoretical assimilation of the world. Each separate step in the analysis, each individual act of reduction of the concrete to the abstract, must from the beginning be oriented at the whole which '*looms in the notion*', in living contemplation, the reflection of which is the highest goal of theoretical work (of course only as long as we deal with theoretical work, as long as man stands to the world only in a theoretical relation).*

Therein lies the profoundly dialectical meaning of Marx's proposition that it is exactly ascent from the abstract to the concrete that constitutes a trait specifically inherent in the theoretical process and is the only possible and therefore the only scientifically correct mode of developing scientific definitions, a mode of transforming the data of living contemplation and notion into concepts.

That means that all genuinely scientific (not absurd or vacuous) abstract definitions do not emerge in the human head as a result of mindless random reduction of the concrete to the abstract—they appear solely through consistent advancement of cognition in the overall law-governed development of science, through concretisation of the available knowledge and its critical transformation.

It would be wrong to take the view that each science has to go through a stage of one-sided analytical attitude to the world, a stage of purely inductive reduction of the concrete to the abstract, and that only later, when this work is fully

---

[4] V. I. Lenin, Plan of Hegel's Dialectics (Logic), *Collected Works,* Vol. 38, p. 320.

* This separate subject of the role of esthetically developed 'strength of imagination' (*Einbildungskraft*) is considered by the author in another work (*On Idols and Ideals*).

accomplished, can it proceed to link up the abstractions thus obtained in a system, to ascend from the abstract to the concrete.

When Marx refers to the history of bourgeois political economy, to the fact that at its origin it really followed the one-sided analytical path, only later to adopt the scientifically correct path, he does not of course mean that every modern science should follow this example, that is, first go through a purely analytical stage and later proceed to ascend from the abstract to the concrete.

The one-sided analytical method, which is indeed characteristic of the first steps of bourgeois political economy, is by no means a virtue that could be recommended as a model. It was rather an expression of the historical limitations of bourgeois political economy, in particular conditioned by the absence of a well-developed dialectical method of thought. Dialectical logic does not at all recommend modern science first to take up pure analysis, pure reduction of the concrete to the abstract, and later to proceed to pure synthesis, pure ascent from the abstract to the concrete. Concrete knowledge is not to be obtained on this path, and if it is, that can only be due to the same kind of wanderings which the development of bourgeois political economy was subject to before Marx.

The example cited by Marx is rather an argument in favour of the thesis that science in these days should from the very beginning take the road that is scientifically correct rather than repeat the wanderings of the 17th century, it must from the very outset use the dialectical method of ascent from the abstract to the concrete in which analysis and synthesis are closely interwoven, rather than the one-sided analytical method. This is an argument in favour of science working out its abstract definitions, from the very outset, in such a way that each of them should at the same time be a step on the road of advancement towards concrete truth, towards cognition of reality as a unified, coherent, developing whole. Bourgeois political economy took a different road at the beginning, but that is no reason to take it for a model.

Science, if it is genuine science rather than a conglomeration of facts and various data, should from the very beginning reflect its object and develop its definitions in a way that Marx characterised as the only possible and correct one in science, and not leave this method for later use in literary exposition of the already obtained results, as neo-Kantian revisionists like Cunow, Renner and others advised to do. Later we shall discuss in detail these attempts to distort the essence of Marx's thought about the method of ascent from the abstract to the concrete, to present this method only as a literary style of expounding available results allegedly obtained in a purely inductive manner.

Of course, the method of ascent from the abstract to the concrete is seen most clearly in those works of Marx which expound his theory systematically: *Zur Kritik der politischen Ökonomie* (A Contribution to the Critique of Political Economy), *Grundrisse der Kritik der politischen Ökonomie* (Outline of a Critique of Political Economy), and in *Capital*. That does not mean at all, however, that the exposition is here fundamentally different in its method from the investigation, or that the method applied by Marx in the investigation is directly opposed to the manner of exposition of the results of the investigation.

If that were so, the analysis of the 'logic of *Capital*' would contribute nothing to an understanding of the method of research, the method of processing the data of contemplation and notion applied by Marx. *Capital* would in this case be only instructive as a model of literary exposition of results previously obtained and not as an illustration of the method of obtaining them. In this case Marx's method of investigation should not be reconstructed from an analysis of *Capital* but rather from an analysis of the rough notes, excerpts, fragments, and arguments that came into Marx's head in his original study of the economic facts. In that case one would have to agree with the insistence of the author of an anti-Marxist pamphlet, theologian Fetscher, who wrote this: 'The method which Marx followed in *Capital* is essentially the same as the one applied by bourgeois scholars. Dialectics was used by Marx, as he says himself in the Afterword to the second edition of *Capital*, only as a "method of presentation", a method which indeed has a number of advantages and which we shall not consider here in greater detail',[5] as it has no bearing on the problem of the method of cognition.

---

[5] *Christen oder Bolschewisten*, Kröner, Stuttgart, 1957, S. 89.

Fetscher offers here a rather free interpretation of Marx's well-known statement that the presentation of a theory in its developed form cannot but be different from the search that resulted in this theory; but the formal difference between the two, referred to by Marx, does not affect the essence of the method of thinking, of the mode of processing the data of contemplation and notion into concepts. This mode of analysis remained the same, namely, dialectial, both in the preliminary processing of data and in their final elaboration, although, of course, it was perfected as the work went on which culminated in the creation of *Capital*.

The main advantage of the mode of presentation, which is by no means of literary stylistic character, consists in that the author of *Capital* does not dogmatically and didactically present ready-made results obtained in some mysterious manner but rather goes through the entire process of obtaining these results, the entire investigation leading to them, before the reader's eyes. 'The reader who really wishes to follow me will have to decide to advance from the particular to the general,'[6] warned Marx already in his Preface to *A Contribution to the Critique of Political Economy*. The method of presentation leads the reader from a comprehension of certain particulars, from the abstract, to the increasingly more concrete, developed, general, comprehensive view of economic reality, to the general as the result of combining the particulars.

Of course, the process of investigation is not reproduced in all the details and deviations of more than twenty-five years of research but only in those principal and decisive features which, as the study itself showed, really advanced thought along the path of concrete understanding. In the final elaboration of the facts for publication Marx no longer repeated those numerous deviations from the principal theme of investigation that are inevitable in the work of any scholar. In the course of actual investigation facts are often considered that are not directly relevant: it is only their analysis that can show whether they are relevant or not. Besides, the theoretician has to recur, as often as not, to the consideration of facts that once seemed to be exhaustively analysed. As a result, research does not proceed

[6] Karl Marx, *A Contribution to the Critique of Political Economy*, p. 19.

smoothly forward but moves ahead in rather complicated manner with frequent reversions and deviations.

These moments are not, of course, reproduced in the final presentation. Due to this, he process of investigation appears in its genuine form free from accidental elements and deviations. Here it is straightened out, as it were, assuming the character of continuous motion forward, which is in agreement with the nature and motions of the facts themselves. Here thought does not proceed from the analysis of one fact to the analysis of the next one before it has really exhausted this fact; that is why one does not have to recur time and again to one and the same subject in order to tackle what has been left unfinished.

Thus the method of presentation of material in *Capital* is nothing but the 'corrected' method of its *investigation*, the corrections being not arbitrary, but in complete accordance with the requirements and laws dictated by the investigation itself. In other words, the method of presentation is in this case the method of investigation freed from anything in the nature of accessories and any confusing elements—a method of investigation strictly conforming to the objective, logical laws of study. That is a method of investigation in pure form, in a systematic form unobscured by deviations and chance elements.

As for the differences of form, of which Marx speaks in the Afterword to the second edition of *Capital*, they have to do with quite different circumstances, in particular, the fact that *Marx personally* became familiar with the different circles of the capitalist hell in a sequence that is different from the one that corresponds to the law of their own development and is presented in *Capital*.

The method of ascent from the abstract to the concrete does not correspond to the order in which certain aspects of the object under study for some reason or other came into the field of vision of individual theoreticians or the science as a whole. It is oriented exclusively at the order which corresponds to the objective interrelations of various moments within the concreteness under study. This genuine sequence, it goes without saying, is not realised all at once. A justification of the method of ascent from the abstract to the concrete must not be looked for in the scientific careers of theoreticians or even the historical development of science as a whole. Science as a whole also arrives at its genuine starting point through long and arduous search.

Marx, for instance, came to the analysis and comprehension of economic relations from the study of legal and political relations among men. The sphere of law and politics proved for him the starting point of the study of the structure of the social organism. In the presentation of the theory of historical materialism Marx's requirement is to proceed from an understanding of economic, material relations to an understanding of law and politics.

Theoreticians of the Fetscher type might insist, on these grounds, that Marx's thesis according to which the starting point for an understanding of all social phenomena must be economy rather than law or politics, belongs merely to the peculiarities of the literary manner of presentation of Marx's theory, while in the investigation itself Marx and Marxists did the same as any bourgeois scientist.

The point is, however, that although the sphere of law and politics was studied by Marx before he took up economic inquiry, he understood this sphere correctly, from the scientific (materialist) standpoint, only after he had analysed economy, be it in very general outline.

The same is true of Marx's view of political economy. Marx studied the laws of movement of money, profit, and rent much earlier than he succeeded in realising the genuine, dual nature of commodity and of labour producing commodities. However, until he understood the real nature of value, his conception of money and rent was incorrect. In *The Poverty of Philosophy* he still shared the illusions of the Ricardian theory of money and rent. Only a clear conception of the nature of value attained in the 1850s showed both money and rent in the true light. Before that, money could not be understood in principle.

In the early 1850s Marx spent much time trying to understand the confusion and conflicts involved in the circulation of money in times of crisis and 'prosperity'. It is these attempts that led him to the conclusion that the laws of the circulation of money could not be understood unless one worked out in the greatest detail the *concept of value*. Having worked out the value concept, he saw that he had shared a number of Ricardo's illusions.

The method of ascent from the abstract to the concrete as a method of inquiry into facts cannot therefore be justified by references to the order in which the study of data proceeded. It expresses the sequence in which the objectively correct conception corresponding to the object takes shape in the theoretician's mind, rather than the order in which certain aspects of reality for some reason or other draw the theoretician's attention and thus enter the field of science.

The method of ascent from the abstract to the concrete expresses the internal law of the development of scientific understanding which in the course of historical advancement paves its way through a mass of accidental moments, deviations, often in a roundabout way unbeknown to the theoreticians themselves. This law is therefore difficult to discover on the surface of scientific development (that is, in the consciousness of theoreticians themselves). In the consciousness of theoreticians this law may not appear at all for a long time or it may appear in a form that will make it unrecognisable. An individual representative of science, as Marx pointed out, often has quite an erroneous conception of what he actually does and how he does it. In view of this, one must not judge a thinker by what he thinks of himself. It is much more important (and difficult) to establish the objective significance of his views and their role in the development of science as a whole.

For this reason, the *genuine* significance of the facts of a scientist's biography and the *genuine* order of development of scientific definitions cannot be revealed through a purely biographic inquiry. The actual progress of scientific knowledge (that is, systematic advances of thought to concrete truth) often significantly diverges from the ordinary chronological sequence. Lenin in his fragment On the Question of Dialectics pointed out that chronology with regard to persons is unnecessary in the analysis of the logic of the development of knowledge, that it does not always correspond to the actual order of stages by which thought conceives its subject-matter.

Taking all this into account, one can draw the conclusion that all the characteristic features of Marx's method of inquiry appear most clearly and distinctly in *Capital* and not in the rough notes, excerpts and arguments that came into his head as he was studying the economic facts.

That is where the genuine sequence of the development of scientific definitions is revealed, which only gradually came to light in the course of preliminary study of the material and was not always clearly realised by Marx himself. A most characteristic trait of Marx was, at all times, a sober critical attitude to his own achievement: many times he resolutely corrected, '*post factum*', the errors and omissions of the preliminary stage of inquiry. In general it is possible to distinguish, with objective rigorousness, between the kernels of objective truth and the form in which they originally appeared in consciousness only after the event: the rudiments of more advanced forms can only be correctly understood when these more advanced forms are already known.

Thus, if one tried to reconstruct Marx's method of inquiry from the mass of rough notes and fragments from his archives rather than from *Capital*, that would only complicate matters. To understand them correctly, one would all the same have to analyse *Capital* first. Otherwise 'rudiments of more advanced forms' simply cannot be distinguished in them. Besides, it is hard to understand why this inquiry should prefer an early and preliminary form of expression to a later, more refined, and mature form of expression. That would only result in the earlier form of expression being taken for an ideal one, and its later form for a distorted variant. The formulations and the method of their development in *Capital* would indeed have to be attributed to the literary manner of presentation and its perfection rather than to the enlargement of the scope of thought, of perception and method of inquiry.

(This awkward trick is, by the way, assiduously practised by present-day revisionists, who insist that genuine Marxism should be looked for in the manuscripts of the young Marx rather than in his mature works. As a result, *Capital* is presented as a distorted conception of the so-called real humanism developed by Marx and Engels in 1843-1844).

That was why Lenin pointed out that in developing The Great Logic of Marxism one should first of all have in mind *Capital*, and that the method of presentation applied by Marx in *Capital* should serve as a model for a dialectical interpretation of reality and a model for the study and elaboration of dialectics in general. Proceeding from these preliminary considerations, one can undertake a more detailed study of the method of ascent from the abstract to the concrete as a scientifically correct method of forming scientific definitions, as a method of theoretical processing of the data of living contemplation and notion.

Let us recall once again in this connection that the data of contemplation and notion are here taken to mean something different from what an individual personally contemplates and pictures in sensual images. This interpretation, characteristic of pre-Marxist philosophy and of the anthropological conception of the subject of cognition, is quite false and extremely narrow. The data of contemplation and notion were always interpreted by Marx as the entire mass of the socially accumulated empirical experiences, the entire colossal mass of empirical data available to the theoretician from books, reports, statistical tables, newspapers, and accounts. It stands to reason, however, that all these empirical data are stored in social memory in an abridged form, reduced to abstract expression. They are expressed in speech, in terminology, in figures, tables, and other abstract forms. The specific task of the theoretician who uses all this information about reality does not, of course, consist in lending this abstract expression still more abstract form. On the contrary, his work always begins with a critical analysis and revision of the abstractions of the empirical stage of cognition, with the critical overcoming of these abstractions, attaining progress through a critique of the one-sidedness and subjective character of these abstractions and revealing the illusions contained in them, from the standpoint of reality as a whole, in its concreteness. In this sense (and only in this sense) the transition from the empirical stage of cognition to the rational one also appears as a transition from the abstract to the concrete.

Of course, the ascent from the cognition of the simple commodity form to the comprehension of such well-developed forms of bourgeois wealth as interest also appears, from a certain standpoint, as the movement from the concrete to *abstract* forms of its manifestation on the surface of events. Interest, for instance, expresses in its impersonal quantitative language the most complex and profound processes of capitalist production. In interest, surplus-value assumes an extremely abstract form of manifestation. This abstract quantitative form is only explained from its concrete content. But this is also evidence of the fact that any abstract moment of reality finds a real explanation only in the concrete system of conditions which gave rise to it, and it can only be correctly understood through it. Thus interest is *concretely* (scientifically) understood only in the final analysis, as a final result, whereas on the surface of phenomena it appears as a very abstract form.

All of this must also be taken into account.

In view of the fact that Marx formulated his ideas on the method of ascent from the abstract to the concrete in direct polemics with its Hegelian interpretation, it will be appropriate to take a critical look at the latter. The materialist nature of Marx's method will stand out clearly and graphically in comparison with it.

HEGEL'S CONCEPTION OF THE CONCRETE

As we know Hegel was the first to understand the development of knowledge as a historical process subject to laws that do not depend on men's will and consciousness. He discovered the law of ascent from the abstract to the concrete as the law governing the entire course of development of knowledge.

This law is, first of all, shown to be a simple empirically stated fact—the fact of progressive development of the spiritual culture of mankind. Indubitably, man's spiritual culture, his spiritual world, are gradually becoming increasingly rich, complicated, varied, and in this sense, more concrete. Despite all its complexity, however, man's spiritual world remains an integral world governed by the same laws thus constituting a genuine unity in diversity.

Movement from the abstract to the concrete appears in Hegel first and foremost as the empirically indubitable natural form in which the construction of the 'kingdom of the spirit' is completed. At first this kingdom (the sphere of human culture) is naturally uncomplicated, poor in established forms, that is, extremely abstract, becoming in the course of time increasingly more complex, rich, and varied, that is, more concrete.

It is easy to see that there is as yet nothing dialectical or idealist in all this.

Idealism, and at the same time specifically Hegel's dialectics, begin later, when Hegel tackles the question of the motive forces of the development of the 'kingdom of the spirit', the sphere of consciousness. The specific feature of

Hegelian philosophy is the fact that the idea of development is fully applied only to the phenomena of consciousness.

In his view, nature existing outside and independently from the spirit does not develop. It confronts consciousness as a picture frozen in time, identical from the very beginning and for all time to come. Consciousness realises its restless active nature through actively considering this motionless picture, this realm of things eternally standing in the same relations to one another. The activity of realisation as such also contains within itself the mainspring of its own development.

The spirit is the only concreteness, that is, the only developed and developing system of living interacting phenomena passing one into another. This latter trait is, in his view, entirely uncharacteristic of nature. For him, nature is abstract through and through, metaphysical in its very essence: all of nature's phenomena are *side by side* with one another, *isolated* from one another, lying outside one another. As Hegel puts it, nature falls within itself into its abstract moments, into separate things, objects, processes, existing side by side with one another and independently from one another. At best, genuine dialectics is only vaguely reflected or dimly looms in nature.

The idealist nature of Hegel's philosophy is here revealed in a very striking manner: he directly attributes the metaphysical limitations of contemporary natural science, the *knowledge of nature*, to *nature itself* as its *eternal* property.

Where contemporary natural science timidly began to realise the dialectics of the things themselves, he also sees 'rudiments' of real concreteness, of the living dialectical interaction of phenomena. Thus he sees an imperfect form of concreteness in organic life. Here he discovers living interaction linking up all parts of the animal organism in a unified system within which each separate member exists and has a meaning only through its interaction with others: outside this interaction it cannot in general exist. An amputated hand decomposes, ceases to be a hand even in external form and ultimately in name, too. It cannot exist separately in abstraction.

Here Hegel sees a weak resemblance of the concreteness which he regards as the exceptional property of the spiritual world. In the world of chemistry, in his view, internal interaction is even weaker, although there are rudiments of it here as well. Here oxygen, for instance, can and does exist side by side with hydrogen, even if they are not bound as elements of water. This relation is impossible in the organism: the hand cannot exist separately from the head, both hand and head exist only through their interconnection, only within this mutual connection and conditioning. A particle possessing only mechanical properties remains the same particle, which does not change in itself depending on the kind of mechanical bond with other particles of the same kind. Isolated or extracted from this bond, that is, in its abstracted form, it will still remain the same, it will not go bad or decay as the hand 'abstracted' from the body.

The Hegelian system of nature is built as a system of stages beginning with the abstract sphere of mechanism and ending with the relatively concrete sphere of organic life. The whole pyramid is crowned by the spirit, as the sphere whose entire meaning lies in *concreteness*, in the absolute interconnectedness of all its phenomena.

Wherein lies the falsity of this Hegelian construction?

First of all in his taking the historically limited conceptions of contemporary natural science, which did not, indeed, contain conscious dialectics, to be the absolute characteristics of nature itself.

As for the fact that nature as a whole is an actually developing integral system of forms of motion of matter mutually conditioning one another, that nature as a whole, including man, is the real, *objective concreteness*, this fact is mystified by Hegel in his system, in which the abstract, that is, the mechanism, is the manifestation of *spiritual* concreteness.

He credits no form of motion, apart from the motion of thinking reason, the sphere of concepts, with an immanent concreteness, that is, with real mutual conditioning of phenomena within a natural whole.

In the same way Hegel considers the sphere of the economic life of society. For him, that is the sphere of 'want and intellect', a sphere where single individuals isolated one from another interact, each of them connected with others only because he has to preserve himself as a single abstract individual, as a kind of social atom.

It is easy to see here as well that Hegel took the metaphysical limitations of contemporary political economy (he had a fair knowledge of the English theoreticians) for a metaphysical, abstractly intellectual character of the *economic sphere itself*. The sphere of economic life, the sphere of civic society, is supremely governed by *intellect*, that is, in Hegelian terms, the abstractedly one-sided form of consciousness.

In this sphere, opposites remain unmediated, unreconciled, they clash with one another, repulse one another, remaining the same metaphysical opposites. Real development is therefore impossible here. One and the same relation, the eternal relation of need to means of gratifying it, is eternally reproduced here.

Therefore the only possible form of transition to some higher stage in which all abstract extremes of the economic sphere are resolved is the transition to *legal* reality. Law emerges as the highest concreteness which is *manifested* as broken down into its abstract elements in the sphere of economic life.

Here we see that Hegel's logic, his dialectical yet at the same time essentially idealist conception of the concrete and the abstract serves to justify that which exists. In natural science, Hegel's conception perpetuates the given level of knowledge of nature, and in sociology it supports the apologetic attitude both to the economic form of property and to the law that sanctions this property.

Hegel's attitude to political economy should be considered in greater detail. It is instructive in two respects: on the one hand, it is here, in the conception of concreteness, that the opposition between Hegel's idealist dialectics and Marx's materialist dialectics is seen most clearly, and on the other hand, it is seen just as clearly that idealist dialectics fully excuses the metaphysical nature of the thinking of the classics of bourgeois economy (Smith, Ricardo, and others) by negating the genuinely dialectical nature of the subject-matter of political economy itself, declaring it to be a sphere in which abstract intellectual definitions fully correspond to the character of the subject-matter.

In other words, the *idealism* of Hegelian dialectics yields the same result which in Smith, Ricardo and Say is the consequence of the *metaphysical* mode of inquiry.

What is the most striking feature of his approach? The fact that the sphere of economic life for him is not a concrete sphere, it is not a system of interaction of men and things which has developed historically and can be understood as a really concrete sphere.

For Hegel, economy is only one of the many manifestations of the 'concrete spirit', that is, an abstract manifestation of some higher nature of man. This higher nature, also manifested one-sidedly in the form of economic activity, is nothing but *the goal-directedly acting will*—the substance of law and economic life, politics and all the rest. The goal-directed (reasonable) will appears as a concrete substance which is manifested abstractly and one-sidedly in its products, in its modi—economy, law, politics, etc. As long as this is taken for a starting point, as long as goal-directed reasonable will (or simply reason, since will in Hegel is a form of the existence of reason in man) is presented as a universal concrete substance of all forms of social activity, he naturally regards economy only as something that may be interpreted as a *manifestation* of reasonable will, as one of its many revelations, as a one-sided (abstract) manifestation of reason and will of the social individual.

Therefore all definitions of economy, all categories of economic life (value, profit, wages, etc.) appear as *abstract modi of reasonable will*, as particular or specific forms of its social being. In economy, reason emerges in a form which does not correspond to its universal nature but *merely to a single* one-sided abstract manifestation of it. Concrete universal will creates the form that is adequate to its nature only in law and the state. The state is, according to Hegel, the concrete reality of the universal will comprising in itself all the particular, specific, and therefore abstract forms of its manifestation, including economy, the sphere of needs, a 'system of needs'.

Within economy, the universal concrete substance of anything that is human—reasonable will—appears in an extremely one-sided and abstract form. The sphere of men's economic activity is not, therefore, a *concrete* system of interaction of men and things, emerging and developing *irrespective of the will and consciousness* of individuals. It cannot constitute the subject-matter of a special science and can only be considered in a system of universal definitions of reasonable will, i.e. within the philosophy of spirit, within the philosophy of state law. Here it appears as one of the specific spheres of the activity of reason, as an abstract form of revelation of reason acting in history.

It is not difficult to see the diametric opposition between the views of Marx and Hegel of economy, of the nature of its dialectical interconnection with all the other manifestations of social life, and of its role in the social whole.

On this point, Marx opposes Hegel as a *materialist* first and foremost. The most interesting feature here is, however, that it is *materialism* that enables him to develop a more profound view of the dialectics of the subject-matter.

For Marx, the sphere of economic interaction of men is a fully *concrete* sphere of social life with its own specific *immanent* laws of motion. In other words, it appears to be relatively independent of all other forms of social activity of men and precisely for this reason constitutes the subject-matter of a special science. The system of economic interaction between men emerges as a historically arising and historically developed system, all aspects of which are mutually connected with one another through unity of origin (genetically).

It is important to stress that the system of economic relations is a system that is not only *relatively* but also *absolutely* independent of the will and consciousness of individuals, although the latter's will and consciousness do play a most active role in its formation. The very nature of this participation of conscious will in the formation of the system is determined by the system of economic relations itself incorporating men endowed with will and consciousness, rather than by the 'nature of the spirit', beforehand and from the outside. In other words, will and reason themselves appear here as modi of some other substance, as its abstract manifestations and products. All definitions of the will and consciousness of individuals involved in the development of the economic system are literally *deduced* from the nature of internal self-movement of the system as a whole, interpreted as *products* of the movement of this system.

Thus, from this point of view everything looks exactly the reverse as compared to the Hegelian construction: everything is right side up. It is materialism that acts as the principal cause and condition of the fact that dialectics is applied to the understanding of economy in a full measure and much more comprehensively than it is generally possible to do from the Hegelian positions.

For Hegel, the category of concreteness is fully applicable only then and there, when and where we deal with conscious will and its products, only in the sphere of the spirit and its products, its manifestations (*Entäusserungen*).

In Marx's view, this most important category of dialectics is fully applicable *everywhere, in any sphere of natural and social being*, independently of any spirit whatsoever, and on this basis, to the phenomena of life of the spirit itself, that is, to the development of any sphere of social consciousness, including reasoning, the sphere of logic.

According to the Hegelian construction and its idealist starting point, no form of movement in nature can be understood as a *concrete* form, as a historically emerging self-developing system of internally interacting phenomena. Any such sphere acquires some relation to concreteness only when it is involved in the spiritual process, when one succeeds in interpreting it as a product of the spirit, a modus of the spiritual substance. The attribute of concreteness proves to be an exclusive monopoly of the self-developing spirit, while nature in itself (including the material aspect of the human social being) has no concreteness at all in its existence. In the eyes of Hegel, interconnection is in general possible only as ideal interconnection, as posited by the spirit or concept.

The category of concreteness, one of the central categories of dialectics, is therefore emasculated in Hegel's system to such an extent that it is impossible to apply it to natural science or the materialist conception of society. In short, the category of concreteness and consequently dialectics as a whole, which is inconceivable without this category, turns out to be inapplicable to anything but the sphere of the spirit. To everything else it is only applicable insofar as these other things are interpreted purely idealistically, as a manifestation of the universal spirit, as a one-sided (abstract) manifestation of the concrete spirit, of the concrete fulness and richness of the absolute spirit, the absolute idea.

These idealist limitations of Hegel's conception of concreteness, the narrowness of this conception, are indissolubly linked with the notion that nature is something static, that development belongs in the sphere of spirit only.

Concreteness indeed is indissolubly linked with development, and dialectical development at that, with self-development through contradictions. The latter Hegel saw in consciousness and nowhere else. Hence the narrowness of his conception of concreteness, a conception which, *narrow as it is*, is later extended to the entire field of nature.

Connected with this is Hegel's interpretation of the method of ascent from the abstract to the concrete. According to Hegel, that means that the entire reality, including nature and history, is the ascent of the spirit to itself, a process that goes through a number of stages from the 'mechanism', as the sphere of *purely abstract manifestation of spiritualness,* to the concrete human spirit. The ascent to itself is performed by the *absolute,* non-human, divine spirit. As such, this spirit is concrete in itself (*an sich*) even before it has revealed itself as 'mechanism', 'chemism', or 'organism' in a one-sided, abstracted manner.

That is why pure logic in Hegel's system precedes the philosophical consideration of nature, the latter being presented as a number of stages in which the concrete logical spirit *reveals itself (sich entäussert)* ever more fully and concretely in the form of space and time.

Ascent from the abstract to the concrete therefore coincides in Hegel with the generation of the world by the logical idea. Thus the law of spiritual *reproduction* of the world by thought is here directly represented as the law of *production* of this world by the creative power of the concept.

This Hegelian illusion, as Marx showed, is simply based on a one-sided view of the philosopher and logician of reality. Hegel, as logician *ex professo*, is interested everywhere and first of all in 'the matter of logic rather than in the logic of the matter'. From this viewpoint, man is considered only as the subject of logical theoretical activity, and the world, only as object, only as material processed in this activity. This abstraction is, within certain limits, justified in logic, and as long as logic bears these limitations in mind, there is nothing idealistic in this abstraction.

Hegel's approach, however, eliminates these boundaries. He considers thought not only and not simply as one of man's abilities but also as the substantional source of all the other human abilities and kinds of activity, as their essential foundation. He treats the ability to change practically the external world, nature outside man, also as a manifestation of the mental principle in man. The actual process of practical transformation of the world appears in his philosophy as a consequence and manifestation of purely spiritual activity—in the final analysis, of purely logical activity, while the whole of mankind's material culture, as a product of thought, as a 'reifined concept', as the 'other-being of the concept'.

In reality, the immediate basis of the development of thought is not nature as such but precisely the transformation of nature by social man, that is, practice. If this objective practical basis of thought is presented as the product of thought, as thought in its material realisation, one has to conclude that thinking has to do with objectivity only in appearance, while in actual fact, essentially, it deals only with itself, with its own 'other-being'. Logical definitions, that is, those definitions which the external objective world owes to thought, appear as the absolute and only genuine definitions of this world.

The point of view of logic becomes in Hegel absolute and all-embracing. If man's essence is believed to be in thought, and the essence of objective reality, in being a product of thought, an 'alienated concept', the law of development of thought appears as the law of development of the real world. That is why man and thinking in concepts prove to be complete synonyms in Hegel, just as the world and the world in concepts, the logically assimilated world. The law which in actual fact determines only the activity of the theoretically thinking head, is made the supreme law of the development and practice of man and of the objective world.

The actual subject-matter of Hegelian logic remains, despite his illusions, only the process of theoretical assimilation of the world, of mental reproduction of the world. Insofar as Hegel studies this world, he arrives at actual discoveries. Insofar as he takes this subject-matter for something different from what it actually is, for something greater—the formation of the world itself, he takes the path of erroneous comprehension of the world and of thought, too. He deprives himself of any possibility of understanding the process of thinking itself. As long as the actual conditions producing logical activity are presented as its own products and consequences, the logical reasoning is suspended in mid air, or rather in the 'ether of pure thought'. The fact itself of the origin of thought and the laws of its development become quite inexplicable. It has no foundation in anything lying outside it. The foundation is believed to lie in itself. That is why Hegel is compelled in the end to interpret the logical ability, the ability to distinguish between and combine concepts, as a kind of divine gift, as activity of the self-developing concept. The law of ascent from the abstract to the concrete, discovered by Hegel in the movement of theoretical cognition also remains inexplicable. The question as to why thought moves in one way rather than another, is answered by Hegelian philosophy in an essentially tautological way: such is the original and 'non-creatable' nature of thought. Tautology ceases to be a mere tautology here, becoming an idealist lie.

That is the point at which Marx levels his critique, showing that there is no explanation at all here, and the attempt to pass an absence of an explanation for an explanation is tantamount to idealism.

Although Marx discards the Hegelian conception of thought as the demiurge of the objective world, he does not, however, reject the law which Hegel established in the movement of theoretical knowledge although he gave it a false idealistic interpretation. The ascent from the abstract to the concrete, as Marx points out, is in actual fact nothing but a method for human thought to assimilate the concrete reality existing outside of and independently from it. As such, this method assumes, first, the existence of uninterpreted concreteness, second, the practical objective activity of the social man developing independently from thought, and third, an immediate sensual form of reflection of objective concreteness in consciousness, that is, empirical consciousness, contemplation and notion formed quite independently from and prior to special theoretical activity. In other words, theoretical thought is posterior to the existence of the objective world and, moreover, to another form of consiousness formed directly in the course of sensual practical activity—*the practical spiritual mode of assimilation of the world*, as Marx referred to it.

Hegel presents all these premises of theoretical thought as its products and consequences. Marx puts all things in their proper places.

From the materialist viewpoint, as Marx showed, the method of ascent from the abstract to the concrete may and must be understood quite rationally, without any mysticism, as the only method by which thought can reproduce in the concept, in the movement of concepts the historically established concreteness existing outside of and independently from it, a world existing and developing outside of and independently from thought.

MARX'S VIEW OF THE DEVELOPMENT OF SCIENTIFIC COGNITION

As we know, the question of the relation of the abstract to the concrete in thought arose before Marx in the light of another, more general, problem: which scientific method should be used? [7]

This question assumes a view of scientific development as of a natural historical process. In general, Marx has always been decidedly opposed to the Leftist view of the development of spiritual culture which ignores all the previous attainments of human thought. In science, just as in all the other fields of spiritual culture, actual progress is always attained by further development of the values created by previous development, not by starting from scratch; by a theoretically developed head rather than by the Lockean *tabula rasa*.

It goes without saying that the assimilation of the results of previous theoretical development is not a matter of simply inheriting ready-made formulas but rather a complex process of their critical reinterpretation with reference to their correspondence to facts, life, practice. A new theory, however revolutionary it might be in its content and significance, is always born in the course of critical reassessment of previous theoretical development. Lenin emphasised this point in his struggle against the Leftist views of the proponents of the so-called proletarian culture, who insisted that proletarian culture should be developed 'straight from life', while all attainments of human thought should be discarded as useless refuse.

The more revolutionary a theory, the greater its role of the genuine heir of previous theoretical development and the degree in which it assimilates the 'rational kernels' accumulated by science in previous development. That is a necessary law of the development of science, of theory. A

---

[7] See Karl Marx, *A Contribution to the Critique of Political Economy*, p. 223.

new theoretical conception of the empirically given data always emerges in the course of revolutionary critical reassessment of the old theoretical interpretation of these facts.

'Settling critical accounts' with the earlier developed theories is not a matter of secondary importance, but a necessary element in the elaboration of theory itself, an element in the theoretical analysis of facts. It is not accidental that *Capital* has a subtitle, a second title: *A Critical Analysis of Capitalist Production.*

In *Capital*, the analysis of concepts developed in the entire preceding history of political economy organically coincides, in essence, with an analysis of the stubborn facts of economic reality. These two aspects of scientific-theoretical inquiry coincide or merge in one single process. Neither of them is conceivable or possible without the other. Just as critical analysis of concepts is impossible outside an analysis of facts, theoretical analysis of facts is impossible unless there are concepts through which they may be expressed. Marx's dialectical logic fully takes this circumstance into account.

That is why dialectics is the area where conscious, intentional coincidence of the inductive and the deductive moments takes place, the two constituting indissolubly linked and mutually assuming moments of *inquiry*.

Old logic was more or less consistent in interpreting induction as analysis of *empirical facts*, as formation of analytical definitions of the fact. That is why induction appeared the *basic*, if not the only, form of attaining new knowledge. Deduction was mostly considered as analysis of the concept, as the process of establishing distinctions within the concept. As such, it largely appeared to be the process and form of *explication* or *exposition* of already existing knowledge, knowledge that is already there in the head, rather than a form of obtaining new knowledge and new concepts. The point is that man (on condition, of course, that he really forms a conception of facts) never takes up analysis of facts with an empty consciousness but always with a consciousness developed by education. In other words, he always approaches facts having in mind certain concepts. Whether he wants it or not, he cannot actively grasp or conceive facts in general without that condition—he may, at best, only passively contemplate them.

In the simplest generalisation, induction is indissolubly linked with deduction: man expresses facts in a *concept,* and that means that a new analytical definition of facts is at the same time formed as a new, and more concrete, definition of that concept which serves as the basis for interpreting these facts. If that is not the case, an analytical definition of the fact is not formed at all.

Whether man wants it or not, each new inductive definition of the fact is formed by him in the light of some ready-made concept which he at some time learnt from society, in the light of some conceptual system or other. He who believes that he expresses facts 'without any bias whatsoever', without any 'preconceived ideas', is not actually free from them. On the contrary, he often proves to be slave to the most banal and absurd ideas.

Here as well as anywhere else freedom lies in *conscious* mastering of necessity rather than in trying to escape from it. A genuinely unprejudiced person does not express facts without any 'preconceived ideas' whatsoever, he does it with the aid of consciously assimilated *correct* concepts.

With regard to philosophical categories, this was demonstrated quite convincingly by Engels in his critique of empiricism: a natural scientist who prides himself on his freedom from any logical categories proves to be a captive of the most banal conceptions of them. By himself, he cannot form them out of facts—that would be equivalent to a claim to do something that can only be done by mankind in its development. He therefore in effect always borrows logical categories from philosophy. The only question is, from what philosophy he will borrow them: from a good-for-nothing fashionable system or one that is actually the peak of development, a system based on the study of the entire history of human thought and its attainments.

This is true, of course, not only of the concepts of philosophy: the same thing happens with the categories of any science. Man never begins reasoning 'from scratch', 'straight from the facts'. The great Russian scientist Ivan Pavlov said once that without an idea in the head you can't see facts. Mindless contemplation and induction without ideas are products of the imagination, just as 'pure thought'.

Empiricism assuming that it 'operates only with undeniable facts ... operates predominantly with traditional notions, with the largely obsolete products of thought of its predecessors'.[8] That is why an empiricist easily confuses abstractions with reality, reality with abstractions, and takes subjective illusions for objective facts and objective facts and concepts expressing them, for abstractions and illusions. As a rule, he posits abstract truisms as definitions of facts.

It follows that 'empirical induction' itself takes the form of concretisation of notions and concepts that serve as the basis for considering facts, that is, the form of deduction or process of filling the original concepts with new and more detailed definitions obtained from facts through abstraction.

The old opposition of deduction and induction is rationally sublated in materialist dialectics. Deduction ceases to be a means of formal derivation of definitions contained a priori in the concept, becoming a means of actual development of knowledge of facts in their movement, in their internal interaction. This deduction organically includes an empirical moment: it proceeds through a rigorous analysis of empirical facts, that is, through induction. In this case, however, the names 'induction' and 'deduction' express only an external, formal resemblance between the method of materialist dialectics and the corresponding methods of ratiocinative, intellect-oriented logic. In actual fact, that is neither induction nor deduction but rather a third method including the other two as sublated moments. Here they are realised simultaneously, as mutually assuming opposites, resulting in a new and higher form of logical development precisely through their reciprocal action.

This higher form, an organic combination of analysis of facts with analysis of concepts, is exactly the method of ascent from the abstract to the concrete of which Marx speaks. That is the only logical form of the development of knowledge which corresponds to the objective nature of the thing. The point is that no other method can reproduce the objective concreteness in thought as reality that emerged and developed historically. One cannot do it in any other way.

As such, the method of ascent from the abstract to the concrete is by no means merely a method for expounding available knowledge obtained in some other way, as Marx's teaching has often been presented by revisionists who dis-

---

[8] Frederick Engels, *Dialectics of Nature*, p. 138.

torted the method of *Capital* in the spirit of banal neo-Kantianism.

That is the way in which the method of ascent from the abstract to the concrete is interpreted by Rudolph Hilferding. Quoting the Preface to Marx's economic MSS of 1857-58 ('On the first path the full idea will evaporate until it becomes an abstract definition; on the second, abstract definitions lead to reproduction of the concrete through thinking'), Hilferding makes this comment: 'It is clear from this already how false it is to equate deduction and induction as sources of knowledge of the same value. Rather, deduction is only a *scientific method of presentation* which, however, must be preceded in the spirit by induction if it should really arrive, in the final analysis, from the general to the presentation of the particular.'[9] Hilferding calls the method of ascent from the abstract to the concrete deduction and interprets it in an extremely one-sided manner, only with regard to its external resemblance to deduction as it is traditionally conceived, denying that it has any advantages as a method for the study of real facts and reducing it merely to a form of systematic presentation of available knowledge, which must in his view be obtained in some other way in advance, namely, the inductive way.

Karl Renner, the well-known Austrian Marxist, author of *Economy as a Whole and Socialisation* follows the same avenue of thought in the Preface to his work. He reduces the essence of the method of ascent from the abstract to the concrete applied in *Capital,* to the manner of presentation characteristic of German philosophers, which Marx, according to Renner, learnt from his contemporaries. Insofar as this manner of presentation has allegedly become quite alien to the modern reader, Renner believes it appropriate to replace it with quite a different one. 'I know no book grown out of such a great mass of empirical data as Marx's *Capital*, and only a few books whose method of presentation is as deductive and abstract.'[10] Therefore Renner believes it expedient to present the content of Marx's theory in another manner, one which 'proceeds from the visual evidence of the facts of experience, arranges them in a certain order, and

[9] *Die Neue Zeit,* Bd. 2, Nr. 43, 29, Jahrgang, 1910/1911, S. 578 (italics ours—*E. I.*).

[10] Karl Renner, *Die Wirtschaft als Gesamtprozess und die Sozialisierung,* Dietz Verlag, Berlin, 1924, S. 5-6.

thus gradually advances to the abstract concept',[11] that is, inductively. In this case, Renner believes, the method of presentation will correspond to the method of investigation, whereas in *Capital* the two are in contradiction.

As a result, Renner generalises, quite uncritically, the empirical phenomena of modern capitalism as they appear on the surface, passing off his generalisations for a theoretical expression of the essence of these phenomena. Following this path he discovers, for instance, that a worker buying shares thereby becomes owner of the social means of production, which results in automatic 'democratisation of capital' and 'socialisation' of social production, making revolution unnecessary. Thus Renner supplants Marx's *method* of studying phenomena by the method of apology, disguising it as a different manner of presentation.

The method of ascent from the abstract to the concrete can just as little be interpreted as a method of purely logical synthesis of available abstractions (previously obtained in a purely analytical manner) in a system. The notion that cognition involves at first 'pure' analysis producing numerous abstractions followed by just as 'pure' synthesis, is the same kind of invention in metaphysical epistemology as the idea of induction without deduction.

In substantiating this view, the development of science in the 17th and 18th centuries is often taken as an example, but the facts are often violated, unwittingly. Even if one should agree that characteristic of that time was indeed the analytical attitude towards facts (although synthesis, despite the illusions of theoreticians, was carried out here as well), one must not forget that that was not the initial stage in the scientific development of mankind and that the 'one-sided analysis' characteristic of that epoch assumed ancient Greek science as a prerequisite. And ancient Greek science, the real initial stage in the scientific development of Europe, is much more characterised by a generalised synthetic view of things. In referring to the history of metaphysics of the 17th and 18th centuries, one should bear in mind that it is not the first but rather the second great epoch in the development of thought. In that case, it is synthesis rather than analysis that emerges historically as the first stage in the processing of facts in thought.

---

[11] Karl Renner, op. cit., S. 5.

The example referred to thus shows something diametrically opposed to what it was intended to show.

Analysis and synthesis are (and have always been) just as indissoluble internal opposites of the process of thinking as deduction and induction. If at certain epochs one was overestimated to the detriment of the other, this should not be raised to a law that thought should be subject to in the future, a logical law, a precept according to which each science must first pass through a purely analytical stage of development later to proceed, on this basis, to a synthetic one.

But that is exactly the conception on which the opinion is based that the method of ascent from the abstract to the concrete can be applied only then and there where the concrete has previously been 'distilled' into the abstract.

The method of ascent from the abstract to the concrete is first of all a method of analysis of real empirical facts. As such, it organically comprises in itself the reverse motion as its internally necessary opposite: each step on this path is exactly an act of ascent from the sensually given concreteness to its abstract theoretical expression. That is why the ascent from the abstract to the concrete in thought is at the same time continually renewed movement from the concrete in contemplation and notion to the concrete in the concept.

Abstract definitions of sensually given facts, that are synthesised on the path of ascent towards the concrete truth, are formed in the process of motion itself. They are by no means taken ready-made as products of the previous, allegedly purely analytical, stage of logical cognition.

If there is any sense in the assertion that ascent from the abstract to the concrete assumes a purely analytical reduction of the sensually empirical concreteness to abstract expression, as a special stage of logical development interior in time and essence, this meaning would appear to be that theoretical consideration of reality assumes the existence of a well-developed vocabulary, a spontaneously formed terminology, and a system of abstract general conceptions. This 'purely analytical' stage in the reflection of objective reality in consciousness is only a prerequisite of logical theoretical activity rather than its first stage.

Thus we may sum up the above as follows: the method of ascent from the abstract to the concrete is a specific form of the activity of thought, of logical transformation of contemplation and notion into concepts. It is by no means an artificial procedure, a manner of presentation of already existing knowledge, or a formal method for combining available abstractions in a system.

This is first and foremost a natural law of the theoretical development of mankind established by philosophy and, in the second place, a consciously applied method of development of theory.

Each inductive generalisation taken separately (according to the formula 'from the concrete in contemplation to the abstract in thought) is in fact always realised in the context of the overall advance of cognition and is in this sense only a 'disappearing moment' in the general movement to concrete truth. Thereby ascent from the abstract to the concrete in thought and the dialectics of thought are indissolubly linked.

It is not for nothing that Lenin, having carefully copied a lengthy definition of the path from the abstract to the concrete given by Hegel in the last section of his greater Logic, describes it as follows:

'This extract is not at all bad as a kind of summing up of dialectics.'

The definition quoted by Lenin characterises reasoning as ascent from the abstract to the concrete:

'...Cognition rolls forward from content to content. This progress determines itself, first, in this manner, that it begins from simple determinatenesses and that each subsequent one is *richer* and *more concrete*. For the result contains its own beginning and the development of the beginning has made it the richer by a new determinateness. The universal is the foundation; the progress therefore must not be taken as a flow from Other to Other. In the absolute method the Notion *preserves* itself in its otherness, and the universal in its particularisation, in the Judgement and in reality; it raises to each next stage of determination the whole mass of its antecedent content, and by its dialectical progress not only loses nothing and leaves nothing behind, but carries with it all that it has acquired, enriching and concentrating itself upon itself....'[12]

---

[12] V. I. Lenin, Conspectus of Hegel's Book *The Science of Logic, Collected Works,* Vol. 38, p. 231.

It is these sections of Hegel's Logic, where the idea is expounded of ascent from an abstract universal definiteness of the object to its increasingly more concrete embodiment, that Lenin singles out in his conspectus as the sections in which idealism is felt least of all and where the dialectical method is in the foreground.

'It is noteworthy that the whole chapter on the "Absolute Idea" scarcely says a word about God (hardly ever has a "divine" "notion" slipped out accidentally) and apart from that—*this NB*—it contains almost nothing that is specifically *idealism,* but has for its main subject the *dialectical method.* The sum-total, the last word and essence of Hegel's logic is the *dialectical method*—this is extremely noteworthy. And one thing more: in this *most idealistic* of Hegel's works there is the *least* idealism and the *most materialism.* "Contradictory", but a fact!'[13]

In the dialectical view of the process of cognition, the method of ascent from the abstract to the concrete, from the universal theoretical definition of the *object* given in contemplation and notion, to its increasingly more concrete definitions, appears as a form of theoretically correct transformation of empirical facts in a concept. That is the view taken by Marx, in the Preface to his *Contribution to the Critique of Political Economy* and by Lenin in his notes on and evaluation of the last chapter of Hegel's Logic.

THE MATERIALIST SUBSTANTIATION OF THE METHOD OF ASCENT FROM THE ABSTRACT TO THE CONCRETE IN MARX

The method of ascent from the abstract to the concrete as a universal law to which scientific development is subject, was formulated by Hegel. But it became an actual method of development of *concrete scientific* knowledge only in the hands of Marx who gave it a materialist substantiation, whereas in Hegel, owing to the idealist interpretation and application of it, it appeared exclusively as a method for constructing a speculative science of sciences, an absolute system of the 'world as a whole'.

Marx not only substantiated this law on the general theoretical plane—he actually applied it to the development of

[13] Ibid., p. 234.

a concrete science, political economy. *Capital*, created with the aid of this method, contains a concrete and extensive practical proof of the necessity of this method, its real materialist substantiation as the only method that agrees with the dialectics of the objective reality.

Analysis of *Capital* with reference to the method of inquiry applied in it should also show the concrete essence of the method of ascent from the abstract to the concrete. It should be shown as the only method that can ensure the solution of the central task of scientific investigation as it is seen in materialist dialectics—the task of tracing the concrete reciprocal conditioning of phenomena creating, through their interaction, a *system* that emerged and developed historically, and still continues to develop new forms of its existence and internal interaction.

This task cannot be solved in any other way. Any other method does not correspond to the objective nature of the object reproduced with its aid in the spirit.

It would be quite erroneous to derive the need for the method of ascent from the abstract to the concrete merely from the fact that man's consciousness is incapable of grasping the object in its entire complexity so that it has to ascend, willy-nilly, from incomplete one-sided (abstract) notion of the object to ever more complete and comprehensive knowledge of it. This explanation would simply be quite inadequate. To be more precise, that is not an explanation but a reference to a well-known fact. It is self-obvious that consciousness is indeed such. But all properties and specific features of consciousness themselves require materialist explanation. Besides, such a reference to the nature of consciousness would explain nothing, generally speaking, about the specificity of the method of ascent from the abstract to the concrete as a method of scientific theoretical inquiry. Familiarisation with an object, phenomenon, or system of phenomena also takes the form of gradual and ordered assimilation of new details, of transition from a one-sided and meagre notion of an object to a comprehensive (though still empirical) notion of it. Accumulation of empirical information through which reality becomes *familiar* but not yet *cognised*, also proceeds as development from one-sided to comprehensive knowledge.

This interpretation would thus take into account only those abstract identical features which theoretical reproduction of concreteness in the concept has in common with simple empirical familiarisation with phenomena, and would express the specificity of neither.

The method of ascent from the abstract to the concrete is merely a method of *reflection* of concrete reality in thought rather than a method of *creation* of it by the power of thought, as it was presented by Hegel. That is precisely why it does not depend on thought at all where logical development of concepts by this method will begin and in what direction it will proceed. As Marx showed, it depends only on the relation in which the various aspects of the concrete whole stand to each other. The method of logical development must therefore correspond to the method of internal division of this whole, to the dialectics of the formation of concreteness outside thought, that is, in the final analysis, to the historical development of this concreteness, although, as will be shown later, this coincidence is by no means simple, dead, or mirrorlike, being concerned only with universal moments of development.

The formula of materialism in epistemology and logic is the reverse of what has just been formulated: the object is such that only the given rather than some other form of activity of consciousness corresponds to it; the object is such that it can be reflected in consciousness only with the aid of the given method.

In other words, the discussion of the mode of logical activity here, too, becomes the study of the *objective nature of the objective reality*, a further elaboration of the category of concreteness as an *objective* category expressing the universal form of the existence of reality.

Here, too, the principle of coincidence of logic, epistemology, and dialectics is the dominant one: a question that is purely logical at first sight is essentially a question of universal forms in which objective concreteness emerges and develops.

A materialist substantiation of the correctness and necessity of the method of ascent from the abstract to the concrete may only consist in demonstrating the real universal laws that equally dominate the formation of any concrete system of interacting phenomena (whether it be the capitalist system of social relations or the solar system, the chemical or the biological form of interaction, etc.).

Here again we run into the familiar dialectical difficulty:

the approach to dialectics is dialectical in itself. It is apparently impossible to establish and theoretically express the universal laws of the formation of *any* concreteness on the path of inductive generalisation, of abstraction of the general and identical features which the capitalist system has in common with the solar planetary system and the biological form of interaction in nature with the electromagnetic or chemical one.

Formulating the question in this manner means setting a task absolutely insoluble in its very nature. Mankind as a whole does not know all cases of concrete interaction in infinite nature, let alone the present author. Nevertheless we face the task of establishing exactly the *universal* (that is, logical) laws of the formation of any objective system of concrete interaction. In other words, we recur to one of the eternal problems of philosophy—whether it is possible to work out a really universal, *infinite* generalisation on the basis of studying a limited and necessarily *finite* series of facts, and if it is, how is one to approach the task.

Luckily, philosophy has never even tried to obtain this understanding within the inductive approach. The actual development of science and philosophy has long found a *practical* way of solving this antinomy, which only seems insoluble in principle as long as it is formulated metaphysically.

In actual fact, mankind has always obtained universal, 'infinite' generalisations and conclusions, not only in philosophy but in any area of knowledge as well, through *analysis* of at least one typical case rather than through *abstraction* of those identical features that all possible cases have in common.

Suffice it in this connection to remember the words from Engels' *Dialectics of Nature*:

'A striking example of how little induction can claim to be the sole or even the predominant form of scientific discovery occurs in thermodynamics: the steam-engine provided the most striking proof that one can impart heat and obtain mechanical motion. 100,000 steam-engines did not prove this more than *one*, but only more and more forced the physicists into the necessity of explaining it. Sadi Carnot was the first seriously to set about the task. But not by induction. He studied the steam-engine, analysed it, and found that in it the process which mattered does not appear in *pure form* but is concealed by all sorts of subsidiary processes. He did away with these subsidiary circumstances that have no bearing on the essential process, and constructed an ideal steam-engine (or gas engine), which it is true is as little capable of being realised as, for instance, a geometrical line or surface, but in its way performs the same service as these mathematical abstractions: it presents the process in a pure, independent, and unadulterated form.'[14]

It is not induction directed at the search of abstractions expressing the general features of all the particular cases but in-depth *analysis* of one particular case aimed at revealing the process under study in its pure form that has been the method of philosophy whenever and wherever it really arrived at objective discoveries. It is only men like Comte and Spencer who tried to follow the path of induction and abstraction—with suitably meagre results.

Philosophy has always been concerned with its own specific problems essentially different from the desire to find the abstract general features which a crocodile has in common with Jupiter and the solar system with wealth. Philosophy has always had its own serious problems, the solution of which brought it closer to the establishment of the universal laws of everything that exists, to revealing the content of categories.

Marx, as is well known, gave a critical analysis of the Hegelian system of universal categories, but he did not do that by comparing these categories with the features which mankind has in common with the atomic nucleus or both of them with the structure of the great Universe.

Hegel's system was critically overcome through its critical comparison mostly with one instance of dialectical development (but, what is most important, a most typical one)—with the dialectics of social production relations at one stage of their development.

A critical overcoming of the universal categories historically developed by philosophy, with reference to at least *one* typical case, is the real path always taken by the evolution in understanding the content of universal categories.

The basic task of the theoretical analysis of the universal is always actually reduced to the analysis of the in-

---

[14] Frederick Engels, *Dialectics of Nature,* p. 229.

dividual from the standpoint of the universal. One must only be able to single out in the individual that which constitutes the universality of this case rather than its individuality or specificity. It is at this point that one most requires a conscious attitude to abstraction and the methods of its obtaining. For the most ordinary error of theoretical inquiry is made when that which actually refers to the given concurrence of transient circumstances in which a real universal form is contemplated, is taken for the universal form itself of the individual fact.

To reveal the content of such a universal category as concreteness, one may and must study at least one typical case of a living dialectically developed system of internally interacting objective phenomena.

The system of capitalist relations between men is a most typical instance of such a self-developing relatively independent system (concreteness). We shall consider it as an immediate particular case of concreteness in general, in which the universal outlines of any concreteness may and must be revealed. Materials from other fields will be considered to the extent in which they are characteristic in themselves.

The choice of this material is determined by reasons other than subjective caprice or personal inclination. A much more weighty consideration in favour of this choice is that no other concreteness has been comprehended as profoundly as this one. No other system of concrete interaction has been presented to the mind in the entire complexity and fulness of its internal dialectics, in the entire complexity of its structure as the system of capitalist relations revealed in *Capital* and other works of the founders of Marxism-Leninism, and that is exactly why it is most expedient to use this material as the basis for considering the universal characteristics of any concreteness, for explicating the category of concreteness in general.

This mode of consideration fully coincides with what Marx himself did in his cognitive practice.

When Marx set himself the task of revealing the universal law of capitalism as such, as a historically determined system of social production, he did not take the path of inductive comparison of all cases, without exception, of capitalist development that took place on the planet in his time. He acted differently, as a dialectician: he took the *most characteristic* and *best developed case*, namely, capitalist reality in England and its reflection in English economic literature and worked out a *universal* economic theory, mostly on the basis of detailed investigation of this *single* instance.

He understood that the universal laws of the development of capitalism are the same for any country, and that England, having advanced farther than any other country along the path of capitalist development, demonstrated all phenomena in their most distinct form. All that which in other countries was present as a very weak and hardly distinguishable rudiment, as a tendency that was not yet fully formed, obscured and complicated by secondary external circumstances, existed here in the most developed and classically clearcut form. On some occasions only did Marx use materials concerning the capitalist development of other countries (in his analysis of rent, for instance, he used numerous materials from the economic development of the Russian village). This way, the way of establishing the immediately common features of different instances of capitalist development, was not a royal road for arriving at a *universal* theory of capitalist development. The royal road of his inquiry was invariably the study of English economic reality and a constructive critique of English political economy.

The same considerations should apparently be taken into account in tackling the problem of the categories of dialectics as logic and epistemology, as the science of thought. It is capitalist reality theoretically revealed in *Capital* and other works of the same cycle (both by Marx and by his best pupils and followers, in the first place by Engels and Lenin) that provides the most comprehensive picture of a historically emergent and developed concreteness, as a most typical instance of concreteness in general. It is *Capital* that we regard as heretofore unsurpassed model of *conscious application of the dialectical method*, of dialectical *logic* in the fulness of its content. It shows many sciences their own future, demonstrating in classically clearcut form all those aspects of the method that have not yet been realised in other sciences in the same consistent manner.

It should also be pointed out that constructive critique of previous theories—a necessary moment of the theoretical elaboration of the scientific problems of our times—assumes that critically assimilated is the best-quality theoretical (mental) material, the really best models of theoretical comprehension of the actuality which appears in the given case as the object of attention and inquiry.

As Marx developed his economic theory, the principal theoretical opponents with whom he argued in working out his comprehension of reality, were the *classic* representatives of bourgeois political economy rather than the contemporary representatives of vulgar economy and of the 'professorial form of decay' of theory. The latter were Marx's contemporaries only chronologically, not from the standpoint of theoretical comprehension of the subject-matter. In regard to theory they were infinitely inferior to the classics and were by no means a theoretical opposition worthy of serious argument. Unfolding his theoretical comprehension of reality in the form of serious argument with the classics, Marx merely ridicules, whenever the occasion warrants, such 'theoreticians' as Senior, Bastiat, MacCulloch, Roscher, etc. Criticising these latter was only appropriate when the theoretical comprehension of the subject-matter had already been unfolded in its essence.

As far as philosophical categories, the categories of dialectics are concerned, *classical* bourgeois philosophy still remains the only worthy and serious theoretical opponent of the philosophy of dialectical materialism, which, however, does not at all eliminate the task of fighting against modern bourgeois systems but, on the contrary, helps to lay bare their desire to escape the great philosophical problems.

The attitude of Marx, Engels and Lenin to Hegel or Feuerbach was fundamentally different from their attitude to Schopenhauer, Comte, Mach, or Bogdanov. Sharply criticising the speculations of petty idealists, they never even tried to look for a rational kernel in their writings.

In denouncing the mixed-up sophistic argumentation of Machists, Lenin first of all reduces it to the classically transparent and principled expression which these views were given by Berkeley and Fichte. That is not merely a polemic manoeuvre but the best way of *theoretically* uncovering the essence of their position. On the other hand, when Lenin faces the task of further elaboration of materialist dialectics, he leaves aside Machists as Berkeley's *theoretical* adherents and goes back to a critical analysis of Hegel's *The Science of Logic* as the real peak of bourgeois thought in comprehending the universal laws of nature, society, and human thought.

The above may be summed up as follows: a genuinely concrete substantiation of the method of ascent from the abstract to the concrete as the only scientifically correct method of logical development, as the only method corresponding to the objective dialectics, should be looked for in Marx's *Capital*, in the analysis of its logical structure.

Logic, epistemology, and dialectics consistently coincide in *Capital*, and this systematic coincidence, the coincidence of induction and deduction, of analysis and synthesis, characterising the method of ascent from the abstract to the concrete, is the distinguishing feature of Marx's method of inquiry. Let us first consider the problem in its concrete economic expression, and then proceed to general methodological and logical conclusions.

Let us pose this question: is it in general possible to understand theoretically (to reproduce conceptually) the objective essence of such phenomena as surplus-value and profit if the category of value has not been previously and independently analysed? Can money be understood if the laws governing the movement of simple commodity market are not known?

Those who have read *Capital* and are familiar with the problems of political economy are aware that this is an insoluble task.

Can one form a concept (a concrete abstraction) of capital through purely inductive generalisation of the abstract features observed in any of the various kinds of capital? Will such an abstraction be satisfactory from the scientific point of view? Will such an abstraction express the inner structure of capital in general, as a specific form of economic reality?

As soon as we pose the question in this form, the need for a negative answer to it becomes apparent.

This abstraction will of course express the identical features that industrial, financial, commercial, and usurious capital have in common. It will indubitably free us from repetitions. But that will exhaust its actual cognitive potential. It will not express the concrete essence of any of these kinds of capital. It will just as little express the concrete essence of their mutual connection, their interaction. These are precisely the features from which an abstraction is made. But, from the standpoint of dialectics, it is exactly the concrete interaction of concrete phenomena that constitutes the subject-matter and goal of thinking in concepts.

The meaning of the general is contradictory, as Lenin pointed out; it deadens living reality but at the same time is the only possible move towards its comprehension. In the given instance, however, it is easy to see that the general *does nothing* but deaden the concrete, moving away from it and being in no way at the same time a step towards it. It is *from the concrete*, as from the 'inessential', that this general is an abstraction.

Neither does this abstraction express the universal nature of capital (of any capital—industrial, financial, or commercial).

Marx's *Capital* demonstrates in a very graphic manner that the concrete economic nature of commercial capital, as a concrete aspect of the capitalist whole, cannot in principle be understood or expressed in theoretical abstraction unless industrial capital is previously understood in its inner structure.

To consider the immanent definitions of industrial capital is the same as to reveal the essence of capital in general. It is just as undoubted that industrial capital cannot be understood before value.

'...The rate of profit is no mystery, so soon as we know the laws of surplus-value. If we reverse the process, we cannot comprehend either the one or the other.' [15]

Let us stress that the point here is *understanding* (expressing in a *concept*), for it is of course quite possible to create the abstraction of profit in general. In the latter case it is sufficient to reduce the empirically observed phenomena of profit to an abstract expression. This abstraction will be quite adequate for *distinguishing* with certainty between the phenomena of profit and other phenomena, for 'recognising' profit. This is quite successfully done by every entrepreneur, who can very well distinguish between profit and wages, money, and so on.

In doing so, the entrepreneur *does not understand*, however, *what profit is*. He does not need it, either. In practice, he acts as an instinctive adherent of positivist philosophy and empirical logic. He merely lends a generalised expres-

[15] Karl Marx, *Capital,* Vol. I, pp. 207-08.

sion to phenomena that are important and essential from his point of view, from the standpoint of his subjective goals, and this generalised expression of phenomena excellently serves him in practice as a concept permitting him to distinguish with certainty profit from non-profit. As an honest-to-goodness positivist, he sincerely believes all talk about the inner nature of profit, about the essence and substance of this phenomenon, so dear to his heart, to be metaphysical sophistry, philosophising divorced from life. Under conditions of capitalist production, the entrepreneur does not have to know any of this. 'Anyone can use money as money without necessarily understanding what money is.'[16]

The narrow practical intellect, as Marx emphasised, is basically alien and hostile to *comprehension* (cf. the remark about Friedrich List in Chapter One of *A Contribution to the Critique of Political Economy*).

It may even be harmful to the entrepreneur to philosophise on the problem of profit. While he is trying to understand it, other, smarter and more practical and pushful operators, will snatch his share of profit. A businessman will never exchange real profit for an understanding of what profit is.

In science, in reasoning, however, *comprehension* is important. Science as thinking in concepts begins only where consciousness does not simply express in other words the conceptions of things spontaneously thrust upon it but rather attempts to analyse both things and conceptions of things in a goal-directed and critical manner.

To *comprehend* a phenomenon means to establish its place and role in the concrete system of interacting phenomena in which it is necessarily realised, and to find out precisely those traits which make it possible for the phenomenon to play this role in the whole. To *comprehend* a phenomenon means to discover the mode of its origin, the rule according to which the phenomenon emerges with necessity rooted in the concrete totality of conditions, it means to analyse the very conditions of the origin of phenomena. That is the general formula for the formation of a *concept* and of *conception*.

To *comprehend* profit means to establish the universal and necessary nature of its origin and movement in the system

[16] Karl Marx, *Theories of Surplus-Value*, Part III, Progress Publishers, Moscow, 1975, p. 163.

of capitalist production, to reveal its specific role in the overall movement of the system as a whole.

That is why a concrete concept can only be realised through a complicated system of abstractions expressing the phenomenon in the totality of conditions of its origin.

Political economy as a science historically begins where recurrent phenomena (profit, wages, interest, etc.) are not merely registered, in terms of generally understood and generally acceptable designations (that takes place before science and outside science, in the consciousness of the practical participants of production) but are comprehended concretely, through analysis of their place and role in the system.

Thus, it is in principle impossible to *comprehend* (express in a concept) profit unless surplus-value and the laws of its origin are comprehended previously and independently from the former.

Why is that impossible? If we answer this question in a general theoretical form, we shall thereby show the real necessity of the method of ascent from the abstract to the concrete, its applicability to any field of knowledge.

We shall therefore turn to the history of political economy.

ADAM SMITH'S INDUCTION AND DAVID RICARDO'S DEDUCTION. THE VIEWPOINTS OF LOCKE AND SPINOZA IN POLITICAL ECONOMY

The logical conflicts in the development of political economy would be incomprehensible if we did not establish real connections between it and contemporary philosophy. The categories in which English economists consciously comprehended empirical facts were rooted in the philosophical systems current at the time.

A characteristic fact that had a profound effect on the development of economic thought in England was that one of the first theoreticians of political economy turned out to be none other than John Locke, the classical representative of empiricism in philosophy.

'Locke's view is all the more important because it was the classical expression of bourgeois society's ideas of right as against feudal society, and moreover *his philosophy served as the basis for all the ideas of the whole of subsequent English political economy.*' [17]

Locke's views proved to be the intermediate link between the philosophy of English empiricism (with all the weaknesses of the latter) and the emerging theory of wealth. Through Locke, political economy assimilated the basic methodological principles of empiricism, in particular and especially the one-sided analytical and inductive method, the standpoint of the reduction of complex phenomena to their elementary constituents.

However, just as in the natural sciences of that epoch, the actual cognitive practice of the study of economic phenomena even in Locke himself differed essentially from the kind of epistemology that could be and was recommended by consistent empiricism. The method which was actually used by theoretical economists to form theoretical definitions of things, despite their one-sided epistemological illusions, did not tally with empirical inductive logic. While consciously applying the one-sided analytical method, the theoreticians proceeded in fact, without realising it clearly, from a number of theoretical assumptions which essentially contradicted the principles of the narrow empirical approach.

The logic of pure empiricism was incapable of coping with the task of working out a theoretical view of the phenomena of economic reality for the simple reason that actual economic reality was a most complex interlacing of bourgeois capitalist forms of property with the feudal ones.

Under those conditions direct inductive generalisation of empirical facts would have yielded, at best, only a correct description of the results of interaction of two not merely different but diametrically opposed and hostile principles of ownership. Locke's empirical-deductive method would not have permitted to go deep into the inner 'physiology' of bourgeois private ownership.

It is well known that Locke himself did not merely generalise what he saw but actively singled out in the empirical facts only those forms and moments which, in his view, corresponded to man's eternal and genuine nature.

In other words, the very task of abstract analytical extraction of the elementary constituents, the task of analys-

[17] Karl Marx, *Theories of Surplus-Value*, Part I, p. 367 (italics ours—*E. I.*).

ing empirical facts here as well implied a certain universal criterion according to which some forms of economy are described as 'genuine', as 'corresponding to man's nature', while others are eliminated as 'un-genuine'. The bourgeois individualistic conception of 'man's nature' was used by all the bourgeois theoreticians as such a criterion. Locke was one of the originators of this view.

Clearly, this universal and fundamental principle of bourgeois science, used as a yardstick to measure empirical facts, could as little be obtained by empirical induction as the concept of atom. In Locke's time, bourgeois capitalist form of ownership was by no means universal and dominant. It was not an empirically universal fact, and the conception of wealth as the starting point of bourgeois political economy could not itself be formed by inductive generalisation of all the particular instances and kinds of ownership without exception.

It was formed with the aid of considerations quite different than the purely logical ones. The spontaneous social reason here too proved to be stronger than the cannons of ratiocinative, intellectual logic.

In other words, from its birth political economy faced the same logical problem as Newton did in his field: to make even a single inductive generalisation, an economist would have to have some conception, at least implied, of the universal genuine nature (substance) of the phenomena under consideration.

Just as Newton based all his inductions on the idea that only the geometrically definable forms of facts are the solely objective forms, economists silently assumed that only those forms of economy which corresponded to the principles of bourgeois private ownership were the genuine forms.

All other forms of economic relations were silently eliminated as subjective errors of men, as forms that do not correspond to the genuine, natural, and therefore objective nature of man. Only those definitions of facts were incorporated in theory which were an immediate and direct outcome of man's 'eternal nature'—in actual fact, of the specific nature of the private proprietor, the bourgeois.

All theoreticians of bourgeois political economy thus had to proceed and really did proceed from quite a definite universal basic principle, from a clear conception of the substance, the general objective nature of the particular cases and forms of economy.

This conception of substance, just as in natural science, could not be obtained through empirical induction. But Lockean epistemology was silent on just this point—on the question of the ways of cognition of substance, of the ways of formation of the universal original foundation of science. This foundation, the conception of the substance of wealth, had to be worked out by economists (Locke included) in a purely spontaneous way, without a clear understanding of the ways of obtaining it.

However it may be, English political economy practically solved this difficulty when William Petty discovered this universal substance of economic phenomena, the substance of wealth, in *labour producing commodities*, in labour performed with the objective of alienating the product of labour in the free market.

Insofar as economists actually proceeded from this more or less clearly realised conception of the universal substance of wealth, their generalisations were theoretical in nature and differed from the purely empirical generalisations of any merchant, usurer, or market woman.

But this meant that a theoretical approach to things coincided with the desire to understand different particular forms of wealth as modifications of one and the same universal substance.

The fact, however, that classical political economy was linked up, in its conscious methodological convictions, with Locke's philosophy, made itself felt directly, and in a very instructive form. As a result, theoretical investigation of facts proper was continually interlaced with simple uncritical reproduction of empirical conceptions.

This is most clearly seen in the work of Adam Smith. The first economist to express clearly the concept of labour as the universal substance of all economic phenomena, he unfolded a theory in which properly theoretical consideration of facts was continually interwoven with extremely untheoretical descriptions of empirical data from the standpoint of a man forcibly involved in production and accumulation of value.

'Smith himself moves with great naïveté in a perpetual contradiction. On the one hand he traces the intrinsic connection existing between economic categories or the obscure structure of the bourgeois economic system. On the other, he simultaneously sets forth the connection as it appears in the phenomena of competition and thus as it presents itself to the unscientific observer just as to him who is actually involved and interested in the process of bourgeois production. One of these conceptions fathoms the inner connection, the physiology, so to speak, of the bourgeois system, whereas the other takes the external phenomena of life, as they seem and appear and merely describes, catalogues, recounts and arranges them under formal definitions. With Smith both these methods of approach not only merrily run alongside one another but also intermingle and constantly contradict one another.'[18]

Smith himself did not of course notice the contradiction between the two modes of reflection of reality in abstractions. It is easy to recognise here a scientist who pictures the process of cognition in a purely Lockean manner. It was Locke's epistemology that ignored the distinction between theoretical abstraction (concept) and simple empirical abstraction, simple expression in speech of the sensually stated similarities and distinctions.

David Ricardo, as is well known, made a decisive step forward, as compared to Adam Smith. The philosophical-historical significance of this step consisted first and foremost in that he was the first to distinguish, consciously and consistently, between the task of properly theoretical consideration of empirical data (the task of expressing these data in concepts) and the task of simple description and cataloguing of phenomena in the form in which they are immediately given in contemplation and notion.

Ricardo understood very well that science (thinking in concepts) dealt with the same empirical facts as simple contemplation and notion. In science, however, these facts have to be considered from a higher point of view—that of their inner connection. This requirement was not consistently and rigorously satisfied in Smith, whereas Ricardo strictly insisted on it.

Ricardo's view of the nature of scientific inquiry is much more reminiscent of Spinoza's method than the epistemology of the empiricist Locke; he consistently adheres to the

---

[18] Karl Marx, *Theories of Surplus-Value*, Part II, Progress Publishers, Moscow, 1968, p. 165.

substantive standpoint. Every individual economic formation, each separate form of wealth must be understood as modifications of one and the same universal substance rather than simply described.

In this respect, too, Ricardo and Spinoza are right where Smith and Locke are wrong.

Marx assessed Ricardo's role in the development of the theory of political economy with classical clarity and decisiveness: '...Ricardo steps in and calls to science: Halt! The basis, the starting point for the physiology of the bourgeois system—for the understanding of its internal organic coherence and life process—is the determination of *value by labour-time*. Ricardo starts with this and forces science to get out of the rut, to render an account of the extent to which the other categories—the relations of production and commerce—evolved and described by it, correspond to or contradict this basis, this starting-point; to elucidate how far a science which in fact only reflects and reproduces the manifest forms of the process, and therefore also how far these manipulations themselves, correspond to the basis on which the inner coherence, the actual physiology of bourgeois society rests or the basis which forms its starting-point; and in general, to examine how matters stand with the contradiction between the apparent and the actual movement of the system. This then is Ricardo's great historical significance for science.' [19]

In other words, Ricardo's view did not consist in the reduction of complex phenomena to a number of their elementary constituents but rather in the deduction of all complex phenomena from one simple substance.

But that brought Ricardo face to face with the need for consciously abandoning the method of forming theoretical abstractions recommended for science by Lockean logic. Empirical induction did not correspond to the task facing Ricardo, the task of *deducing* theoretical definitions from one rigorously applied principle—the conception of the nature of value as determined by labour.

Adam Smith, to the extent in which he actually produced something more significant than mere description of facts, spontaneously and unconsciously contradicted at every step his own philosophical premises borrowed from Locke, doing

[19] Ibid., p. 166.

something quite different from what he thought he was doing, whereas Ricardo quite consciously chose the path of theoretical deduction of categories.

The rigorously deductive character of his reasoning has long become proverbial among political economists. But it was Marx alone who correctly evaluated the significance of this deduction, showing it as the natural logical expression of the greatest merit of Ricardo's theoretical approach—his desire to understand all forms of bourgeois wealth without exception as more or less complex and remote products of labour producing commodities, of labour producing value, and all categories of political economy, as modifications of the value category.

What distinguishes him from Smith is his desire to regard empirical facts consistently and without waverings from one and the same viewpoint rigorously formulated in the definition of the basic concept—from the labour theory of value.

This standpoint is also present in Smith, and that makes him a theoretician. But it is not the *only* point of view with him, and on this score Ricardo is decisively at variance with Smith. In the latter, theoretical consideration of facts (that is, their analysis from the standpoint of the labour theory of value) all too often gives way to their purely empirical description.

Ricardo found, spontaneously and by trial and error, the correct view of the nature of theoretical analysis of facts. Hence his desire for a strictly deductive consideration of phenomena and categories.

This conception of deduction, as is easy to see, does not yet contain anything metaphysical or idealistic or formal logical. In this conception, deduction is tantamount to a negation of eclecticism with regard to facts. That means that a conception of the universal nature or substance of all the particular and individual phenomena, once established, must remain the same throughout the investigation, providing guidance for the understanding of any particular or individual phenomenon.

In other words, deduction in this interpretation (and in this interpretation only!) is a synonym of a really *theoretical* attitude to empirical facts.

The first formal indication of decline of Ricardo's school of political economy was the giving up of the attempt to develop the entire system of economic categories from one established principle (the labour theory of value). Representatives of the 'vulgar economy', and still more of hotchpotch compilation that Marx branded contemptuously as the professorial form of the decay of theory, rebelled first of all against the teacher's deductive manner of inquiry. They rejected that which was Ricardo's chief virtue as a theoretician—his desire to understand each particular category *as a converted form of value*, as a complex modification of labour creating commodities.

The principle of the vulgar and professorial form of theorising was this: if one could not deduce a conception of real phenomena from one basis common to them all (in this case from the labour theory of value) without running at once into a contradiction, one had to abandon the attempt in general, one had to introduce still another principle of explanation, one more 'point of view'. If that did not help, one merely had to introduce a third and a fourth principle, taking into account this, that, and the other.

Supposing one could not explain the real market value (price) of a capitalistically produced commodity in terms of the necessary time spent on its production. That only meant that one need not persist in one-sidedness. Why not assume that value comes from many different sources rather than from one single universal source, as Ricardo believed? From labour too, but not only from labour. One must not underestimate the role of capital and the role of natural fertility of soil; one had to take into account the whims of fashion, accidents of demand, the effect of the seasons (felt boots cost more in winter than in summer), and a host of other factors, including the effect on the market situation of the periodical changes of the number of spots on the Sun that have an undoubted effect on crops and therefore on the price ('value') of grain and bread. Marx was never more sarcastic than in criticising the manner of theorising characteristic of the vulgar and professorial pseudotheory. This eclectic manner of explaining a complex phenomenon by a number of factors and principles without any inner connection between them is, in Marx's apt phrase, a real grave for science. There is no more theory, science, no more thinking in concepts here, only a translation of the widely spread superficial notions into the doctrinaire language of economic terminology and their systematisation.

John M. Keynes, an acknowledged classic of the entire present-day official science of the capitalist world, no longer permits himself to speak of value in general. In his view, that is an empty word, a myth. The only reality he recognises is market price. The latter, according to his theory, is determined by a concurrence of most diverse circumstances and factors, where labour plays a very insignificant role. Keynes insists, for instance, that the interest rate entirely depends on the emotions of the owners of capital and is therefore a purely psychological factor. But that is not strong enough for Keynes: 'It might be more accurate, perhaps, to say that the rate of interest is a highly conventional, rather than a highly psychological, phenomenon.'[20] 'Slumps and depressions', according to Keynes, are 'the mere consequence of upsetting the delicate balance of spontaneous optimism. In estimating the prospects of investment, we must have regard, therefore, to the nerves and hysteria and even the digestions and reactions to the weather of those upon whose spontaneous activity it largely depends.'[21]

There can be no question of theory or science here, of course. Where vulgar economy was mostly busy translating popular superficial conceptions into the doctrinaire language, assuming that it elaborated concepts, modern bourgeois science passes off the capitalist's irrational emotions in their scholastic expression for concepts. That is the limit, as the saying goes.

Marx showed clearly that after Ricardo, the height of bourgeois political economy, the latter entered the phase of degradation. This degradation is certainly camouflaged by high-sounding verbiage and appeals for sober, inductive empirical study of facts, etc. In opposing their induction to Ricardo's deductive method, the representatives of the decaying bourgeois political economy merely advocate eclecticism as against rigorous theory.

His desire to comprehend all categories without exception from the consistent position of the labour theory of value is unacceptable to them for, as they might have occasion to see, this position, when one considers its tendency of development, inevitably leads to the conception of the system

[20] John M. Keynes, *The General Theory of Employment, Interest and Money*, Macmillan, London, 1936, p. 203.
[21] Ibid., p. 162.

of bourgeois economy as a system of insoluble antagonisms and contradictions. The motive force behind this attitude to Ricardo and his deductive method is simply an apologetic attitude towards reality.

Thus, Ricardo does not come to the choice of the deductive method of considering empirical facts out of a loyalty to rationalism. He applies this method of developing theoretical definitions, because it is the only one that answers his desire to understand the system of bourgeois economy as an integral system coherent in all its manifestations rather than as a totality of more or less accidental relations of men and things. Ricardo wants to deduce any particular, specific form of relations of production and distribution of wealth out of the labour theory of value, out of a theory expressing the universal substance, the real essence of all economic phenomena.

This desire of Ricardo is his absolute merit as a theoretician. The giving up of this desire is in general tantamount to a rejection of theoretical attitude to empirical facts. Here we see already that the method of reasoning which proceeds from a universal theoretical expression of reality as a rigorously tested basic principle, can ensure a theoretical attitude to empirical facts. Otherwise thought inevitably slides into eclectic empiricism.

Ricardo by no means rejects the empirical element in investigation. On the contrary, he realises that a genuine understanding of empirically given facts, genuine (rather than eclectical) empiricism, can only be carried through if empirical facts are considered from a standpoint in itself substantiated as the only correct and objective one, rather than from an arbitrary standpoint.

Spontaneously obeying the logic of things, Ricardo thus comes to the starting-point of theory that was later chosen by Marx consciously. Yet the fact that Ricardo arrived at this view of reality and of ways of reproducing it conceptually in a purely spontaneous manner, having no clear idea of the dialectics of the universal, the particular, and the individual, with which he had to deal in reality, this fact left its imprint on his theory.

The conscious philosophical conceptions that were at his disposal—those of the relationship of deduction and induction, the universal and the particular, of essence and appearance, etc., had a direct bearing on the process of cognition as it was actually carried out by him. They had a significant effect on his inquiry and in some cases were directly responsible for the failure of his search.

What Ricardo actually did was not at all deduction in the sense in which it was interpreted by the metaphysical logic of his epoch; it was by no means speculative deduction of one concept from another concept. In his hands it is, in the first place, a method for theoretical expression of empirical facts, of empirical phenomena in their inner unity. As such, this method includes empirical induction. But he does not go unscathed by the purely spontaneous manner in which induction and deduction coincide in his method. Where he has to take a clear view of his method of studying facts, he is compelled to accept the contemporary conception of deduction and induction, of the relation of the universal to the particular, of the law to forms of its manifestation, etc. The metaphysical conception of the categories of logic and of ways of reproducing reality in thought directly disorients him as a theoretician.

Let us analyse Ricardo's line of reasoning to show this more clearly. His method is as follows. He proceeds from the definition of value by the quantity of labour time, taking it as a universal basic principle of his system. Then he attempts to apply this universal basic principle, directly and immediately, to each of the particular categories with the aim of checking whether they agree with this universal basic principle or not.

Everywhere he endeavours to show direct coincidence of economic categories with the law of value.

In the spirit of contemporary metaphysical logic and philosophy, Ricardo assumed that the universal definition on which he based his deduction was a direct generic concept, that is, an abstract general concept comprising in itself the features that were directly common to all phenomena comprehended by it, and nothing more. The relation of the value concept to the concepts of money, profit, rent, wages, interest, etc., appeared to him a genus-to-species relation between concepts. According to this conception based on a metaphysical notion of the relation of the universal to the particular and the individual, the concept of value must include only those features that are equally common to money, profit, rent, and any of the other categories. In the same spirit, he believed that any specific category was not exhausted by traits expressed in the definitions of the universal concept, and that each specific category possessed, apart from these definitions, additional features expressing precisely the specificity of each particular category.

Consequently, it is by no means enough to subsume any category under a universal principle or definition of a universal concept (in this case, the value concept). This operation will show only that in the particular category which is already expressed in the definitions of the universal concept. It is then necessary to find out what definitions are present in it over and above that—the definitions expressing the distinctive rather than the common, identical features.

This logical conception, applied to the categories of political economy, appears as follows. Money, just as all the other categories, is a particular form of value. It follows that real money is subject in its motion to the law of value, first and foremost. It follows that the labour theory of value is directly applicable to money; in other words, definitions contained in the value concept must above all be included in the theoretical definition of money. That is the way in which the first definition of money is deduced.

It is quite clear, however, that this does not exhaust the concrete nature of money. The question then naturally arises what is money *as money,* what is money over and above the fact that it is the same kind of value as all other kinds, why money is money rather than simply value.

At this point in the study of the nature of money and the formation of the necessary theoretical definitions of money as a separate economic phenomenon, all deduction naturally stops. Deduction permitted to distinguish only those definitions of the nature of money which were previously contained in the concept of value.

And what is one to do next? How is one to discover in the actual empirical phenomena of money circulation theoretical definitions that would express just as necessary properties of money as those that are deduced from the value concept? How is one to read in the real money those characteristics that belong to it as necessarily as the universal value definitions yet at the same time constitute the difference of money from all the other forms of the existence of value?

Deduction becomes impossible at this point. One has to resort tc induction, the goal of which is the singling out of definitions that are equally inherent in all the cases of the movement of money—the specifically general properties of money.

That is the way Ricardo is compelled to act. He constructs further theoretical definitions of the money form through immediate empirical induction, through singling out those abstract general properties which all phenomena of money circulation without exception have in common. He directly generalises the phenomena of the money market, in which simultaneously diverse forms of money circulate—metal coins, bullion, paper money, etc. He looks for the features that are common to metal coins, paper banknotes, gold and silver bullion, bank vouchers, promissory notes, etc. That is the fatal weakness of his theory of money.

Following this line, Ricardo confuses theoretical definitions of money as money with those properties which money actually owes to capital, whose specific movement in money has nothing in common with the phenomena of money circulation as such. As a result, he takes the laws of movement of financial *capital* for the laws of money movement and vice versa—he reduces the laws of financial capital to those of simple circulation of metal coins. Money as such, as a specific economic phenomenon, is not comprehended theoretically, just as before, or rather it is conceived erroneously.

Ricardo himself sensed that this method was inadequate. He understood that the purely empirical induction to which he had to resort at this point did not and could not by its very nature yield the necessary conclusion about the nature of money. This understanding did not come from purely logical considerations. The fact is that he continually argues with heads of banks and financiers who, in his view, handle money in a way that contradicts the value nature of money rather than agrees with it. He regards this as the cause of all unpleasant conflicts and disfunctions in the sphere of money circulation. That is what compels him to look for the genuine essence and nature of money, not the philosophical and logical interest.

The empirically given picture of money circulation presents something directly opposed to the genuine nature of money—the handling of money that does not correspond to the nature of money, the results of incorrect handling of money by banks. So, purely empirical induction, as Ricardo himself understood quite clearly, will at best yield a generalised expression of untrue movement of money, one that does not correspond to the nature of money, and will never yield a generalised expression of movement of money corresponding to the law of its existence.

In other words, he wants to find a theoretical expression of the kind of movement of money (gold, coins, papers, vouchers, etc.) which directly answers the requirements of the universal law of value and does not depend (as in the empirical reality) on the ill will, cupidity, and caprice of heads of banks. He searches for the genuine nature of money with the aim in view that the practical financier should act differently from the way he has acted previously—in accordance with the needs flowing from the nature of money.

He endeavours to solve this task by deducing the theoretical definitions of money from the law of value, which alone can show the necessary characteristics contained in the very nature of money.

But he will not be able to deduce the specific features of money as such, those that are not contained in the theoretical definitions of the universal law of value but constitute the specificity of money *as a particular kind of value*. No sophisticated procedures will help to deduce the specific properties of money from the definitions of value. Willy-nilly they have to be obtained not through deduction from a universal principle of the theory but through purely empirical induction, by extraction of the abstract general from all forms of money circulation without exception, including metal coins, paper money, state banknotes, and all the rest.

The conception of money therefore remained one of the weakest points of the theory of the Ricardian school.

Ricardo's deduction actually remains purely formal, enabling one to single out in the phenomenon only that which was already contained in the definitions of the universal concept, while induction remains purely empirical and formal rather than theoretical; formal induction does not permit to abstract from the phenomenon those of its aspects which necessarily belong to it, being bound to the nature of the phenomenon as its attributes rather than emerging in it through the influence of external circumstances unconnected with its nature.

The formal nature of deduction in Ricardo's system was still more apparent when he attempted to include such phenomena as profit and surplus-value in the sphere of the law of value.

In including profit in the universal category of value, Ricardo came face to face with the paradox that profit, on the one hand, could be included in the category of value but, on the other hand, profit contained, over and above the established universal definitions, something that proved to contradict the universal law if one attempted to express this 'something' through the category of value.

The situation here is somewhat similar to a hypothetical case where one would apply the dictum 'All men are mortal' to a certain Caius and see that, on the one hand, the dictum does apply to him but, on the other, his individual special trait is precisely that he is—immortal.

That is exactly the kind of absurd situation in which Ricardo found himself when he tried to deduce theoretical definitions of profit from the law of value, when he tried to apply the law of value *directly* to profit. True, Ricardo himself did not notice this contradiction although it was he who discovered it. But it was immediately noticed by enemies of the labour theory of value, in particular by Malthus.

Ricardo's adherents and followers tried hard to prove what could not be proved—that this contradiction in his system did not actually exist, and if it did, it resulted merely from the teacher's vagueness of expression, deficiency of his terminology, etc., and could therefore be eliminated by purely formal means—through changes in the terms, more precise definitions, expressions, etc., etc.

These attempts signified the beginning of the decline of Ricardo's school and factual rejection of the principles of the labour theory of value despite formal agreement with them. Precisely because the *logical* contradiction between the universal law of value and the law of the average rate of profit established by Ricardo's theory is a quite *real contradiction*, all attempts to present it as non-existent, as the product of vague expression and imprecise definition, could not result in anything but factual rejection of the very essence of the theory, of its rational kernel.

The first and principal indication of the decline of Ricardo's school was the factual discarding of the objective of developing the entire system of economic categories from one universal principle, from the principle of defining value by the quantity of labour time, from the conception of labour creating value as the real substance and source of all the other forms of wealth.

At the same time the development of theory after Ricardo directly led to the need for a firm grasp on the dialectics of the relation of the universal law to developed forms of its realisation, to the particular. The development of Ricardo's theory led to the problem of contradiction in the very essence of the definitions of the subject-matter of theoretical investigation. Neither Ricardo himself nor his orthodox followers could cope with the difficulties through which the actual dialectics of reality manifested itself to thinking. Their reasoning remained essentially metaphysical and naturally could not conceptually express dialectics without rejecting its own fundamental logical notions, including the metaphysical understanding of the relation of the abstract to the concrete, of the universal to the particular and the individual.

Inability and unwillingness to consciously express in concepts the contradictions, the dialectics inherent in things was manifested in reasoning as obvious logical contradictions within theory. Metaphysics in general knows only one way of solving logical contradictions—*elimination of them from reasoning*, interpretation of contradictions as products of vagueness of expression, definitions, etc., as a purely subjective evil.

Although Ricardo approached facts and their theoretical expression in a spontaneously correct way, *consciously* he remained on the positions of the metaphysical method of reasoning. Deduction for him was still a method of development of concepts which permitted to see in a particular phenomenon only that which was already contained in the major premise, in the original universal concept and its definitions, while induction contained thereby to be one-sidedly empirical. It offered no opportunity for singling out those traits of phenomena which necessarily belong to them and for forming a theoretical abstraction that would express phenomena in their pure form, in their immanent content.

Deduction and induction, analysis and synthesis, universal concept and concept expressing the specificity of a phenomenon—all these categories still remained metaphysical opposites in Ricardo, which he could not link up.

Deduction continually came into conflict with the task of inductive generalisation of facts in his system; in trying to bring analytical abstractions into a system, i.e. to synthesise them he ran into the insurmountable difficulties of logical contradiction; a universal concept (value) proved to be in mutual contradiction with a particular concept (profit) in his system, etc., etc. Under enemy fire, these internal rifts widened and the whole labour theory of value decayed, turning into compilation work without any system, which could only plume itself on empirical comprehensiveness totally unaccompanied by a theoretical understanding of the actual concreteness.

Philosophy and logic of Ricardo's time did not (and could not) provide any correct indications concerning a possible way out of all these difficulties. What was required here was conscious dialectics combined with a revolutionary critical attitude to reality—a mode of reasoning that was not afraid of contradictions in definitions of objects and was alien to an apologetic attitude to the existing state of things. All these problems met at one point—the need to understand the system of capitalist production as a concrete historical system, as a system that emerged and developed towards its end.

DEDUCTION AND THE PROBLEM OF HISTORICISM

While he viewed the subject-matter of inquiry, capitalist economy, as a single whole coherent in all its manifestations, as a system of mutually conditioning relations of production and distribution, Ricardo at the same time did not regard this system as a *historically emerging and developing* integral totality of relations between men and things in the process of production.

All the merits of Ricardo's method of inquiry are closely connected with the substantive viewpoint, that is, with the conception of the object as a single whole coherent in all its manifestations. Contrariwise, all the defects and vices of his mode of unfolding his theory are rooted in complete failure to understand this whole as a historically formed one.

The capitalist form of production seemed to him to be the natural, eternal form of any production whatever. That explains the non-historical (and even anti-historical) character of his abstractions and lack of historicism in the method of obtaining them. Deduction of categories, where it is combined with a non-historical comprehension of the object reproduced with its help in the concept, inevitably becomes purely formal.

It is easy to see that deduction in its very form corresponds to the conception of *development*, of movement from the simple, undivided, and general to the complex, divided, individual and particular. Now, if objective reality reproduced in concepts deductively is in itself understood as non-developing reality, as an eternal and natural system of interacting phenomena, deduction, naturally and inevitably, appears only as an artificial procedure in the development of thought. In this case, too, logic necessarily recurs to the view of the nature of deduction which was expressed in classically clear form by Descartes.

As he set about the construction of his system of the world, the deduction of all the complex forms of interaction in nature from the movements of the elementary particles of matter definied exclusively in geometrical terms, Descartes justified his mode of theory construction in the following way: 'And its nature (of the world—*E.I.*) is much more easily conceived if one thus watches its gradual origin than if one considers it as ready made.'[22] Unwilling to come into open conflict with the theological teaching of the creation of the world, Descartes immediately qualified this statement: 'At the same time I did not wish to infer from all this that our world was created in the way I suggested; for it is much more likely that from the beginning God made it in the form it was intended to have.'[23]

It was obvious to Descartes that the form of deduction which he consciously applied was closely akin to the conception of development and emergence of things in their necessity. That was why he faced the ticklish problem of reconciling deduction and the idea that the object was eternally equal to itself and had not come from anywhere in particular, being once created by God.

Ricardo found himself in the same kind of situation. He understood quite well that only deductive movement of thought could express phenomena in their inner connection, and that one could only cognise this connection in considering the gradual emergence of divers forms of wealth from one substance common to them all—from commodity-producing

---

[22] René Descartes, *Philosophical Writings*, Fletcher and Son Ltd., Norwich, 1971, p. 40.

[23] Ibid.

labour. But how was one to link up this mode of reasoning with the idea that the bourgeois system was a natural and eternal system that could neither emerge nor develop in reality? Still, Ricardo reconciled these two conceptions, in their essence absolutely incompatible. This was reflected in his method of reasoning, in the method of forming abstractions.

The fact that the construction of theory begins with the category of value, later to proceed to the consideration of other categories, may be justified by the category of value being the most general concept which implies profit, interest, rent, capital, and all the rest—a generic abstraction from these real particular and individual phenomena.

The movement of thought from an abstract general category to the expression of specific features of real phenomena therefore appears as movement entirely in thought but by no means in reality. In reality all categories—profit, capital, rent, wages, money, etc.—exist simultaneously with one another, the category of value expressing what is common to them all. Value as such actually exists in the abstraction-making head only, as a reflection of the features which commodity has in common with money, profit, rent, wages, capital, etc. That generic concept comprising in itself all the particular categories, is value.

Here Ricardo reasoned in the spirit of contemporary nominalist logic rebelling against medieval realism, against creationist conceptions according to which the general, say, animal in general, existed before the horse, the fox, the cow, the hare, before the particular species of animals and was subsequently transformed or 'split' into the horse, the cow, the fox, the hare, etc.

According to Ricardo, value as such can only exist *post rem*, only as a mental abstraction from the particular kinds of value (profit, rent, wages, etc.), by no means *ante rem*, as an independent reality chronologically preceding its particular species (capital, profit, rent, wages, etc.). All these particular species of value eternally exist side by side with one another and by no means originate in value, just as the horse does not actually derive from the animal in general.

The trouble was, however, that the nominalist conception of the general concept, justifiably attacking the principal proposition of medieval realism, in general eliminated from the real world of individual things, along with that proposition, the idea of their real development.

Inasmuch as Ricardo held the bourgeois view of the essence of bourgeois economy, the one-sided and extremely metaphysical conception of nominalism in logic appeared to him to be most natural and appropriate. Only individual phenomena belonging to the particular species of value existed eternally—commodity, money, capital, profit, rent, etc. As for value, it was an abstraction from these individual and particular economic phenomena—*universalia post rem*, by no means *universalia ante rem*. That was why Ricardo did not study value as such, value in itself, most rigorously abstracted from profit, wages, rent, and competition.

Having formulated the concept of value, he proceeded directly to the consideration of developed particular categories, directly applying the value concept to profit, wages, rent, money, etc.

That is the most natural logical move if one conceives reality reproduced by means of it as an eternal system of interaction of particular species of value.

If the content of the universal concept underlying the entire system of the theory is to be understood as a sum of features abstractly common to all particular and individual phenomena, one will necessarily act as Ricardo did. If the universal is understood as the abstract feature common to all individual and particular phenomena without exception, to obtain theoretical definitions of value one will have to consider profit, rent, etc., and abstract what is common to them. That was the way Ricardo acted. And that was what Marx sharply criticised him for, since here Ricardo's *anti-historical* approach to value and its species was particularly apparent.

The greatest defect of Ricardo's method of inquiry, according to Marx, lay in that he did not study specially the theoretical definitions of value as such completely independent from the effects of production of surplus-value, competition, profit, wages, and all the other phenomena. The first chapter of Ricardo's principal work treats not only of exchange of one commodity for another (that is, of the elementary form of value, value as such), but also of profit, wages, capital, the average rate of profit, and the like.

'One can see that though Ricardo is accused of being too abstract, one would be justified in accusing him of the opposite: lack of the power of abstraction, inability, when dealing with the values of commodities, to forget profits, a factor which confronts him as a result of competition.'[24]

But this requirement, the requirement of objective completeness of abstraction, is impossible to satisfy unless, first, one gives up the formal metaphysical conception of the universal concept (as a simple abstraction from the particular and individual phenomena to which it refers), and second, one accepts the standpoint of historicism in the conception, in this instance, of the development from value to profit.

Marx demands from science that is should comprehend the economic system as a system that has emerged and developed, he demands that the logical development of categories should reproduce the actual history of the emergence and unfolding of the system.

If that is so, value as the starting point of theoretical conception should be understood in science as an objective economic reality emerging and existing before such phenomena as profit, capital, wages, rent, etc., can emerge and exist. Therefore theoretical definitions of value should also be obtained in quite a different manner than mere abstraction of the features common to commodity, money, capital, profit, wages, and rent. All these things are assumed to be *non-existent.* They did not exist eternally at all, but somehow and at some point did emerge, and this emergence, in its necessity, should be discovered by science.

Value is a real, objective condition without which neither capital nor money nor anything else is possible. Theoretical definitions of value as such can only be obtained by considering a certain objective economic reality capable of existing before, outside, and independently of all those phenomena that later developed on its basis.

This elementary objective economic reality existed long before the emergence of capitalism and all the categories expressing its structure. This reality is *direct exchange of one commodity for another commodity.*

We have seen that the classics of political economy worked out the universal concept of value exactly through considering this reality, although they had no idea of the real philosophical and theoretical meaning of their acts.

---

[24] Karl Marx, *Theories of Surplus-Value,* Part II, p. 191.

One would assume that Ricardo would have been not a little perplexed if someone were to point out the fact that both his predecessors and he himself did not work out the *universal* category of his science by considering an abstract general rule to which all things having value are subject—on the contrary, they did so by considering *a very rare exception from the rule*—direct exchange of one commodity for another without money.

Inasmuch as they did so, they obtained a really objective theoretical conception of value. But, since they did not adhere strictly enough to the consideration of this particular mode of economic interaction extremely rare in developed capitalism, they could not fully grasp the essence of value.

Herein lies the *dialectics* of Marx's conception of the universal—the dialectics in the conception of the method of elaborating the universal category of the system of science.

It is easy to see that this conception is only possible on the basis of an essentially *historical* approach to the study of objective reality.

Deduction based on conscious historicism becomes the only logical form corresponding to the view of the object as historically emerging and developing rather than ready made.

'Owing to the theory of evolution, the whole classification of organisms has been taken away from induction and brought back to "deduction", to descent—one species being literally *deduced* from another by descent—and it is impossible to prove the theory of evolution by induction alone, since it is quite anti-inductive.'[25]

The horse and the cow did not of course descend from the animal in general, just as the pear and the apple are not products of self-alienation of the concept of fruit in general. But the cow and the horse undoubtedly had a common ancestor in the remote past epochs, while the apple and the pear are also products of differentiation of a form of fruit common to both of them. This actual common ancestor of the cow, the horse, the hare, the fox and all the other now existing species of animals did not of course exist in divine reason, as an idea of the animal in general, but in nature

---

[25] Frederick Engels, *Dialectics of Nature,* p. 227.

itself, as a quite real particular species, from which divers other species descended through differentiation.

This universal form of animal, animal as such, if you wish, is by no means an abstraction comprising in itself only that feature which is common to all the now existing particular species of animals. This universal was at the same time a particular species possessing not only and not so much those traits that were preserved in all the descendants as features common to them all, but also its own specific features, partly inherited by the descendants, partly entirely lost and replaced by new ones. The concrete image of the universal ancestor of all the species existing at present, cannot in principle be constructed out of those properties that these species have in common.

Doing this sort of thing in biology would mean taking the same wrong avenue by which Ricardo hoped to arrive at a definition of value as such, of the universal form of value, assuming that these definitions were abstractions from profit, rent, capital, and all the other particular forms of value that he observed.

The idea of development as real descent of some phenomena from others determines the dialectical materialist conception of deduction of categories, of ascent from the abstract to the concrete, from the universal (which is in itself quite a definite particular) to the particular (which also expresses a universal and necessary definition of the object).

The basic universal foundation of a system of theoretical definitions (the basic concept of science) expresses, from the standpoint of dialectics, concrete theoretical definitions of *quite a specific* and *definite* typical *phenomenon* sensually and practically given in empirical contemplation, in social practice and experiment.

This phenomenon is specific in that it is really (outside the theoretician's head) the starting-point of development of the analysed totality of interacting phenomena, of the concrete whole which is, in the given case, that concrete whole that is the object of logical reproduction.

Science must begin with that with which real history began. Logical development of theoretical definitions must therefore express the concrete historical process of the emergence and development of the object. Logical deduction is nothing but a theoretical expression of real historical development of the concreteness under study.

To understand this principle correctly, one must take a concrete, essentially dialectical view of the nature of historical development. This most important point of Marx's logic—his view of the relation of scientific development to historical one (the relation of the logical to the historical)—must be considered specially. Without it, the method of ascent from the abstract to the concrete remains inexplicable.

Chapter 4

LOGICAL DEVELOPMENT AND CONCRETE HISTORICISM

ON THE DIFFERENCE BETWEEN THE LOGICAL AND THE HISTORICAL METHODS OF INQUIRY

We have already commented on the most significant circumstance that theoretical analysis of empirical facts always naturally coincides with critical analysis of concepts, with creative development of the available, historically established categories, and that novel theoretical conception of facts (a new system of categories) never emerges out of nowhere, never 'straight from the facts', as positivists and vulgar scientists would have it, but through a most rigorous scientific critique of the available system of categories.

The problem of creative continuity in the development of theory (the problem of the historical development of science) is always pushed into the foreground when the question arises of the relation of scientific (logical) development to historical.

In his reviews of Marx's *Contribution to the Critique of Political Economy* Engels showed clearly that the problem of the relation of the logical to the historical directly emerges before the theoretician as the question of *the way of criticising available theoretical literature*: 'Even after the determination of the method, the critique of economics could still be arranged in two ways—historically or logically.' [1]

However, inasmuch as a novel theoretical conception of facts can only be worked out through critique of available theoretical literature, the mode of critique of theoretical literature coincides essentially with the attitude to facts. Theoretical categories are criticised by comparing them with

[1] Karl Marx, *A Contribution to the Critique of Political Economy*, p. 225.

actual empirical facts. In this respect, there is no difference between the logical and the historical modes of analysis of concepts and facts, and neither can there be.

The difference lies elsewhere. In the so-called historical mode of critique of previous theories, they are collated with the same historical facts on the basis of which they were created. For instance, if Marx had chosen the historical mode of critique of Ricardo's theory, he would have had to compare this theory with facts of Ricardo's time—that is, the facts of capitalist development of the late 18th-early 19th century.

The theory of Ricardo, its categories and laws would have been critically compared with facts of more or less remote past, with facts of undeveloped stage of capitalist reality. Yet this mode of critique assumes that the facts themselves have been studied well or must be studied well, whereas in this case the facts were not studied or comprehended scientifically, moreover, they had not been even collected and summed up. Under these conditions, the historical method of critique was apparently inexpedient. It would have merely delayed work.

Therefore Marx preferred the so-called logical mode of critique and correspondingly the logical mode of considering reality.

In this mode, a historically preceding theory is not critically compared with those very facts on the basis of which it emerged but with facts existing at a different historical stage in the development of the object—with the facts directly observed by Marx himself.

This mode has two decisive advantages: first, the facts from Marx's own time were better known to him and, if need be, could be thoroughly checked out, and second, they revealed the tendencies of capitalist development much more distinctly and acutely than the facts of Ricardo's time.

Everything that emerged rather vaguely in the early 19th century, assumed a much more mature form of expression by the mid-19th century—suffice it to mention here the economic crises.

The logical mode therefore enables one to consider each economic phenomenon (insofar as we are dealing with political economy) precisely at that point where it reaches a maximal expression and development.

Clearly, logical comparison with the actual facts of developed capitalism revealed with greater facility both the falsity of some of Ricardo's theoretical propositions and their rational kernel. At the same time, the reality of Marx's own times was directly expressed. These are the two decisive advantages of the logical mode of analysis of concepts and facts as compared to the historical one.

Still, these advantages would not be apparent and the method of logical analysis itself would not be justified from the philosophical standpoint if we had not shown why and in what way analysis of a higher stage of development can give a historical conception of reality without recourse to a detailed study of the past (for in some cases it is extremely difficult while in others impossible at all, as for instance in the study of cosmogony).

In other words, we have to know why and in what way theoretical (systematical logical) analysis of the present can *simultaneously* disclose the mystery of the past—of the history that led to the present.

Let us first analyse two relations, that may in principle exist between the development of science and the history of its subject-matter.

In the first instance theory develops within a period of time that is too short for the object itself to undergo any significant changes. This relation is more characteristic of the natural sciences—astronomy (cosmogony), physics, chemistry, etc.

In this case, application of the logical mode of analysis of concepts and facts is not only justifiable but even the only possible way. The different stages in the development of the science deal with the same historical stage in the development of the object, with the same object at the same stage of development. Thus, Newton, Laplace, Kant, and Otto Schmidt described the same stage in the development of the solar-planetary system.

Application of the logical way of criticising categories (as well as, correspondingly, the mode of theoretical expression of facts) is in this case naturally justified. The old theory and its categories are conceived as an incomplete, one-sided, and abstract expression of the truth. The new theory appears as a more comprehensive and concrete theoretical expression of the essence of the same facts, the same object. The rational kernel of the previous theory is included in the new one as its abstract component. What is discarded is the conception that the old theory comprised in itself an *exhaustive* expression of the essence of facts. The old theory (of course, not all of it but the rational kernel of it only) becomes in the process one of the shades of the new theory, a particular instance of the universal principle of the new theory.

The theoretician's right to apply the logical mode of critique of previous theories is here based on the fact that theories and categories analysed with reference to actually given facts reflected *the very same object* which he now has before his eyes. The theoretician therefore arranges a confrontation between theories constructed hundreds of years ago and the facts observed at present, usually without any doubts as to his right to do so.

Matters are more complicated in the second case, where different stages in the development of science deal with different historical stages in the development of the object. Here the history of science itself serves as a kind of mirror for the history of the object. Changes in the science reflect major historical changes in the structure of the object itself. The object develops fast enough, and the historical periods in its development coincide with those of the development of the science and its categories.

It goes without saying that this case is more characteristic of the social sciences. A typical example here is political economy. Esthetics, ethics, epistemology, the science of law are all in much the same situation.

The doubt may naturally arise whether the logical mode of development of theory is in general applicable here.

How can one compare the theory and categories developed hundreds (or even dozens) of years ago with facts observed at present? In this case, the object has changed considerably during these years; will the logical mode of critique of categories be effective in this case? Or will it merely lead to misunderstandings, to expression of different things in the same categories, to theoretically fruitless debate?

The dialectical-materialist conception of development disperses these doubts. It should be taken into account that in this case, too, science throughout its development deals with facts *referring to one and the same object,* although this object appears at different stages and phases of its maturity. That means that those really universal and necessary laws that make up the 'elementary essence' of the object under study, the abstract outlines of its inner structure, remain the same throughout its historical development. On the other hand, those phenomena and categories which appear at the early stages of development but disappear without a trace at the higher ones, objectively prove, by the very fact of their disappearance, that they are not attributive, internally necessary forms of being of the object.

In his analysis of economic theories and categories developed by his predecessors (not only by Adam Smith and David Ricardo but even by Aristotle), Marx confidently applies the logical mode of critique, using the historical mode only occasionally, as an auxiliary one.

This mode of analysis of the theories of the past is not only admissible but also the most expedient in the development of the *general theory* of some subject, as it leaves aside all those moments that are of historical significance only, characterising as they do more or less accidental circumstances within which the development of the object that is of interest for the general theory, proceeded. The logical mode of critique and development of theory gives Marx an objective criterion for distinguishing between categories pertaining to the inner structure of the capitalist organism and all those moments that are connected with forms of production ousted out or destroyed in the course of its development, with the purely local traits of capitalist development in that particular country where the analysed theory emerged, etc.

The advantages of the logical mode of critique of previous theories stem from the fact that the more mature stage in the development of the object, with which the theories of the past are directly compared, reveals the attributive forms of its structure with greater clarity and distinctness, showing them in their quite pure form. The advantage of the logical mode is pointed out by Engels in his review of Marx's *Contribution to the Critique of Political Economy:* '... each factor can be examined at the stage of development where it reaches its full maturity, its classical form.'[2]

For this reason, we can critically analyse Hegel's Logic taking into account the facts of development of *modern*

[2] Karl Marx, *A Contribution to the Critique of Political Economy*, p. 225.

science rather than those of Hegel's times, and this critique will result in dialectical elucidation of these facts as well as in materialist conception of the categories of Hegelian dialectics, of their rational kernel.

Taking this into account, Marx believes it to be not only justifiable but also most expedient to choose the logical mode of critique of previous theories and of developing their rational kernel, in the socio-historical fields of knowledge as well as in the natural sciences where the object remains immutable throughout the development of science. There is no gap, in principle, between the natural and social sciences in this respect. Besides, the situation in the natural sciences is not so simple as it may appear at first sight: although Einstein dealt with 'the same' object as Newton did, the immediate facts from which he proceeded in his critique of Newtonian mechanics were different. The sensual-practical experimental activity of the social man showed him the same object much more fully and comprehensively. Thus from this side, too, the right to apply the logical mode of critique and development of theory in the social sciences is substantiated just as well as in the natural ones.

In both types of sciences, the social man's sensual-practical activity proves to be the mediating link between the object 'in itself' and the theoretician's thought. For this reason, *practice* appears as the decisive argument in the analysis of the relation between the natural and social sciences, which refutes the neo-Kantian idea of the abyss that in principle exists between the methods of the natural and the socio-historical sciences.

Of course, Marx does not rule out the historical method of critique of his predecessors at all. Marx continually resorts to it, revealing the historical circumstances within which the theory that he criticises emerged. Still, the historical method of critique plays but a subordinate, auxiliary role with him. The principal method of the critique and development of theory remains the logical one.

'To develop the laws of bourgeois economy, it is not necessary to write *the real history of the production relations*. But the correct view and deduction of the latter as relations that grew historically, always leads to certain first correlations—like the empirical numerical data in the natural sciences—which point to the past lying behind this system. These indications, together with correct conception of the present, offer then the key to the understanding of the past,'[3] wrote Marx in 1858.

LOGICAL DEVELOPMENT AS EXPRESSION OF CONCRETE HISTORICISM IN INVESTIGATION

In the above, we formulated the question as follows: why and in what way the theoretical analysis (analysis of facts through a critique of categories) proceeding *from the results* of the historical process, can in itself yield an essentially historical (though logical in form) expression of reality even where real (empirical) history leading to these results is not directly studied in detail.

The answer to this question can only be obtained through considering the real dialectical laws which govern any actual development in nature, society, and in cognition itself, in thought. If, in studying the results of a certain historical process, we can discover the history of their emergence and development sublated in them, if we can, proceeding from the results of history, theoretically reconstruct the general outline of their emergence, this possibility is based in the first place on the fact that the objective result of the development preserves in itself its own history in a changed, sublated form.

Here again, a logical problem is transformed into the problem of law-governed correlation between historical development and its own results. As we pointed out in the above, the really universal and necessary moments characterising the object as a concrete historical whole are preserved in it throughout its existence and development, constituting the law of its concrete historical development.

The problem, then, is to find out in what shape and form the historical conditions of the object's emergence and development are preserved at the higher stages of its development. Here we confront the fact of dialectical relation between the historically preceding conditions of the emergence of the object and their later consequences that have developed on this basis.

The dialectics of this relation consists in a kind of inversion of the historically preceding into the subsequent and

[3] K. Marx, *Grundrisse der Kritik der politischen Ökonomie (Rohentwurf). 1857-1858,* S. 364-65.

vice versa, the transformation of the condition into the conditioned, of the effect into a cause, of the complex into the elementary, etc.

Owing to this objective dialectics, a situation arises which appears to be paradoxical at first sight: a logical presentation of the laws of the historical process (a conception of facts that is logical in form and concrete historical in essence) is a reversal of the picture that appears to be natural and corresponding to the empirically stated order of the development of the object.

To understand this dialectics, the following fact should be taken into account. Any real process of concrete development (in nature, society, or consciousness) never begins from scratch or in the ether of pure reason but on the basis of premises and conditions created by different processes subject to different laws, and ultimately, by the entire previous development of the universe.

Thus man begins his specific history on the basis of premises and conditions created before him and independently from him by nature. The emergence of life (a specifically biological development) implies very complex chemical combinations formed independently from life. Any qualitatively new form of development emerges within the context of circumstances arising independently from it and, moreover, its entire subsequent development takes place within the same context, a very complex interaction with them. That much is clear. But then we run into a difficulty—the dialectical nature of relations between lower and higher forms of development, and objective changes of their role in this relationship.

The point is that a historically posterior result arising from the entire preceding development does not remain merely a passive result, merely a consequence. Each newly arisen (higher) form of interaction becomes a new universal principle dominating all historically preceding forms, transforming them into secondary external forms of its specific development, into 'organs of its body', as Marx put it in connection with one instance of this kind. They begin to move according to laws characteristic of the new system of interaction in which they now function.

The new and higher (historically later) system of concrete interaction begins to preserve and actively reproduce, by its own movement, all the really necessary conditions of its movement. It generates, as it were, out of itself everything that was originally created by the previous development and not by itself.

In this case, too, development takes the spiral-like form which we analysed in the first part of the work as a most characteristic feature of internal interaction, of concreteness in the genuine sense of the concept.

The necessarily assumed condition of historical emergence of the object becomes in this case the necessarily posited consequence of its specific development.

In this form, the historically necessary conditions of the emergence of the object are preserved in its structure throughout its development, its specific movement. All those moments which, though present at the birth of the new form of development, were not absolutely necessary conditions of this birth, are not, in the final analysis, preserved or reproduced. These forms are not observed at the higher stages of development of the object—they disappear in the course of its historical maturing, becoming lost in the darkness of the past.

For this reason, a logical consideration of the higher stage of development of an object, of an already developed system of interaction, reveals a picture in which all the really necessary conditions of its emergence and evolution are *retained* and all the more or less accidental, purely historical conditions of its emergence are absent.

Logical analysis does not therefore have to free from the purely historical accidentals and from the historical form the presentation of those really universal and absolutely necessary conditions under which the given system of interaction could only emerge and, having emerged, could continue to exist and develop. The historical process itself does the work of this purification instead of and before the theoretician.

In other words, the objective historical process itself carries out the abstraction which retains only the concrete universal moments of development freed from the historical form dependent on the concurrence of more or less accidental circumstances.

Theoretical establishment of such moments results in concrete historical abstractions. That was the principle by which Marx was confidently guided in analysing the categories of political economy.

Labour force as such, as ability for work in general, one of the historical premises of the origin of capital, in the same way as land, air, and mineral deposits. As such, it remains a mere premise of the emergence of capital without being at the same time its consequence or product. On the other hand, capital actively reproduces (engenders as its product) *labour force as commodity*, that is, as the concrete historical form in which labour force functions in the capacity of an element of capital.

The same thing occurs with commodities, money, commercial profit, rent, etc.: as such, they belong to 'antediluvian' premises of capitalist development, to its 'prehistoric' conditions. As concrete historical forms of being of capital, reflecting in their movement its specific history, they are products of capital itself.

As a result, all the really necessary conditions for the emergence of capital are observed on the surface of developed capital as its secondary forms and they are observed in a form that is free from its historical integument. Reproducing them as its product, capital erases all vestiges of their original historical image. Simultaneously, logical analysis provides indications for historical inquiry, too. In its conclusions it guides the historian towards the search for the really necessary conditions and premises of the emergence of a certain process, providing a criterion for distinguishing between the essential and the merely striking, the necessary and the purely accidental, etc.

The dialectics described here does not, of course, take place in the case of capital only. That is a universal law.

The same thing may be observed, for instance, in the formation of the biological form of the movement of matter. Originally, the elementary protein body emerges independently of any biological processes, simply as a chemical product, and a very instable product at that.

Even now we do not know with sufficient precision in what way and under what concrete conditions this elementary biological formation emerged. Chemistry cannot as yet create a living protein body artificially, it cannot create conditions in which such a body would necessarily emerge. That means that chemists do not yet know what those conditions were.

What is reliably known and objectively established, is the fact that within a developed biological organism these conditions (the entire necessary totality of these conditions) are actually present, they are actually realised as long as the organism lives. The conditions under which matter coming from the outside is transformed into protein, into living matter, can here be determined quite objectively and strictly. At the same time the original products of the chemism may be discovered which are capable of becoming a living body under proper conditions, taking into account that not any substance can be assimilated by the organism.

Thus the study of processes taking place in the organisms living at present, can and does give a key to an understanding of the origin of life on the earth—true, in the most general outline only.

We can conclude that the logical development of categories presenting the internal structure of the object in the form in which it is observed at the higher stages of its development, leads in the first approximation to a conception of the history of its origin, of the law of the formation of this structure. Logical development therefore coincides with historical development internally, in the essence of things. But this coincidence is profoundly dialectical, and it cannot be achieved without a comprehension of this dialectics.

ABSTRACT AND CONCRETE HISTORICISM

A concrete understanding of reality cannot be attained without a historical approach to it. The reverse is also true—historicism devoid of concreteness is pure fiction, pseudohistoricism. In these days, one can hardly find a scientist who would reject the idea of development in its general abstract form. But the standpoint of historicism, unless it is combined with the dialectical idea of concreteness, inevitably becomes empty verbiage. Non-concrete, that is, abstract historicism, far from being alien to the metaphysical mode of reasoning, constitutes a most characteristic feature of it. Metaphysicians always expostulate willingly and at length on the need for a historical approach to phenomena, making excursion into the history of the object, and working on 'historical substantiations' of their theoretical constructions. Distinguishing between the concrete historicism of the method of materialist dialectics and the abstract historicism of metaphysicians is not as easy as might seem at first sight.

It is very easy to slide to the standpoint of abstract historicism (or pseudohistoricism). Moreover, this standpoint appears to be the most natural one. Indeed, isn't it natural to consider the history which created an object if one wants to form a historical conception of the object?

But this simple and natural view quickly leads to insoluble difficulties. To begin with, any historically emerging object has behind it, as its past, the entire infinite history of the Universe. Therefore, an attempt to understand a phenomenon historically through tracing out all the processes and premises preceding its birth inevitably leads into bad infinity and for this reason, if not for any other, will not result in anything definite or concrete.

Whether one wishes to do so or not, but in going back one will have to stop somewhere, to begin at some point. Now, what is one to begin with? Abstract historicism sets no limits here for subjectivism and arbitrariness.

But that is not all. The standpoint of abstract historicism leads, inevitably and irrespectively of one's desires, to crude antihistoricism, under the guise of the historical approach. It is not difficult to see why that is so. Bourgeois economists, who interpret capital as accumulated labour in general, quite logically and naturally consider the hour of its historical birth to be the hour in which the primitive man picked up a club. If capital is conceived as money bringing new money from circulation, the historical beginnings of capital will inevitably be found somewhere in Phoenicia. An antihistorical conception of the essence or nature of the phenomenon is in this case justified by 'historical' arguments. There is nothing surprising about it—the comprehension of the past is closely linked with the comprehension of the present. Before one considers the history of the object, one is obliged to form a clear conception of the nature of the object whose history is to be studied.

The result of application of the principle of abstract historicism is this: the history of a certain phenomenon is described in terms of facts pertaining to the history of quite different phenomena, those that merely prepared the emergence of the former phenomenon historically. By this trick, the given concrete historical phenomenon appears to the theoretician either eternal or in any case very ancient, much more ancient than it actually is.

A most striking example of this abstract historical approach, of conception that is historical in appearance and antihistorical in essence, is the bourgeois economists' explanation of the primitive accumulation.

The bourgeois economist also views this process 'historically'. He will easily agree that capital is not an eternal phenomenon, that it must have emerged somewhere and in some manner. The history of its origin consists in that the means of production were in some way concentrated in the hands of a few persons. How did that happen historically?

These ways are extremely varied. In any case, the fact remains that the means of production were first concentrated in the hands of the future capitalist in any manner but exploitation of wage labour, through frugality, the future capitalist's own labour, successful commercial operations, simple robbery, feudal legacy, and so on and so forth.

From this, the bourgeois economist draws the conclusion that in its origin, and consequently in its essence, capital is not the product of unpaid-for labour of the wage worker. As for the worker himself, he descended 'historically' from the serf who ran away to town from a cruel landlord, or a craftsman impoverished through inability, or a lazy vagabond. In other words, the wage labourer was created by processes other than capitalist exploitation. The capitalist offering him work now appears as a benefactor.

It is quite apparent here that a formally historical explanation is made into a means of shameless apology for the existing state of things. Historical substantiation becomes an argument in favour of an antihistorical conception of both the process of primitive accumulation and of the nature of capital. Historical arguments are used to present capital as an 'eternal' and 'natural' relation. The secret of the trick is in the history of the origin of the historical premises of capital being directly presented as the history of capital itself as a concrete historical phenomenon.

The real historical beginning of the development of capital, as Marx showed, was the point at which capital began to build its body out of the unpaid-for labour of the wage worker. Only at this point does its specific concrete history begin. As for the original concentration of the means of production in the hands of the future capitalist, it may take any form whatever—that has no significance for the history of capital as capital and no relevance to the being of man, possessing it, as the being of a capitalist.

Originally, man's mode of appropriation is not that of a capitalist, and the ways in which he appropriates the product of labour has no bearing on his history as a capitalist. They lie somewhere below the lower boundary of the history of capital, just as processes that created the premises of life, the chemical processes, lie below the lower limit of the history of life, pertaining to the field of chemistry rather than of biology.

The same thing has to be borne in mind in logic, in order not to take the history of the premises of a concept (abstractions in general, words expressing the general in their meaning, etc.) for the history of the concept itself.

Thus the significance becomes apparent of the principle of *concrete historicism* which imposes the requirement of establishing, in a strictly objective manner, the point at which the real history of the object under consideration begins, the genuinely concrete starting-point of its origin.

The problem is the same whether we are dealing with the emergence of the capitalist system or the historical origin of man or the point at which life was born on the earth or the ability to think in concepts.

The precepts of abstract historicism merely disorientate the theoretician in this decisive field of theoretical analysis. As is well known, scientists often took the biological prehistory of human society for an undeveloped form of human existence, and biological laws, for abstract, elementary, and universal laws of human development. Examples of the same kind are attempts to deduce man's esthetic feeling from certain externally similar phenomena of the animal world—the beauty of the peacock's tail, the colours of the butterfly's wing and other purely biological adaptive phenomena.

The historicism of the logical method of Marx, Engels, and Lenin is concrete. It means that the concrete history of a concrete object should be considered in each particular case rather than history in general. The former is of course more difficult than the latter. But scientific research cannot be guided by the principle of ease, the principle of 'economy of intellectual effort', despite the neo-Kantian illusions. Scientific development can only be guided by the principle of correspondence with the object, and where the object is complex, there simply is nothing to be done.

The logical development of categories, in the form of

which the construction of the system of science is completed, must coincide with the historical development of the object, in the same way as reflection coincides with that which is reflected. The sequence of the categories itself must reproduce the real historical sequence in which the object of investigation and its structure are formed.

That is the main principle of dialectics. The whole difficulty lies in the fact that the concrete history of the concrete object is not so easy to single out in the ocean of the real facts of empirical history, for it is not the 'pure history' of the given concrete object that is given in contemplation and immediate notion but a very complicated mass of interconnected processes of development mutually interacting and altering the forms of their manifestation. The difficulty lies in singling out from the empirically given picture of the total historical process the cardinal points of the development of this particular concrete object, of the given concrete system of interaction. Logical development coinciding with the historical process of the formation of a concrete whole should rigorously establish its historical beginning, its birth, and later trace its evolution as a sequence of necessary and law-governed moments. That is the whole difficulty.

The capitalist system, for instance, does not emerge out of nothing but on the basis of and within historically preceding forms of economic relations, its concrete development involving the struggle and overcoming of these forms. Having originally emerged as a rather inconspicuous but more viable mode of economic relations, this system gradually transforms all types of production existing at the time of its birth in accordance with its own requirements and in its own image. It gradually converts earlier independent and even alien forms of economy into forms of its own realisation, subordinating them, partly breaking them down so that there is not a trace of them left, partly continuing to drag (sometimes for a very long time) the debris that it had no time to destroy, and partly developing into full flowering something that had previously existed only as a tentative tendency.

As a result, the historical development of a concrete whole, conceived in its essence and expressed in logical development, does not coincide with the picture that is to be found on the surface of events, that is open to the theoretically naked eye. The essence and the phenomena here also coincide only dialectically, only through contradiction.

Therefore the logical development of categories intended to reflect the real historical sequence of the formation of the analysed system of interacting phenomena, cannot be directly guided by the sequence in which certain aspects of the whole in the process of formation appeared or played the decisive role on the surface of the historical process open to empirical contemplation. 'It would be inexpedient and wrong therefore to present the economic categories successively in the order in which they have played the dominant rôle in history'[4]—that was the way in which Marx categorically summed up the methodological significance of this real circumstance.

The theoretician who accepts abstractly interpreted historicism is guided by the principle of analysis which Marx defines as inexpedient and wrong. When he considers phenomena in the sequence in which they follow one another in the historical time, in the sequence which appears at first sight as the most natural one, in actual fact he considers them in a sequence that is the reverse of the real and objective one.

The apparent and imaginary correspondence between the logical and the historical here conceals from the theoretician an actual absence of correspondence. Very often (much more often than the empiricist believes) the genuine objective cause of a phenomenon appears on the surface of the historical process later than its own consequence.

For instance, the general crisis of overproduction in the capitalist world is empirically manifested first of all in the form of disturbances in the sphere of bank credits, as a financial crisis, later it involves commerce and only at the very end does it reveal itself in the sphere of direct production as a real general crisis of overproduction. The superficial observer, who takes succession in time for the only historical principle, concludes from this that misunderstandings and conflicts in bank clearances are the cause, the basis, and the source of the general crisis. In other words, he takes the most abstract and derivative effect for the real basis of events, while the objective basis inevitably begins to seem the effect of its own effect.

[4] Karl Marx, *A Contribution to the Critique of Political Economy*, p. 213.

In this way crude empiricism yields the same absurd result as the most refined scholasticism. Crude empiricism in general inevitably becomes the worst kind of scholasticism when it is raised to the principle of theoretical explanation of events.

From the standpoint of science and of genuine historicism it is quite obvious however that overproduction had taken place before it had time to manifest itself in disturbances and confusion in the sphere of bank clearance, these disturbances merely reflecting in their own way the actually accomplished fact and in no way creating it. Logical development of categories in the system of science corresponds to the genuine historical sequence concealed from empirical observation, but it contradicts the external appearance, the superficial aspect of this sequence.

The correctly established logical order of development of categories in the system of science discloses the secret of the real objective sequence of development of phenomena, of the aspects of the object, permitting to understand the chronological sequence itself just as scientifically rather than empirically, from the standpoint of the man in the street. Logical development of categories in science contradicts temporal sequence exactly because it corresponds to the genuine and objective sequence of the formation of the concrete structure of the object under study. Herein lies the dialectics of the logical and the historical.

The 'historically anterior' continually becomes the 'logically posterior' in the course of development, and vice versa. Phenomena that emerged earlier than others as often as not become forms of manifestation of processes that started much later. The beginning (the genuine beginning) of a new branch of development, of a novel concrete historical system of interaction, cannot be understood as a product of a smooth evolution of the historically preceding forms. What takes place here is a genuine leap, a break in the development, in which a fundamentally new concrete historical form of development begins.

This new direction of development can only be understood out of itself, from its intrinsic contradictions. Each newly appearing concrete historical process has its own concrete historical beginning. In regard of economic development Marx expressed this circumstance in these terms: 'There is in every social formation a particular branch of production which determines the position and importance of all the others, and the relations obtaining in this branch accordingly determine the relations of all other branches as well. It is as though light of a particular hue were cast upon everything, tingeing all other colours and modifying their specific features; or as if a special ether determined the specific gravity of everything found in it.' [5]

Clearly this law is not restricted in its action to social development or social phenomena in general. Development in nature also takes this form and cannot take any other. Here too, a new concrete form of development emerges on the basis of and within the framework of those that precede it, becoming a concrete universal principle of a new system and as such involving these chronologically preceding forms in its specific concrete history.

From this point on the historical destiny of these historically preceding phenomena comes to be determined by entirely new laws. The chemical substances involved in the development of life behave in this process in quite a different manner from the way they had behaved before and independently from it. They are subject to the universal law of this higher new form, and their movement can only be understood from the laws of life, from the concrete universal laws of this higher and chronologically later form of the motion of matter.

The laws of these elementary forms cannot, of course, be violated, abolished or altered. But they become here subordinate laws, abstract universal laws that can explain absolutely nothing in the movement of the concrete whole the external manifestations of which they became. The development of organic life also results in the formation of 'a special kind of ether' which determines the share of any being that exists in it.

This 'specific ether', that is, the concrete universal principle of a new and higher form of movement that emerges chronologically at a later stage but becomes the dominant principle, must be understood in science before any other and first of all on its own merits, from the internally inherent concrete universal contradictions.

The historically preceding elements that, owing to the dialectics of development, became a secondary, auxiliary

[5] Karl Marx, *A Contribution to the Critique of Political Economy*, p. 212.

moment of the new form of movement, a kind of material in which some new concrete historical process is realised, may indeed be understood only from the concrete universal law of the higher form in whose movement they are involved.

These historically preceding elements may long pre-exist the logically prior ones, they may even constitute the condition of origin of this logically anterior, concrete universal phenomenon, later becoming its manifestation or product.

Rent as a form of capitalist economy cannot be comprehended before capital is comprehended, while capital may and must be understood in its internal contradictions before rent, though rent historically emerged earlier than capital and even served as a historical condition of its origin. Quite a few landlords, having accumulated feudal rent, later began to use it as capital. The same is true of commercial profit.

The historical destiny of rent and commercial profit as elements of the capitalist whole, as forms of manifestation and modifications of capital may be compared, for graphic effect, to the destiny of a block of marble, out of which the statue of a man is sculptured.

The concrete form of marble can in no way be explained from the properties of marble itself. Although it is the form of marble, in its real substance it is by no means the form of marble as a product of nature. Marble owes its form not to itself, not to its own nature, but to the process in which it is involved—the process of man's artistic development.

For millions of years marble lay in the ground, it appeared long before man, not only before the sculptor's time but also before mankind as a whole. But the concrete form in which it is displayed in the hall of a museum is the product of man's development, which commenced much later than marble as such, marble as mineral, appeared. That is an active form of some quite different process, a process that is realised in marble and through marble but naturally cannot be understood in terms of marble alone.

The situation is the same with the concrete historical form of the existence of rent, interest, commercial profit and similar forms and categories. In capitalist production, they are secondary, subordinate forms of economy, forms of manifestation of surplus-value, of a form that appeared much later than they themselves did.

This concrete universal form should be understood in science before and quite independently from all the others.

Their concrete history as the history of forms of being of surplus-value began when and where they were involved in the production and accumulation of surplus-value, so that they became organs of its body and a mode of its realisation. Before that point, their destinies had no internal relation whatever to the history of capitalism, to the history expressed in the sequence of categories of political economy. They had existed before that moment outside the history of capital, side by side with it but quite independently from it. But they became involved in the formation of the capitalist system, turning into concrete historical forms and elements of the given system, only in those areas where the concrete universal form of capital, which had developed independently from them, expressed its movement through them.

Thus logical development does not reproduce history as a whole, but rather the concrete history of the given concrete historical whole, of the given concrete system of phenomena interacting in a specific manner.

The logical order of the categories of science directly corresponds to this history and its sequence; it is the latter that is expressed in a theoretically generalised form. Logical development of categories and their concrete definitions cannot therefore be guided by the principle of abstract historicism (or pseudohistoricism), the principle of temporal sequence of the emergence of diverse forms of the analysed whole in history.

Contrariwise, it is only logical development of categories that is guided by the relation in which the elements of the analysed concreteness stand to one another in the developed object, in the object at the highest point of its development and maturity, that discovers the mystery of the genuine objective sequence of the formation of the object, of the moulding of its internal structure.

Following this path, we can always discover the genuinely natural (rather than the seemingly natural) order of development of all the aspects of the analysed concrete historical whole. In this case we shall attain a real coincidence of the logical and the historical. Otherwise we can only arrive at a divergence between the two, at an empirical scholastic expression of history, but not at its objective theoretical reflection in concept.

The inquiry into the system of capitalist production in *Capital* was a splendid confirmation of the correctness of this methodological principle, of Marx's and Engels' philosophical view of the dialectics of the historical process and its theoretical reproduction.

To form a genuinely historical conception of the capitalist formation, of the laws of its historical emergence, development, and decline, Marx studied first of all the *existing* state (*Dasein*) of this formation, proceeding from the contemporary situation, from the relation in which the diverse elements of its necessary structure stand to one another. Proceeding from this existing factually stated situation, he analysed the concepts and categories of political economy, studied these concepts critically, and unfolded, on the basis of this analysis, his theoretical conception of the facts, a system of theoretical definitions.

Each of the aspects and elements of the structure of the capitalist organism found therefore its concrete theoretical expression, and was reflected in a concrete historical abstraction.

The theoretical definitions of each category of political economy were formed by Marx through tracing the history of its emergence—not the empirical history but the history 'sublated' in its results.

This inquiry led him directly to a conception of the real historically necessary premises of the emergence of bourgeois economy, offering thereby a key to a theoretical understanding of the empirical history of its emergence and evolution. On the other hand, owing to this method of inquiry, the bourgeois formation itself emerged as a system of historically maturing premises of the birth of another, new, and higher system of social relations—of socialism, into which the capitalist system of production of material life inevitably develops under the pressure of the internal contradictions of its evolution.

Chapter 5

THE METHOD OF ASCENT FROM THE ABSTRACT TO THE CONCRETE IN MARX'S 'CAPITAL'

CONCRETE FULNESS OF ABSTRACTION AND ANALYSIS AS A CONDITION OF THEORETICAL SYNTHESIS

We shall now turn to a consideration of the logical structure of *Capital*, comparing it both with the logic of Ricardian thought and the theoretical views of Marx's predecessors in the field of logic; this discussion should reveal Marx's logic in its actual practical application to the analysis of facts, to the analysis of empirical data.

Our task is that of singling out the universal logical elements of Marx's treatment of economic materials, the logical forms that are applicable, due to their universality, to any other theoretical discipline.

Capital, as is well known, begins with a most thorough and detailed analysis of the category of value, i.e., of the real form of economic relations that is the universal and elementary form of the being of capital. In this analysis, Marx's field of vision encompasses a single and, as we have already noted, extremely rare, in developed capitalism, factual relation between men—direct exchange of one commodity for another. At this stage of his inquiry into the capitalist system, Marx intentionally leaves out of account any other forms—money or profit or wages. All of these things are as yet believed to be non-existent.

Nevertheless, analysis of this single form of economic relations yields, as its result, a theoretical expression of the objectively universal form of all phenomena and categories of developed capitalism without exception, an expression of a developed concreteness, a theoretical expression of value as such, of the universal form of value.

The elementary type of the existence of value coincides with value in general, and the real actually traceable development of this form of value into other forms constitutes the objective content of the deduction of the categories of *Capital*. Deduction in this conception, unlike the Ricardian one, loses its formal character: here it directly expresses the real descent of some forms of economic interaction from others.

That is precisely the point missing in the systems of Ricardo and of his followers from the bourgeois camp.

The conception of a universal concept underlying the entire system of the categories of science, applied here by Marx, cannot be explained by the specificity of the subject-matter of political economy. It reflects the universal dialectical law of the unfolding of any objective concreteness—natural, socio-historical, or spiritual.

This conception is of great significance for any modern science. To give a concrete theoretical definition of life as the basic category of biology, to answer the question of what is life in general, life as such, one ought to act in the same way as Marx acted with value in general, that is, one should undertake a concrete analysis of the composition and mode of existence of an elementary manifestation of life—the elementary protein body. That is the only way of obtaining a real definition and of revealing the essence of the matter.

Only in this way, and not at all by abstraction of the general features of all phenomena of life without exception, can one attain a really scientific and materialist conception of life, creating the concept of life as such.

The situation is the same in chemistry. The concept of chemical element as such, of chemical element in general, cannot be worked out through abstraction of the general and identical features that helium has in common with uranium or silicon with nitrogen, or the common features of all the elements of the periodic table. The concept of chemical element may be formed by detailed consideration of the simplest element of the system—hydrogen. Hydrogen appears in this case as the elementary structure in the decomposition of which chemical properties of matter disappear in general, whether the analytical decomposition is performed in an actual experiment or only mentally. Hydrogen is therefore a concrete universal element of chemism. The universal necessary laws that emerge and disappear with it, are the simplest laws of the existence of the chemical element in general. As elementary and universal laws they will occur in uranium, gold, silicon, and so on. And any of these more complex elements may in principle be reduced to hydrogen, which, by the way, happens both in nature and in experiments with nuclear processes.

In other words, what takes place here is the same living mutual transformation of the universal and the particular, of the elementary and the complex which we observed in the categories of capital, where profit emerges as developed value, as a developed elementary form of commodity, to which profit is continually reduced in the real movement of the economic system and therefore in thought reproducing this movement. Here as everywhere else, the concrete universal concept registers a real objective elementary form of the existence of the entire system rather than an empty abstraction.

'Value in general' (value as such), 'life in general', 'chemical element'—all these concepts are fully concrete. This means that the reality reflected in them is the reality objectively existing at present (or at any time in the past), existing by itself as an elementary and further indivisible instance of the given concreteness. That is exactly why it can be singled out as a specific object of consideration and may be studied and obtained by experiment.

If one were to conceive value (just as any other universal category) only as a reflection of abstract universal features existing in all *developed* particular phenomena without exception, it could not be studied as such, all these developed phenomena strictly ignored. Analysis of the universal would in this case be impossible in any other form except that of formal analysis of the concept. In the sensually given world, there can be no 'animal in general' or 'chemical element as such' or 'value'—as reflections of abstract general features they indeed exist only in the head.

Ricardo had not the slightest inkling that value should be studied concretely in its form, that it might in general be studied as such, in strictest abstraction from profit, rent, interest, capital, and competition. His abstraction of value therefore is, as Marx showed, doubly defective: 'On the one hand, he (Ricardo) must be reproached for not going far enough, for not carrying his abstraction to completion, for instance, when he analyses the *value* of the commodity, he at once allows himself to be influenced by consideration of all kinds of concrete conditions. On the other hand one must reproach him for regarding the phenomenal form as *immediate and direct* proof or exposition of the general laws, and for failing to *interpret* it. In regard to the first, his abstraction is too incomplete; in regard to the second, it is formal abstraction which in itself is wrong.'[1]

It is not difficult to formulate Marx's own view of the universal category assumed by this evaluation. Abstraction must be, first, *complete*, and second, *meaningful* rather than formal. Only then will it be correct and *objective.*

What does that mean, however?

We have shown already that fulness of abstraction assumes that it directly expresses something quite different from abstract universal features inherent in absolutely all particular phenomena to which this universal abstraction refers; rather it expresses the concrete characteristics of the objectively simplest further indivisible element of a system of interaction, a 'cell' of the analysed whole.

In the capitalist system of interaction between men in social production of material life, this cell turned out to be a commodity, the elementary commodity form of interaction. In biology, this cell is apparently the simplest protein structure, in the physiology of the higher nervous activity, the conditioned reflex, etc.

At this point, the question of 'the beginning of science', of the basic universal category underlying the entire system of the concrete categories of science, is closely linked with the question of concreteness of analysis and of the objectively admissible limits of analytical division of the object.

Concrete theoretical analysis means that a thing is divided into internally connected, necessary forms of its existence specific to it rather than into components indifferent to its specific nature.

Marx's analytical method is diametrically opposed in this respect to the so-called one-sided analytical mehod, as illustrated by the practice of the classical bourgeois political economy. The one-sided analytical method, inherited by the economists of the 17th and 18th centuries from contemporary mechanistic natural science and the philosophy of empiricism (through Locke), fully corresponds to the conception of objective reality as a kind of aggregate of eternal

[1] Karl Marx, *Theories of Surplus-Value,* Part II, p. 106.

and immutable constituent elements, identical in any object of nature. According to this conception, cognising a thing means analysing it into these eternal and immutable constituents and then comprehending the mode of their interaction within this thing.

'Labour', 'need', 'profit' in the theory of Smith and Ricardo are in this respect just as striking an example of one-sided analytical abstractions, in which the entire concrete historical definiteness of the object is extinguished, as 'the particle' of Cartesian physics, Newton's 'atom' and similar categories of the science of that time. Both Smith and Ricardo endeavoured to understand the capitalist system of interaction as a complex whole whose component parts are eternal realities identical for any stage of the development of mankind: labour, labour implements (capital), needs, surplus product, etc.

This operation of analytical division of the object can always be performed both experimentally and mentally. A living rabbit may be analytically decomposed into chemical elements, into mechanical 'particles', etc. But, having thus obtained an aggregate of analytically singled out elements, we shall not be able to perform a reverse operation, even after a most detailed consideration of these elements—we shall never understand why their combination before the analytical dismemberment existed as a live rabbit.

In this case analysis killed and destroyed exactly that which we intended to understand in this way—the living and concrete interaction specific for the given thing. Analysis made synthesis impossible.

Bourgeois classical economics, the theory of Smith and Ricardo, ran into the same difficulty.

Synthesis, a comprehension of the necessary connection between the abstractly considered constituent elements of the object (labour, capital, profit, etc.), proved to be impossible exactly because analysis that singled out these categories was *one-sided* analysis: it broke up that very concrete historical form of connection of these categories.

The difficulty of the problem of analysis and synthesis was noted already by Aristotle. He saw quite well that one-sided analysis could not by itself solve the problems of cognition. In his *Metaphysics* he comes to the conclusion that the task of cognition is dual: it is not enough to find out of what parts a thing consists—one must also discover why these constituent parts are interconnected in such a way that their combination constitutes the given concrete thing rather than some other one.

A thing given in contemplation is not difficult to analyse into its constituent elements: the chair is black, made of wood, with four legs, heavy, with a round seat, etc., etc. That is an elementary example of empirical analysis and at the same time an example of empirical synthesis of abstract definitions in a judgement about a thing.

It should be noted that a direct coincidence of analysis and synthesis takes place in this case, too. In the proposition 'This chair is black' one can discern both. On the one hand, that is pure synthesis, a combination of two abstractions in a proposition. On the other hand, it is just as pure analysis—a singling out of two different definitions in a sensually given image. Both analysis and synthesis take place *simultaneously* in an utterance of an elementary proposition (judgement) concerning a thing.

In this example, however, the guarantee and basis of correctness of analysis and synthesis is direct contemplation: in it, the features synthesised in the proposition appear as combined and at the same time distinct. Contemplation itself is the basis and criterion of correctness of the analytic singling out of abstractions linked in the proposition.

It is thus easy to understand the coincidence of analysis and synthesis in a proposition concerning an individual fact, in an utterance expressing the actual state of things. It is much more difficult to understand the relation between analysis and synthesis in a *theoretical* proposition that has to be based on better grounds than mere indication of the fact that a thing appears in contemplation in a certain aspect rather than some other one.

The proposition 'All swans are white' does not present any difficulties for comprehension from the point of view of logic precisely because it does not express the necessity of the connection between the two definitions. The proposition 'All objects of nature are extensive' is quite a different matter. A swan may just as well be non-white, whereas the proposition 'All objects of nature are extensive' implements a necessary synthesis of two definitions. Unextended objects of nature are non-existent—and contrariwise, there can be no extension that would not be an attribute of an object of nature.

In other words, a theoretical proposition is a linking of abstractions each of which expresses a definiteness without which the thing ceases to be what it is, it ceases to exist as a given thing.

A swan may be painted any colour other than white—it will not cease to be a swan.

But extension cannot be taken away from an object of nature without destroying that object itself.

A theoretical proposition must therefore contain only those abstractions which express the forms of existence of the given object necessarily inherent in it.

What is to guarantee that a proposition connects precisely these abstract definitions?

Empirical contemplation of a thing cannot answer this question. To separate the necessary form of the being of a thing from one that may or may not exist, without impairing the existence of a thing as the given concrete thing (a swan, a body of nature, labour, etc.), one should proceed from contemplation *to the sensually practical experiment, to man's social practice in its historical entirety.*

It is only the practice of social mankind, that is, the totality of historically developing forms of actual interaction of social man with nature, that proves to be both the basis and the verification criterion of theoretical analysis and synthesis.

How does this real problem present itself in the development of political economy?

This can be easily traced by considering the category of labour and the category of value connected with it.

Inasmuch as the value category forms the foundation of the entire theory and the theoretical basis of all other generalisations, the conception of labour *as the substance* of value determines the theoretical understanding of all other phenomena of the capitalist system.

Is the proposition 'The substance of value is labour' true? It is not. This theoretical proposition (judgement) is tantamount in its theoretical significance to the proposition 'Man is by nature a private proprietor'—an assertion that being a private proprietor is the same kind of attribute in man's nature as extension in a body of nature.

In other terms, a consideration of the empirically given situation reveals abstract characteristics none of which is necessarily contained in the nature of labour and value.

Marx gave a lucid explanation of the whole matter. A historically transient property of labour is here taken for a characteristic expressing its absolute inner nature. By far not all labour creates value, not *any* historically concrete form of labour, in the same way that it is not man as such that is an owner of private property but a historically concrete man, man within a definite, historically concrete form of social being.

But how is one to distinguish between that which is inherent in a historically definite form of man's existence, and that which is inherent in man in general?

This can only be done by a detailed analysis of the reality on which a theoretical judgement is passed from the standpoint of the entire practice of mankind. The latter is the only criterion which permits confidently to abstract or analytically reveal a definition that would express the form of being that is the object's attribute.

Both at the time of Smith and Ricardo and in Marx's time man's being as a private proprietor was an empirically universal fact. The ability of labour to create commodities and value rather than merely a product was also an empirically universal fact.

The classic representatives of political economy recorded this empirically universal fact in the proposition 'The substance of value is labour'—labour in general, without further theoretical qualifications expressing its concrete historical definiteness within which it creates commodity rather than product, value rather than use-value.

Insofar as the classics of political economy worked out abstract theoretical definitions with the aid of the one-sided analytical method, they were unable to understand why labour appeared now as capital, now as wages, now as rent.

This logical task that was common both to the natural scientists of the 17th and 18th centuries and to Smith and Ricardo is essentially insoluble. The former attempted to understand why and in what way atoms, particles and monads could form in different combinations now a cosmic system, now the body of an animal; the latter endeavoured to comprehend why and in what way labour in general generated now capital, now rent, now wages.

Neither the former nor the latter could attain a theoretical synthesis—exactly because their analysis was not concrete but rather divided the object into indifferent parts common to any objective sphere or any historical form of production.

Labour in general is an absolutely necessary condition of the emergence and development of rent, capital, wages, and all the other specifically capitalist categories. But it is also a condition of their non-being, their negation and destruction. Labour in general is just as indifferent to the being of capital as to its non-being. It is a universal necessary condition of its emergence, but it is not an *internally* necessary condition, a condition that is at the same time a *necessary sequence.* The form of inner *reciprocal* action, inner *reciprocal* conditioning is absent here.

Concerning this defect of one-sided analytical abstractions worked out by the classics of bourgeois science, Marx remarked: 'It is just as impossible to pass directly from labour to capital as directly from different human races to a banker or from nature to a steam-engine.'[2]

This is an echo of Feuerbach's well-known aphorism, 'You cannot directly deduce even a bureaucrat from nature'; Marx draws the same conclusion from this aspect of the matter, too: all difficulties of theoretical analysis and synthesis are solved in reality on the basis of the category of concrete historical *reciprocal* action, *reciprocal* conditioning of phenomena within a definite historically developed whole, within a concrete historical system of interaction.

To put it differently, both analysis/synthesis and deduction/induction cease to be metaphysically polar and therefore helpless logical forms only on the basis of a *conscious historical view* of the analysed reality, on the basis of the conception of any objective reality as a historically emergent and developed system of interacting phenomena.

This view gave Marx a clear criterion which he, proceeding from the entire rationally comprehended history of the practice of mankind, confidently applied to the solution of the difficulties of theoretical analysis and synthesis and theoretical deduction and induction.

The practice of mankind in its historical entirety was used by Marx as a criterion for distinguishing between empirical synthesis and *theoretical synthesis*, of analytical abstractions reflecting the universal empirical state of things

---

[2] K. Marx, *Grundrisse der Kritik der politischen Ökonomie (Rohentwurf). 1857-1858,* S. 170.

and *theoretical abstractions* the interconnection of which reflects the internally necessary connection of the phenomena which they express.

In Smith and Ricardo (and even Hegel) purely empirical synthesis is often set up as theoretical one; they continually set up the historically transient form of the phenomenon for its inner structure (for its eternal nature), deducing the justification of the crudest empirical facts from the nature of things, whereas Marx's method raises the most rigorous logical and philosophical barriers in the way of such movement of thought.

Deduction and induction, analysis and synthesis prove to be powerful logical means of processing empirical facts exactly because they are consciously used in the service of an essentially historical approach to research, being based on the dialectical materialist conception of the object as a historically emergent and developing system of phenomena interacting in a specific way.

For this reason, Marx's analytical method, the method of ascent from the whole given in contemplation to the conditions of its possibility, coincides with the method of *genetic deduction* of theoretical definitions, with logical tracing of real descent of some phenomena from others (of money from the movement of the commodity market, of capital from the movement of commodity-money circulation in which labour force becomes involved, etc.). This essentially historical view of things and of their theoretical expression enabled Marx to formulate clearly the question of the real substance of the value properties of the labour product, of the universal substance of all the other concrete historical categories of political economy.

It is not labour in general but the concrete historical form of labour that was conceived as the substance of value. In this connection, new light was thrown on theoretical analysis of the form of value: it emerged as the concrete universal category which permits to understand theoretically (to deduce) that real concrete historical necessity with which value is transformed into surplus-value, into capital, wages, rent and all the other developed concrete categories.

In other words, for the first time an analysis was given of the starting-point from which one can really develop the entire system of theoretical definitions of the object, the system that logically reflects the necessity of the real genesis of the capitalist formation.

What did concrete analysis of the form of value consist in, that very analysis which David Ricardo failed to conduct? The answer to this question should give us the key to an understanding of the method of ascent from the abstract to the concrete.

Ascent from a universal theoretical definition of the object to an understanding of the entire complexity of its historically developed structure (concreteness) assumes a concrete and comprehensive analysis of the *basic universal category of the science*. We have seen that insufficient concreteness of Ricardo's analysis of value determined the failure of his intention to develop the whole system of theoretical definitions, to construct the entire building of science on a single solid foundation; it did not permit him to deduce even the proximate category, money, not to mention all the other categories.

Wherein lies the specific quality of Marx's analysis of value, which forms the solid foundation of theoretical synthesis of categories, enabling him to proceed in a most rigorous manner from the consideration of value to the consideration of money, capital, etc.?

Thus formulated, this question compels logic to face the problem of contradiction in the definitions of a thing, a problem which ultimately contains the key to everything else. Contradiction as the unity and coincidence of mutually exclusive theoretical definitions was discovered by Marx to be the solution of the riddle of the concrete and a way to express theoretically the concrete in concepts. We are now passing on to the analysis of this point.

CONTRADICTION AS THE CONDITION OF DEVELOPMENT OF SCIENCE

Logical contradiction—the existence of mutually exclusive definitions in the theoretical expression of a thing—has long interested philosophy. There has never been one single philosophical or logical doctrine that would not consider this question in one form or another and solve it in its own way. It always interested philosophy exactly because contradiction in definitions is first and foremost a fact independent from any philosophy, a fact that is continually and with fatal necessity reproduced in scientific development, in mankind's thought, including philosophy itself. Moreover, contradiction most unambiguously reveals itself as a form in which thought about things moves, always and everywhere.

Ancient Greeks understood full well that truth was only born in the struggle of opinions. Critique of any theory was always directed at discovering contradictions in it. A new theory always asserted itself ~~through~~ demonstrating a method by which contradictions were solved that had been insoluble within the framework of the principles of the old theory.

However, if this empirical fact is simply described as a fact, it will appear that a contradiction is something intolerable, something that thought always tries to get rid of in one way or another. At the same time, despite all attempts to get rid of it, thought reproduces it again and again.

Inasmuch as philosophy and logic study this fact, not content with simply stating and describing it, the question arises of the causes and sources of its origin in thought, of its real nature. In philosophy, this question arises in the following form: is contradiction admissible or inadmissible in the genuine expression of a thing? Is it something purely subjective, created only by the subject of cognition, or does it necessarily emerge as the outcome of the nature of things expressed in thought?

That is the boundary between dialectics and metaphysics. In the final analysis, dialectics and metaphysics are two fundamentally opposed methods of solving contradictions which inevitably arise in scientific development, in the development of theoretical knowledge.

The difference between them, expressed in a most general form, is that metaphysics interprets contradiction as a mere *subjective* phantom which regrettably recurs in thought due to the imperfections of the latter, while dialectics considers it as the *necessary logical* form of the development of thought, of the transition from ignorance to knowledge, from an abstract reflection of the object in thought to an ever more concrete reflection of it.

Dialectics regards contradiction as a necessary form of development of knowledge, as a universal logical form. That is the only way to consider contradiction from the point of view of cognition and thought as a natural historical process controlled by laws independent from man's desires. *

The development of knowledge and science compels philosophy to recur to the problem of logical contradiction again and again. The question of contradiction, of its real significance, its source and the cause of its emergence in thought arises in those areas where science approaches the stage of systematic expression of its subject-matter in concepts, where reasoning has to construct a system of theoretical definitions. In cases of unsystematic recounting of phenomena, there is no question of contradiction. An elementary attempt to systematise knowledge immediately leads to the problem of contradiction.

We have already noted the points at which the development of the labour theory of value necessarily ran into this problem: in Ricardo, despite his wishes, a system of theoretical contradictions arises exactly because he attempts to develop all categories out of one principle—that of determining value by the quantity of labour time. He noticed some logical contradictions in his system himself, others were maliciously pointed out by the opponents of the labour theory of value.

The main type of logical contradiction that was the focal point of the struggle for and against the labour theory of value, proved to be the contradiction between the universal law and the empirical universal forms of its own realisation.

Attempts to deduce from the universal law theoretical definitions of developed concrete phenomena that regularly recur on the surface of the capitalist production and distribution of commodities, resulted in paradoxical conclusions at every step.

A phenomenon (say, profit) is, on the one hand, included in the sphere of action of the law of value, its necessary theoretical definitions are deduced from the law of value; but, on the other hand, its specific distinctive feature proves

---

* It should be borne in mind that here and in the following we mean those contradictions in definitions which arise in the course of movement of thought that is correct from the standpoint of the logic of the object, that is, we mean dialectical contradictions in reasoning. As Lenin pointed out, in any inquiry there must be no logical contradictions in the narrow sense of the word, that is, verbal, forced, or subjective contradictions. Rules barring these contradictions must be worked out by formal logic.

to be contained in a definition which directly contradicts the formula of the universal law.

This fatal contradiction manifested itself all the more clearly, the more efforts were made to get rid of it.

Contradictions are by no means a 'privilege' of political economy that studies the antagonistic reality of economic relations between classes.

Contradictions are inherent in any modern science. Suffice it to recall the circumstances of the birth of the theory of relativity. Attempts to explain certain phenomena established in the Michelson experiments in terms of the categories of classical mechanics resulted in the appearance, within the system of concepts of classical mechanics, of absurd, paradoxical contradictions in principle insoluble in these terms, and Einstein's brilliant hypothesis was put forward as a means of solving these contradictions.

The theory of relativity did not, of course, eliminate contradictions from physics. For example, one may point out to the well-known paradox contained in the theoretical definitions of the rotating body. The theory of relativity, linking up the spatial characteristics of bodies with their motion, expressed this connection in a formula according to which the length of a body is reduced in the direction of motion proportionately with the speed of the body's motion. This expression of the universal law of the motion of a body through space became a firmly established theoretical attainment of the mathematical arsenal of modern physics.

However, an attempt to apply it to a theoretical elaboration or assimilation of such an actual physical phenomenon as rotation of a hard disc round its axis results in a paradox: the circumference of a rotating disc diminishes with an increase of the speed of rotation, while the length of the radius, according to the same formula, remains unchanged.

Let us note that this paradox is no mere curiosity but an acute test of the *physical reality* of Einstein's universal formulas. If the universal formula expresses an objective law of objective reality studied in physics, one should assume the existence in the reality itself of an objectively paradoxical relation between the radius and the circumference of a rotating body (even in the case of the spinning top), for the infinitely small decrease in the extent of the circumference changes nothing in the fundamental approach to the problem.

The conviction that physical reality itself cannot contain such a paradoxical correlation, is tantamount to a rejection of the physical reality of the universal law expressed in the Einstein formula. And that is a way to a purely instrumental justification of the universal law. If law serves theory and practice that is all to the good, and one should not bother about the vacuous problem whether it has anything to correspond to it in the 'things in themselves' or not.

One can cite quite a number of other examples showing that objective reality always reveals itself to theoretical thought as contradictory reality. The history of science from Zeno of Elea down to Albert Einstein, independently from any philosophy shows this circumstance to be an incontestable empirically stated fact.

Let us go back to the reality of capitalist economy and its theoretical expression in political economy. This is a good example because it is extremely typical: it shows graphically the cul-de-sacs in which metaphysical thought inevitably lands itself in trying to solve the prime task of science—that of unfolding a systematic expression of the object in concepts, in a system of theoretical definitions of the object, a system developed from one general theoretical principle. That is the first reason. And the second and probably most important reason is that in Marx's *Capital* we find a rational way out of the difficulties and contradictions, a dialectical materialist solution of the antinomies which destroyed the labour theory of value in its classical Ricardian form.

THE CONTRADICTIONS OF THE LABOUR THEORY OF VALUE AND THEIR DIALECTICAL RESOLUTION IN MARX

Let us recall that the logical theoretical contradictions of Ricardo's system are the result of his effort to express all phenomena through the category of value, to understand them from one principle only.

Where this effort is not made, no contradictions arise. The formula of vulgar science (capital—interest, land—rent, labour—wages) does not contradict either itself or the obvious empirical facts. However, precisely because of that it does not contain a single grain of theoretical comprehension of things. There are no contradictions here for the simple reason that this formula does not establish any inner connection at all between capital and interest, between labour and wages, between land and rent, also because vulgar science does not even attempt to deduce definitions of all these categories from a single principle. They are not shown to be necessary distinctions necessarily arising within a certain common substance, they are not understood as modifications of this substance. It is not surprising that there is no inner contradiction here but merely an external contradiction between different internally non-contradictory things. And that is a situation with which a metaphysician will be easily reconciled. They do not contradict each other simply because they do not stand in any internally necessary relation at all. That is why the formula of vulgar science has approximately the same theoretical value as the favourite maxims of the proverbial school teacher from a short story by Chekhov: 'Horses eat oats' and 'the Volga flows into the Caspian'.

Unlike vulgar economists, Ricardo tried to develop the entire system of theoretical definitions from the principles of the labour theory of value. And that is exactly why the whole reality, as he describes it, appears as a system of conflicts, antagonisms, antinomical mutually exclusive tendencies, diametrically opposed forces whose opposition creates the whole which he considers.

Logical contradictions which economists and philosophers from the bourgeois camp regarded as an indication of weakness, of lack of development of Ricardo's theory, actually expressed quite the reverse—the strength and objectiveness of his method of theoretical expression of things. What Ricardo aimed at, first and foremost, was correspondence of theoretical propositions and conclusions to the actual state of things, and only in the second place, their correspondence to the metaphysical postulate that an object cannot contradict itself and neither can its separate theoretical definitions contradict one another.

He expressed the actual state of things in a bold (and even, as Marx put it, cynical) manner, and the actually contradictory state of things was reflected in his system as contradictions in definitions. When his pupils and followers made it their principal concern not so much theoretical expression of facts as formal coordination of already available definitions, subject to the principle forbidding contradictions in definitions as the supreme principle, from that point on the disintegration of the labour theory of value set in.

In his analysis of the views of James Mill, Marx states: 'What he tries to achieve is formal, logical consistency. The *disintegration* of the Ricardian school "therefore" (therefore!—*E.I.*) begins with him.' [3]

In itself, the desire for justifying Ricardo's theory in terms of the canons of formal logical sequence does not of course spring from a platonic love for formal logic. This preoccupation is stimulated by a different motive—a desire to present the capitalist system of commodity production as an everlasting form of production eternally equal to itself, rather than as a historically emergent system that can therefore turn into another, higher system.

If a certain phenomenon, expressed and conceived in terms of the universal law of value, suddenly enters into a relation of theoretical (logical) contradiction with the formula of the universal law (determination of value by the quantity of labour time), to a bourgeois theoretician this appears as evidence of its deviation from the eternal and immutable foundations of economic being. All effort is directed at proving that the phenomenon directly corresponds to the universal law, which in itself is conceived as existing without contradiction, as an eternal and immutable form of economy.

More acutely than anything else, bourgeois economists feel the contradiction between Ricardo's universal law of value and *profit*. An attempt to express the phenomena of profit in terms of the category of value, to apply the labour theory of value to profit, reveals, already in Ricardo, contradictions in the definition. Inasmuch as profit is the holy of holies of the religion of private property, economists direct their theoretical efforts at coordinating the definitions of profit with the universal law of value.

There are two ways of directly coordinating theoretical definitions of value with the theoretical definitions of profit as a specific form, as a specific modification (kind) of value.

The first way is to change the expression of *profit* in such a manner that it might be included without contradiction in the sphere of application of the category of value, of its

---

[3] Karl Marx, *Theories of Surplus-Value,* Part III, p. 84.

universal definitions. The second way is to change the expression of *value*, to qualify it in such a way that definitions of profit might be included in it without contradiction.

Both of these ways led to the disintegration of the Ricardian school. Vulgar political economy preferred the second way, that of qualifying definitions of value, for the motto of empiricism has always been, 'Bring the *universal* formula of a law in agreement with the empirically unquestionable state of things, with that which is identical in the facts', in this case, with the empirical form of the existence of profit.

This philosophical position appears at first glance to be the most obvious and sensible. Its realisation, however, is impossible unless the universal theoretical propositions of the labour theory of value, the very *concept* of value, are sacrificed.

Let us consider in detail why and in what way this necessarily comes about.

The paradoxical relation between the theoretical definitions of value and profit is a stumbling-block for Ricardo himself. His law of value says that live labour, man's labour, is the only source of value, while the time spent on the production of an article constitutes the only objective measure of value.

What do we observe, however, if we apply this universal law that cannot be either violated or abolished or altered (expressing as it does the universal intimate nature of any economic phenomenon) to the empirically unquestionable fact of the existence of profit?

Ricardo realised quite well that profit could not be explained by the law of value alone and that the entire complexity of the structure of profit was not exhausted by this law. Ricardo took the law of the average rate of profit, the general rate of profit, as the second decisive factor whose interaction with the law of value could explain profit.

The general rate of profit is a purely empirical and therefore unquestionable fact. Its essence is this: the magnitude of profit depends exclusively on the aggregate magnitude of capital and in no way depends on the proportion in which it is divided into fixed and circulating capital, constant and variable capital, etc.

Ricardo applies this empirically universal law to the explanation of the mechanism of profit production, treating it as a factor which modifies and complicates the action of the law of value. Ricardo did not inquire into the nature of this factor, its origin, its inner relation to the universal law. He assumed its existence absolutely uncritically, as an empirically unquestionable fact.

Any more or less close analysis will reveal at once that the law of the average rate of profit directly contradicts the universal law of value, the determination of value in terms of labour time, the two laws being mutually exclusive.

'Instead of *postulating* this *general rate of profit*, Ricardo should rather have examined in how far its *existence* is in fact consistent with the determination of value by labour-time, and he would have found that instead of being consistent with it, *prima facie*, it *contradicts* it....'[4]

The contradiction here is as follows: the law of the average rate of profit establishes the dependence of the magnitude of profit solely on the magnitude of capital as a whole; it stipulates that the magnitude of profit is absolutely independent from the share of capital spent on wages and transformed into the live labour of the wage worker. But the universal law of value states directly that new value can only be the product of live labour, it can by no means be the product of dead labour, for dead labour, (that is, labour earlier materialised in the form of machines, buildings, raw materials, etc.) does not create any new value, merely passively transferring its own value, bit by bit, onto the product.

Ricardo saw the difficulty himself. However, entirely in the spirit of metaphysical thinking, he expressed and interpreted it as an exception from the rule rather than a contradiction in the definitions of the law. Of course, that does not alter the situation, and Malthus points out quite correctly in this connection that, as industry develops, the rule becomes an exception and an exception the rule. [5]

Thus a problem arises that is completely insoluble in metaphysical thought. From the point of view of the metaphysically thinking theoretician, a universal law can only be justified as an empirically universal rule to which all phenomena without exception are subject. In the given case it turns out, however, that something directly opposing the universal law of value, a negation of the law of value, becomes a universal empirical rule.

[4] Karl Marx, *Theories of Surplus-Value*, Part II, p. 174.

[5] See ibid., p. 191.

A theoretically established universal law and an empirical universal rule, the empirically universal element in the facts, come here into an antinomy, an insoluble contradiction. If one continues the attempts to bring into agreement the universal law with the immediately general features abstracted from facts, a problem arises that is 'much more difficult ... to solve than that of squaring the circle.... It is simply an attempt to present that which does not exist as in fact existing'.[6]

The problem of correlation of the universal and the particular, of a universal law and an empirically obvious form of its own manifestation (of the general in the facts), of *theoretical* and *empirical* abstraction, became one of the stumbling-blocks in the history of political economy that proved insurmountable to bourgeois theory.

Facts are a stubborn thing. Here, too, the fact remains: a universal law (the law of value) stands in the relation of mutually exclusive contradiction to the empirically universal form of its own manifestation, with the law of the average rate of profit. It is impossible to bring them into agreement exactly because such an agreement does not exist in the economic reality itself.

A metaphysically thinking theoretician facing this fact as a surprise or paradox, will inevitably interpret it as a result of mistakes earlier made in reasoning, in the theoretical expression of facts. For a solution of this paradox, he naturally resorts to purely formal analysis of theory, to specification of concepts and correction of expressions. The postulate that objective reality cannot be self-contradictory is for him the supreme and indisputable law for which he is ready to sacrifice anything at all.

Marx denounced the complete lack of the scientific spirit in these attitudes, their absolute incompatibility with a theoretical approach, in these terms:

'Here the contradiction between the general law and further developments in the concrete circumstances is to be resolved not by the discovery of the connecting links but by directly subordinating and immediately adapting the concrete to the abstract. This moreover is to be brought about by a *verbal fiction*, by changing the correct names of things.

---

[6] Karl Marx, *Theories of Surplus-Value*, Part III, p. 87.

(These are indeed "verbal disputes", they are "verbal", however, because real contradictions which are not resolved in a real way, are to be solved by phrases.)'[7]

The law forbidding contradictions in definition triumphs, but theory perishes, degenerating into verbal disputes, into a system of semantic tricks.

Indicating contradictions in the theoretical definitions of the object does not in itself constitute a privilege of conscious dialectics. Dialectics is not merely a desire for piling up contradictions, antinomies, and paradoxes in theoretical definitions of things. Metaphysical thought is much better at this task (true, contrary to its own intentions).

Contrariwise, dialectical thought emerges only at that point where metaphysical thought is hopelessly lost in a maze of contradictions with itself, in the contradictions of some of its conclusions with others.

The desire to get rid of contradictions in definitions through specifying terms and expressions is a metaphysical mode of solving contradictions in theory. As such, it results in disintegration of theory rather than in its development. Since life compels a development of theory all the same, in the end it always turns out that an attempt to construct a theory without contradictions leads to the piling up of new contradictions that are still more absurd and insoluble than those that were apparently got rid of.

To repeat: the task of theory does not consist in merely proving that the objective reality always arises before theoretical thought as a living contradiction demanding a solution, as a system of contradictions. In the 20th century, this fact does not have to be proved, and new examples add nothing. Even the most inveterate and confirmed metaphysician cannot fail to see this obvious fact.

However, the metaphysician of our times, starting out from this premise, directs all his efforts at justifying this fact as resulting from intrinsic defects of man's cognitive ability, from poor development of concepts, definitions, the relative and vague character of terms, expressions, etc. Now, the metaphysician will be reconciled with the existence of contradiction—as with an inevitable subjective evil, not more. Just as in Kant's times, he is still not prepared to admit that this fact expresses inner contradictions of things

---

[7] Ibid., pp. 87-88.

'in themselves', of the objective reality itself. That is why agnosticism and subjectivism of the relativist type resort to metaphysics in these days.

Dialectics proceeds from a diametrically opposite view. Its solution of the problem is based first of all on the assumption that the objective world itself, the objective reality is a living system unfolding through emergence and resolutions of its internal contradictions. The dialectical method, dialectical logic demand that, far from fearing contradictions in the theoretical definition of the object, one must search for these contradictions in a goal-directed manner and record them precisely—to find their rational resolution, of course, not to pile up mountains of antinomies and paradoxes in theoretical definitions of a thing.

The only way of attaining a rational resolution of contradictions in theoretical definition is through tracing the mode in which they are resolved in the *movement of the objective reality, the movement and development of the world* of things 'in themselves'.

Let us go back to political economy, to see how Marx resolves all those antinomies which were recorded by the Ricardian school despite its conscious philosophical intention.

In the first place, Marx gives up any attempts to bring directly into agreement the universal law (the law of value) with the empirical forms of its own manifestation on the surface of events, that is, with the abstract general expression of facts, with the immediately general features that may be inductively established in the facts.

Marx shows that this direct coincidence of the universal law and the empirical forms of its manifestation does not exist in the reality of economic development itself: the two are connected by the relation of mutually exclusive contradiction. The law of value contradicts in actual fact, not only and not so much in Ricardo's head, the law of the average rate of profit.

In an attempt to prove their coincidence, 'crass empiricism turns into false metaphysics, scholasticism, which toils painfully to deduce undeniable empirical phenomena by simple formal abstraction directly from the general law, or to show by cunning argument that they are in accordance with that law'. [8]

---

[8] Karl Marx, *Theories of Surplus-Value*, Part I, p. 89.

Finally realising the impossibility of doing so, the empiricist will in this case draw the conclusion that the formulation of the universal law is incorrect and will proceed to 'correct' it. Following this path, bourgeois science emasculated the theoretical meaning of the Ricardian law of value, losing, as Marx pointed out, the concept of value itself.

This loss of the value concept occurred in the following way: to bring the law of value into agreement with that of the average rate of profit and other irrefutable phenomena of economic reality contradicting it, MacCulloch changed the concept of labour as the substance of value. Here is his definition of labour:

'*Labour* may *properly* be defined to be any sort of action or operation, whether performed my man, the lower animals, machinery, or natural agents, that tends to bring about any desirable result.' [9]

By means of this definition MacCulloch 'gets rid' of the Ricardian contradictions.

Marx has this to say about the argument: 'And yet some persons have had the temerity to say that the miserable Mac has taken Ricardo to extremes, he who ... abandons the very concept of labour itself!' [10]

This 'abandonment of the concept' is inevitable given the desire to construct a system of theoretical definitions without contradictions between a universal law and the empirical form of its own manifestation.

Marx's mode of action is different in principle. In his system, the theoretical definitions do not eliminate the contradictions which horrify the metaphysician who does not know any other logic but the formal one.

If one should take a theoretical proposition from the first volume of *Capital* and confront it with a theoretical proposition from the third volume, it will appear that the two are in logical contradiction with each other.

In the first volume it is shown, for instance, that surplus-value is exclusively the product of that part of capital which is expended on wages, which became the live labour of a wage worker, that is, the product of the variable part of capital and only of that part.

But proposition from the third volume reads as follows: 'However that may be, the outcome is that surplus-value

[9] Ibid., Part III, p. 179.
[10] Ibid., pp. 181-82.

springs simultaneously from all portions of the invested capital.'[11]

The contradiction established by the Ricardian school has not thus disappeared here but is on the contrary shown to be the *necessary* contradiction of the very essence of production of surplus-value. That was precisely why the bourgeois economists, after the publication of the third volume of *Capital,* triumphantly stated that Marx had not been able to resolve the antinomies of the labour theory of value, that he had not made true the promises given in the first volume, and that the entire *Capital* was nothing but a speculative dialectical trickery.

The logical-philosophical basis of these reproaches was again the metaphysical conception that a universal law was proved by facts only when it could be brought into agreement *without contradictions* directly with the general empirical form of the phenomenon, with the general features in facts open to direct contemplation.

That is exactly what we do not find in *Capital*, and the vulgar economist raises a shout that the propositions of the third volume refute those of the first, insofar as they are in relations of mutually exclusive contradiction with them. In the empiricist's eyes that is evidence of the falsity of the law of value, a proof that this law is the 'purest mystification' contradicting reality and having nothing in common with it.

At this point, vulgar empiricism of bourgeois economists was supported by the Kantians. For instance, Conrad Schmidt seemingly agreed with Marx's analysis, with one reservation, however: he 'declares the law of value within the capitalist form of production to be a pure, *although theoretically necessary, fiction*'.[12]

The reason why the Kantians regard this law as a speculative hypothesis or fiction is that it cannot be justified in terms of the immediately general in the empirically unquestionable phenomena.

The general in the phenomena—the law of the average rate of profit—is something diametrically opposed to the law of value, something that contradicts it and excludes it. In the Kantians' view it is therefore no more than an artifi-

[11] Karl Marx, *Capital,* Vol. III, p. 36.
[12] Ibid., p. 895 (italics ours—*E. I.*).

cially constructed hypothesis, a theoretically necessary fiction—by no means a theoretical expression of the objectively universal law to which all pertinent phenomena are subject.

The concrete thus contradicts the abstract in Marx's *Capital,* and this contradiction does not disappear because of the fact that a whole chain of mediating links is established between the two but rather is proved as the necessary contradiction of economic reality itself, not as the consequence of the theoretical drawbacks of the Ricardian conception of the law of value.

The logical nature of this phenomenon may well be demonstrated by means of an easier example which does not require special knowledge in the field of political economy.

In quantitative mathematical description of certain phenomena self-contradictory systems of equations are very often obtained, in which there are more equations than unknown quantities, e. g.:

$$\begin{cases} x+x=2 \\ 50x+50x=103. \end{cases}$$

The logical contradiction is patently obvious here, yet the system of equations is quite real. Its reality will become apparent on condition that x here denotes one kopek, and the addition of kopeks takes place not only and not so much in the head but in the savings bank, too, which puts to an account three per cent interest *per annum.*

Under these concrete, and quite real, conditions, the addition of kopeks is quite precisely expressed by the above 'contradictory' system of equations. Contradiction is here a direct expression of the fact that in reality it is not speculative pure quantities that are added (or substracted, or divided, or raised to a power, etc.) but *qualitatively definite magnitudes,* and that the purely quantitative addition of these magnitudes produces at some point a qualitative leap disrupting the ideal quantitative process and resulting in a paradox in the theoretical expression.

Any science runs into this problem at every step. Let us take an elementary example. It was established that as the temperature of a gas decreases by one degree, its volume diminshes by $^1/_{273}$; within certain limits the behaviour of gases is strictly consistent with this law. At very low temperatures, however, the figures are quite different. The contradiction ('lack of agreement') between the basic law and the mathematical expression of its action at very low temperatures is evidence of the fact that at some point a new factor emerges, caused by the same lowering of the temperature, which effects the proportion; it does not prove at all that the contradictory numerical expressions are wrong. Science has long learnt a way to treat these contradictions properly. Unwillingness or inability consciously to apply dialectics here results, however, in the view of mathematics as a 'theoretically necessary fiction', a purely artificial instrument of the intellect.

Modern positivists speak of mathematics, which runs into these paradoxes at every step, exactly in the same manner in which Conrad Schmidt discussed value. They justify pure mathematics also in an entirely pragmatic, instrumentalist way—only as an artificially invented mode of the subject's spiritual activity which for some (unknown) reason yields the desired result. The grounds for this attitude to mathematics are the real circumstance that direct application of mathematical formulas to the real quantitative-qualitative development of phenomena, to real concreteness, invariably and inevitably leads to a paradox, to a logical contradiction in mathematical expression.

In this case, however (just as in political economy), the contradiction is not at all a result of errors made by thought in the theoretical expression of the phenomenon. It is a direct expression of the dialectics of the phenomena themselves. A real resolution of this contradiction may only consist in further analysis of all the concrete conditions and circumstances in which the phenomenon is realised, and in revealing the qualitative parameters which disrupt the purely quantitative series at a certain point. The contradiction does not in this case demonstrate a falsity of the mathematical expression or its erroneousness but something quite different: the falsity of the view that the given expression defines the phenomenon in an exhaustive manner.

The equations $x+x=2$, $50x+50x=103$ express quite precisely the quantitative aspect of the underlying fact, and seem absurd only until the concrete objective meaning of the unknown quantity is established and the concrete conditions are specified in which addition of these unknown quantities takes place.

One can certainly envisage a case where contradiction in equations of the illustrated type will be an indication and a form of manifestation of imprecision or errors made by the subject. Assume that the real value of x, for instance, equals 1.0286—objectively, independently of the subject performing the measurement, of the scale of measurement and of the resolution of the measuring device; assume also that no qualitative change occurs as a result of addition of the x's. In this case the logical contradiction in the mathematical expression will be quite different from the above in origin and objective meaning: it will merely be evidence of error or imprecision in measurement, of insufficient resolution power of the measuring device, crude scale, etc. The contradiction is here to be blamed on the subject and only on the subject who, in measuring the sum of two x's, was unable to notice and express the difference between 2 and 2.056, and in measuring the sum of a hundred such x's obtained a result in which the difference manifested itself quite clearly. This logical contradiction is naturally solved in quite a different manner from the first case.

However, it is quite impossible to conclude from the formal mathematical structure of the equations alone with which particular case we are dealing and in what way the contradiction must be resolved. Both cases require additional concrete analysis of the reality in the expression of which the contradiction was manifested.

The difference between dialectics and metaphysics on this score does not at all lie in the fact that metaphysics immediately declares any contradiction in the definitions of the object an intolerable evil while dialectics regards it as virtue and truth. That is only true of metaphysical logic, but dialectics does not at all consist in asserting the opposite. That would not be dialectics but merely inverted metaphysics, that is, sophistry.

Dialectics does not at all negate the fact that purely subjective contradictions may and very often do figure in cognition, contradictions that have to be got rid of as soon as possible. However, it is quite impossible to conclude from the external (formal mathematical or verbal syntactical) form of an equation or proposition with what contradiction we are dealing in each particular case. Since metaphysical logic in any case regards contradiction in definitions as a purely subjective evil, as a result of errors and inaccuracies made earlier by thought, contradictions in the way of movement of thought become insurmountable difficulties for it. If a contradiction arises in this framework, metaphysical logic forbids further development of thought, recommending to go back and to find at any cost the mistake in previous reasoning which resulted in contradiction. Until contradiction is shown to be the subject's error, there is a ban on the advance of thought.

Dialectics does not at all negate a certain usefulness of checking and double-checking the previous course of reasoning, neither does it negate that in some cases the checks may reveal the contradiction to be a result of error or inaccuracy.

What dialectics does reject is something different, namely the assumption that a formula may be worked out that would permit to recognise logical (that is, subjective) contradictions resulting from inaccuracy or carelessness without recourse to analysis of knowledge in its real objective content. That is the underlying claim of both classical formulations of 'exclusion of contradictions'—the Aristotelian and the Leibniz-Kantian. According to the first, *any* proposition is forbidden which expresses a contradiction of the object to itself 'at one and the same time and in one and the same relation'. According to the second, *any* proposition or utterance is forbidden which ascribes to a concept a predicate (or attribute) contradicting it.

The ban in its Aristotelian formulation applies, as has long been established, to the proposition expressing the famous paradox of Zeno concerning the flying arrow. That is why all logicians endeavouring to raise the Aristotelian ban to an absolute, have for two thousand years made attempts, as persistent as they have been unsuccessful, to present this paradox as the result of errors in the expression of facts. They run the risk of spending another two thousand years of vain effort, for Zeno expressed in the only possible (and therefore the only correct) form an extremely typical case of the dialectical contradiction contained in any fact of transition, motion, change, or transformation.

On the other hand, the Leibniz-Kantian formula will absolutely forbid a proposition like this: *the ideal is the material* transplanted into the human head and transformed in it. This proposition also expresses a transition of the opposites into each other. It therefore naturally defines the subject through a predicate that cannot be immediately connected with it. *The ideal* as such is not material, it is non-material, and vice versa.

Any utterance expressing the very moment, the very act of transition (and not the *result* of this transition only) inevitably contains an explicit or implicit contradiction, and a contradiction 'at one and the same time' (that is, during transition, at the moment of transition) and 'in one and the same relation' (precisely with regard to the transition of the opposites into each other).

That is exactly why any attempt to formulate the ban on contradiction as an absolutely unquestionable formal rule (that is, a rule formulated irrespective of the concrete content of the utterances) is doomed to failure. This rule will either forbid, along with 'logical contradictory' propositions, all propositions expressing the contradictions of real change, of real transition of opposites, or else it will permit the former along with the latter. That is quite inevitable, for the two cannot in general be distinguished in the form of expression in speech, in the utterance. As often as not, objective reality contains an internal contradiction 'at one and the same time and in one and the same relation', and the utterance expressing this situation is regarded in dialectical logic as quite correct, despite the loud protestations of metaphysicians.

Thus, if a contradiction in definitions of a thing necessarily emerged as a result of the movement of thought by the logic of facts characterising the movement, change of development of the thing, the transition of its different elements into each other, that is not a logical contradiction, though it might have all the formal indications of such, but a quite correct expression of an objective dialectical contradiction.

Contradiction is not in this case an insurmountable barrier in the way of the movement of the investigating thought but, on the contrary, a springboard for a decisive leap forward in a concrete investigation, in further processing of empirical data into concepts.

But this leap, characteristic of the dialectical development of concepts, only becomes possible because contradiction appears in reasoning always as a real problem, the solution of which is attained through further concrete analysis of concrete facts, through finding those real mediating links through which the contradiction is resolved in reality. The really serious problems in science have always been solved in this way.

For instance, the philosophy of dialectical materialism, for the first time in history, was able to formulate and solve the problem of consciousness exactly because it approached this problem with a dialectical conception of contradiction. The old metaphysical materialism ran at this point into an obvious contradiction. On the one hand, the proposition advocated by any kind of materialism asserts that matter (objective reality) is primary, whereas consciousness is a reflection of this reality, that is, it is secondary. But, if one takes abstractly a single isolated fact of man's goal-directed activity, the relation between consciousness and objectiveness is the reverse. The architect first builds a house in his consciousness and then brings objective reality (with the workers' hands) in agreement with the ideal plan he has worked out. If one were to express this situation in philosophical categories, it would apparently contradict the general proposition of materialism, be in 'logical contradiction' to it. What is primary here is consciousness, the ideal plan of activity, while the sensual objective implementation of this plan is something secondary or derivative.

Materialists of the pre-Marxian epoch in philosophy could not, as we know, cope with this contradiction. As far as theoretical consciousness was concerned, they advocated the point of view of reflection, the proposition that being is primary and consciousness secondary. But, as soon as the debate switched to man's goal-directed activity, metaphysical materialism was unable to make head or tail of the situation. It is not accidental that all materialists before Marx were pure idealists in the conception of the history of society. Here they accepted the diametrically opposed principle of explanation in no way connected with the principle of reflection. In the theories of the French Enlighteners, two unreconciled antinomic principles of explanation of human cognition and activity coexisted peacefully.

Marx and Engels showed that metaphysical materialism continually lapsed into this contradiction because it failed to see the real mediating link between objective reality and consciousness—it failed to grasp the role of practice. By discovering this mediating link between thing and consciousness, dialectical materialism solved the problem concretely, explaining the subject's very activity from a single universal principle and thereby fully implementing the principle of materialism in the conception of history. The contradiction was in this way removed, concretely resolved, and explained as necessarily appearing.

This contradiction is eliminated in metaphysical materialism through abstract reduction of definitions of consciousness to definitions of matter. This 'solution', however, leaves the real problem untouched. The facts that were not included directly and abstractly into the sphere of application of the proposition on the primacy of matter (facts of man's conscious activity) were not, of course, thereby eliminated from reality. They were merely eliminated from the consciousness of the materialist. As a result, materialism could not put an end to idealism even within its own theory.

For this reason, metaphysical materialism did not liquidate the real grounds on which, again and again, idealist conceptions of the relationship between matter and spirit emerged.

Only the dialectical materialism of Marx, Engels, and Lenin proved capable of solving this contradiction, retaining the basic premise of any materialism but implementing this premise concretely in the understanding of the birth of consciousness from the practical sensual activity changing things.

In this way, contradiction was shown to be a necessary expression of a real fact in its origin, rather than eliminated or declared to be false and invented. Idealism was thereby dislodged from its most solid shelter—speculation on facts concerning the subject's activity in practice and cognition.

Such is in general the way for solving theoretical contradictions in dialectics. They are not rejected or eliminated but concretely resolved in a new and more profound conception of these facts, in tracing out the entire chain of mediating links which connects the mutually exclusive abstract propositions.

The metaphysician always tries to choose one of the two abstract theses, leaving it as abstract as it was before the choice: that is the meaning of the 'either ... or' formula.

Dialectics imposes the requirement of reasoning according to the 'both ... and' formula, yet it does not at all orientate thought at eclectic reconciliation of two mutually exclusive propositions, as metaphysicians often impute in the heat of the debate. It orientates thought at a more concrete study of the facts in the expression of which the contradiction arose. That is where dialectics seeks a solution of the contradiction—in a concrete study of facts, in tracing out the entire chain of mediating links between the actually contradictory aspects of reality.

In the process, each of the previously abstract propositions is transformed into a moment in a concrete understanding of facts and is explained as a one-sided expression of the real contradictory concreteness of the object, and moreover a concreteness in its development. In development, there is always a point where new reality appears which, though evolving on the basis of previous forms, nevertheless rejects these forms and possesses characteristics contradicting the characteristics of the less developed reality.

CONTRADICTION AS A PRINCIPLE OF DEVELOPMENT OF THEORY

Let us further analyse the fundamental difference between deduction of categories in *Capital* and formal-logical deduction, that is, the concrete essence of the method of ascent from the abstract to the concrete.

We have established that the Ricardian concept of value, that is, a universal category of the system of a science, is an abstraction, an incomplete and formal one, and therefore also incorrect. Ricardo regarded value as a concept expressing the abstract general features inherent in each of the developed categories, each of the concrete phenomena to which it applies, and he therefore does not study value specially, in the strictest abstraction from all the other categories.

Thus the theoretical definitions of the basic universal category and the methods of its definition contain already, as in an embryo, the whole difference between the deduction of categories by the metaphysician Ricardo and the method of ascent from the abstract to the concrete used by the dialectician Marx.

Quite consciously, Marx constructs the theoretical definitions of value by a most thoroughgoing concrete analysis of simple commodity exchange, leaving aside, as irrelevant, a host of phenomena that developed on this basis and the categories that express these phenomena. That is, on the one hand, really complete abstraction, and on the other, really meaningful rather than formal ('generic') abstraction.

Only this conception, assuming a concrete historical approach to things, makes possible special analysis of the form of value, special inquiry into the concrete content of the universal category—analysis of value as a *concrete sensually given reality, as an elementary economic concreteness*, and not as a concept.

Value is not analysed as a mental abstraction of the general but rather as a fully specific economic *reality* actually unfolding before the observer and therefore capable of being specially studied, as reality possessing its own concrete historical content, the theoretical description of which is identical with elaboration of definitions of the *concept* of value.

Marx shows that the real content of the form of value is not, as Ricardo believed, simply abstract quantitative identity of portions of labour but rather dialectical contradictory *identity of the opposites* of relative and equivalent forms of expression of the value of each commodity entering the relation of exchange. The point where Marx's dialectics opposes Ricardo's metaphysical mode of reasoning is the fact that Marx revealed the *inner contradiction* of the simple commodity form.

To put the matter differently, the content of the universal category, of the concerete concept of value is not elaborated by Marx on the basis of the abstract identity principle but rather on the basis of the dialectical principle of the identity of mutually assuming poles, of mutually exclusive definitions.

That means that the content of the value category is revealed through establishing the inner contradictions of the elementary form of value realised as exchange of a commodity for another commodity. Marx presents commodity as a living contradiction of the reality denoted by that term, as a living unresolved antagonism within that reality. A commodity contains a contradiction within itself, in its immanent economic definitions.

Let us note that the inner dichotomy into mutually exclusive and at the same time mutually presupposing moments is characteristic, as Marx shows, of *each* of the two commodities participating in an act of exchange.

Each of them comprises in itself the economic form of

value as its immanent economic definiteness. In an exchange, in the act of substitution of one commodity for another, this inner economic definiteness of each of the commodities is merely *manifested* or *expressed* and in no way *created.*

That is the central point, the understanding of which determines not only the problem of value but also the logical problem of the concrete concept as a unity of mutually exclusive and at the same time mutually presupposing definitions.

The phenomenon of actual exchange presents the following picture: one commodity is replaced in the hands of the commodity owner by another, and this replacement is reciprocal. The replacement can only take place when both mutually substitutable commodities are equated as values. The question therefore arises in this form: what is value?

What is the economic reality the nature of which is revealed in an exchange? How is it to be expressed in a concept? The actual exchange shows that each of the commodities is, vis-à-vis its owner, exchange value only, and in no way use-value. In the hands of the other owner each of the participants in the exchange sees use-value only, that is, a thing that can satisfy his needs. That is the reason why he endeavours to possess it. And this relation is absolutely identical on both sides.

From the point of view of one commodity owner each of the commodities appears in different, and namely in directly opposed forms: the commodity he owns (linen) is *only exchange* value and by no means use-value—otherwise he would not alienate, that is, exchange it. The other commodity (the coat) is, on the contrary, *only* a *use*-value for him, with regard to him, *only an equivalent* of his own commodity.

The meaning of actual exchange lies in mutual substitution of the exchange- and use-values, of the relative and equivalent forms.

This mutual substitution, mutual transformation of polar, mutually exclusive and opposed economic forms of the product of labour is a true and factual transformation taking place outside the theoretician's head and completely independent from it.

Value is realised and implemented in this mutual transformation of opposites. Exchange emerges as the only possible form in which the value nature of *each of the commodities* is manifested or expressed in a phenomenon.

It is factually obvious that this mysterious nature can only be *manifested* or *revealed* through mutual conversion of the opposites—exchange- and use-values, through mutual substitution of the relative and equivalent forms. In other words, the only way is this: one commodity (linen) appears as exchange value, while another (coat), as use-value; one of them assumes the relative form of expression of value, and the other, the opposite, the equivalent form. Both of these forms cannot be combined in one commodity, for in this case the need for exchange disappears. Only that is alienated through exchange which does not constitute a direct use-value but only an exchange value.

Marx gives theoretical expression to this actual state of things: 'A single commodity cannot, therefore, simultaneously assume, in the same expression of value, both forms. The very polarity of these forms makes them mutually exclusive.'[13]

The metaphysician will undoubtedly be overjoyed at reading this proposition. Two mutually exclusive definitions cannot in reality be combined in one commodity! A commodity can only assume one of the mutually exclusive economic forms and by no means both of them simultaneously!

Does that mean that the dialectician Marx rejects the possibility of combining polar definitions in a *concept*? It may appear to be so, at first glance.

However, a closer analysis of the movement of Marx's thought shows that the matter is not so simple as that. The point here is that the passage quoted here crowns an analysis of the empirical form of manifestation of value and merely leads up to the problem of value as immanent content of each of the commodities. The task of working out a concept expressing this latter still lies ahead. Reasoning, which so far registers the mere form of empirical manifestation of value rather than the inner content of this category, indicates the fact that each of the commodities may assume, in this manifestation of value, only one of its polar forms and not both of them simultaneously.

But the form assumed by each of the commodities confronting each other *is not value* at all but merely an ab-

[13] Karl Marx, *Capital*, Vol. I, p. 56.

stract one-sided *manifestation* of the latter. *Value in itself*, the concept of which is yet to be established, is a third quantity, something that does not coincide with either of the polar forms taken separately or with their mechanical combination.

A closer consideration of exchange shows that the above-mentioned impossibility of coincidence in one commodity of two polar mutually exclusive economic characteristics is nothing but a necessary *form of manifestation* of value on the surface of phenomena.

'The opposition or contrast existing internally in each commodity between use-value and value, is, therefore, made evident externally by two commodities being placed in such relation to each other, that the commodity whose value it is sought to express, figures directly as a mere use-value, while the commodity in which that value is to be expressed, figures directly as mere exchange-value. Hence the elementary form of value of a commodity is the elementary form in which the contrast contained in that commodity, between use-value and value, becomes apparent.' [14]

The matter looks quite different, however, when we are not dealing with the external form of manifestation of value but with value as such, as an objective economic reality concealed in each of the commodities confronting each other in an exchange and constituting the hidden, inner nature of each of them.

The principle forbidding direct coincidence of mutually exclusive forms of being in one and the same thing and at one and the same time (and consequently in the theoretical expression of this thing) applies, it appears, to the external empirical form of manifestaion of analysed reality (value, in this case) but is directly rejected with respect to the inner content of this reality, to the theoretical definitions of value as such.

The inner nature of value is theoretically expressed only in the *concept* of value. The distinctive feature of the Marxian *concept* of value is that it is revealed through identity of mutually exclusive theoretical definitions.

The value concept expresses the inner relation of the commodity form rather than the external relation of one

---

[14] Karl Marx, *Capital*, Vol. I, p. 67.

commodity to another (in the latter the inner contradiction is not directly manifested but split into contradictions 'in different relations': in one relation, in relation to the owner, the commodity appears as exchange value only; in another, in relation to the owner of the other commodity, it appears as use-value, although objectively there is one, not two relations, here). To put it differently, a commodity is here considered *not in relation to another commodity but in relation to itself reflected through the relation to another commodity*.

This point contains the mystery of Marxian dialectics, and it is impossible to understand anything either in *Capital* or in its logic unless this point, this kernel of the logic of *Capital*, is properly understood.

Value, the inner essence of each commodity, is only manifested or revealed (reflected) in the relation to another commodity. This value, this objective economic reality, is not created or born in the exchange but only manifested in it, being one-sidedly reflected in the other commodity as in a mirror that is only capable of reflecting that side that is turned to it. In the same way the real mirror reflects only man's face, although he also has the back of the head.

Being reflected outside, value appears in the form of external opposites that do not coincide in one commodity—as exchange- and use-values, the relative and the equivalent forms of expression.

However, each of the commodities, inasmuch as it is a value, is a direct *unity* of mutually exclusive and at the same time mutually assuming economic forms. In the phenomenon (in the exchange act) and in its theoretical expression this concrete dual economic nature always appears divided, as it were, into its two abstract moments confronting each other, each of which mutually excludes the other and at the same time assumes it as a necessary condition of its existence, a condition that is not within but outside it.

In the *concept* of value these opposites, abstractly confronting each other in the phenomenon, are united again, though not in a mechanical way but exactly in the way they are united in the economic reality of the commodity itself—as living mutually exclusive and at the same time mutually assuming economic forms of the existence of *each commodity*, of its immanent content—value.

To phrase it differently, the concept of value registers the inner unrest of the commodity form, the inner stimulus of its movement, its self-development—the economic content that is inherent in a commodity prior to any exchange and in no relation to other commodities.

Proceeding from the established concept of value as a living dialectically contradictory coincidence of opposites within each separate commodity, Marx confidently and clearly reveals the evolution from the elementary commodity form to the money form, the process of generating money by the movement of the elementary commodity market.

What is the crux of the matter here, where does Marx see the necessity for the transition from the simple, direct, exchange of one commodity for another without money to exchange mediated by money?

The need for such a transition is deduced directly from the impossibility to resolve the contradiction of the elementary form of value while remaining within the framework of this elementary form.

The point is that each of the commodities entering an exchange relation is a living antinomy. Commodity *A* can only be in one form of value and not simultaneously in two. But if the exchange is performed in reality, that means that each of the two commodities assumes in the other the very form which the latter cannot take because it already has the opposite form. After all, the other commodity owner did not bring his commodity to the market for someone to measure by it the value of his commodity. He himself must, and wants to, measure the value of his own commodity by the other commodity, that is, he must regard the opposing commodity as an equivalent. But it cannot be an equivalent because it already has the relative form.

This relation is absolutely identical on both sides. The owner of linen regards the commodity—the coat—only as an equivalent, and his own commodity only as a relative form. But the coat owner reasons in precisely the opposite way: for him linen is an equivalent, and the coat only an exchange value, only the relative form. And if the exchange does take place, that means (to express the fact of the exchange theoretically) that both commodities *mutually measure their value* and just as mutually serve as the material in which value is measured. In other words, both coat and linen posit each other as that very form of expression of value which they cannot assume for precisely the reason that they have already assumed the other form.

Linen measures its value in the coat (that is, makes it an equivalent), while the coat measures its value in linen (that is, makes it an equivalent, too). However, as both linen and coat have already assumed the relative form of value, as both measure *their* value in the other, they cannot assume the role of the equivalent. But, if the exchange actually did take place, that means that both commodities mutually measured their value in each other, they mutually recognised each other to be equivalent values, despite the fact that both of them had been before that in the relative form, which excludes the possibility of assuming the opposite, the equivalent form. Thus real exchange is a real, actually occurring coincidence of two polar and mutually exclusive forms of expression of value in each of the commodities.

But this cannot be, the metaphysician will say: it appears that Marx contradicts himself! Now he says that a commodity cannot assume both polar forms of val , and then again he says that in actual exchange it is compelled to be in both at the same time!

Marx answers that this may and actually does take place. That is a theoretical expression of the fact that direct commodity exchange cannot serve as a form of the social exchange of matter that would proceed smoothly, without friction, obstacles, conflicts or contradictions. That is nothing but the theoretical expression of the real impossibility against which the movement itself of the commodity market runs—impossibility of precise establishment of the proportions in which the socially necessary work is spent in diverse branches of the socially divided labour connected only through the commodity market, that is, the impossibility of precise expression of value.

Direct exchange of commodity for commodity cannot express the socially necessary measure of the expenditure of labour in various spheres of the social production. The antinomy of value in the framework of the elementary commodity form therefore remains unresolved and unresolvable. Here commodity both *must* and *cannot* assume both mutually exclusive economic forms. Otherwise exchange *according to value* is impossible. But it cannot be simultaneously in two forms. That is a hopeless antinomy that cannot be resolved in the framework of the elementary form of value.

Marx's dialectical genius showed itself in the fact that he grasped this antinomy and expressed it as such.

But, inasmuch as exchange according to value still has to take place somehow, the antinomy of value has to be somehow resolved in a relative way.

The solution is found by the movement itself of the simple commodity market, generating money, the money form of expression of value. Money in Marx's analysis emerges as the natural form in which the movement of the market itself finds a means for the solution of the contradiction of the elementary form of value, of direct exchange of one commodity for another commodity.

This is a point where the fundamental difference is most graphically demonstrated between the dialectical materialist mode of solving contradictions and all those methods that are known to metaphysical thought.

What is the metaphysician's procedure when a contradiction arises in the definition of a theoretical expression of a certain reality? He always endeavours to solve it by making concepts more precise, by setting stricter limits upon terms, etc.; he will always attempt to construe it as an external rather than an internal contradiction, as a contradiction in different relations, with which metaphysics is well reconciled. In other words, all he does is change the expression of the reality in which a contradiction has arisen.

Marx acts quite differently in a case like this. He proceeds from the assumption that in the framework of the elementary form of value the established antinomy in definitions is not resolved and cannot *objectively* be resolved. One therefore need not search for its solution in the consideration of the elementary form of value. This antinomy is insoluble in direct exchange of commodity for commodity either objectively (that is, by the movement of the commodity market itself) or subjectively (that is, in theory). Its solution must not therefore be looked for in further reflexion on the elementary form of value, but in tracing out the objective spontaneous necessity with which commodity market itself finds, creates, or works out the real means of its relative resolution.

The dialectical materialist method of resolution of contradictions in theoretical definitions thus consists in tracing the process by which the movement of reality itself resolves them in a new form of expression. Expressed objectively, the goal lies in tracing, through analysis of new empirical materials, the emergence of reality in which an earlier established contradiction finds its relative resolution in a new objective form of its realisation.

That is Marx's procedure in the analysis of money. Money is the natural means by which use-value begins to transform itself into exchange value, and vice versa.

Before money appeared, each of the commodities coming together in an exchange had to perform simultaneously, within one and the same individual relation, both of the mutually exclusive metamorphoses (from use-value into exchange value and at the same moment, within the same act, to perform the reverse transfiguration). Now it all looks different. Now the dual transformation is not realised as direct coincidence of the two mutually exclusive forms but as a mediated act—through transformation into money, the universal equivalent.

The transformation of use-value into value no longer directly coincides with the opposite transformation of value into use-value. Exchange of commodity for another commodity breaks up into two different and opposite acts of transformation no longer coinciding in one point of space and time. Commodity is transformed into money, not another commodity. A use-value becomes an exchange value, no more, and somewhere at another point of the market, possibly at a different time, money becomes a commodity, value becomes use-value, is replaced by it.

The coincidence of two transformations in two diametrically opposed directions now falls, in the reality of exchange itself, into two different transformations no longer coinciding in time or place—the act of selling (transformation of use-value into value) and the act of buying (transformation of value into use-value).

Money fully monopolises the economic form of equivalent, becoming a pure embodiment of value as such, while all the other commodities assume the form of relative value. They confront money as use-values only.

The antinomy in the theoretical expression of commodity exchange was apparently resolved: the contradiction (as direct coincidence of two polar mutually exclusive opposites of economic form) now emerged split, as it were, between two different things, between commodity and money.

In actual fact, with the emergence of the money form of value, the contradiction of value did not disappear or evaporate at all—it merely assumed a new form of expression. It continues to be (though only implicitly) an *inner* contradiction permeating both money and commodity and, consequently, their theoretical definitions.

Indeed, a commodity confronting money has apparently become a use-value only, and money, a pure expression of exchange value. But, on the other hand, each commodity appears only as exchange value in relation to money. It is sold for money precisely for the reason that it is no use-value for its owner. And money plays the role of an equivalent precisely because it confronts any commodity as the universal image of use-value. The entire import of the equivalent form lies in that it expresses the exchange value of another commodity as *use*-value.

The originally established antinomy of the elementary commodity exchange has thus been retained both in money and in commodities, it still constitutes the elementary essence of the one and of the other, although on the surface of events this inner contradiction of both money and commodity forms proved to be extinguished.

'We saw [says Marx] . . . that the exchange of commodities implies contradictory and mutually exclusive conditions. The differentiation of commodities into commodities and money does not sweep away these inconsistencies, but develops a *modus vivendi*, a form in which they can exist side by side. This is generally the way in which real contradictions are reconciled. For instance, it is a contradiction to depict one body as constantly falling towards another, and as, at the same time, constantly flying away from it. The ellipse is a form of motion which, while allowing this contradiction to go on, at the same time reconciles it.' [15]

From the *external* contradiction of use-value and exchange value Marx proceeds to the fixing of the *internal* contradiction contained in *each* of the two commodities. The fact that the contradiction first arises as contradiction in different relations (exchange value in relation to one of the commodity owners and use-value in relation to the other) is for him an indication of abstractness, of insufficient completeness and concreteness of knowledge. The concreteness

[15] Karl Marx, *Capital,* Vol. I, p. 106.

of knowledge is manifested in comprehending this external contradiction as a *superficial* mode of revelation of something quite different, namely, an internal contradiction, a coincidence of mutually exclusive theoretical definitions in the concrete concept of value.

Its significance may be explained, e.g., by comparing Marx's analysis of value with a discourse on value in a work by the English empiricist Bailey.

The latter took the external form of manifestation of value in exchange for its genuine and only economic reality, believing all talk about value as such abstract dialectical scholastics; he declared: 'Value is nothing intrinsic and absolute'. His substantiation of this assertion was this: 'It is impossible to *designate*, or *express the value* of a commodity, except by *a quantity of some other commodity*.' To this, Marx answered: 'As impossible as it is to "*designate*" or "*express*" a thought except by a quantity of syllables. Hence Bailey concludes that a thought is—syllables.' [16]

In this case Bailey aimed at presenting value as a relation of one commodity to another, as an external form of a thing posited by its relation to another thing, whereas Ricardo and Marx endeavoured to find an expression of value as an *inner content* of each exchanged thing, of each thing entering the relation of exchange. The proper immanent value of a thing is only manifested, by no means created, in the form of a *relation* of one thing to another.

Bailey, being an empiricist, tries to present the inner relation of a thing within itself as an external relation of one thing to another.

Ricardo and Marx endeavour (and therein lies the *theoretical* nature of their approach) to see through the relation of one thing to another the *inner* relation of a thing *to itself*—value as the essence of a commodity, which is only manifested in an exchange through an external relation of this commodity to another one.

The metaphysician always attempts to reduce an inner contradiction of a thing to an external contradiction of this thing to another thing, to a contradiction in different relations, that is, to a form of expression in which this contradiction is eliminated from the concept of a thing. Marx, on

16 Karl Marx, *Theories of Surplus-Value*, Part III, p. 146.

the contrary, always endeavours to discern in the external contradiction only a superficial manifestation of an inner contradiction immanently inherent in each thing confronting its counterpart in the relation of external contradiction. Therein lies the difference between a genuinely theoretical approach and an empirical description of phenomena.

Dialectics consists exactly in the ability to discern the inner contradiction of a thing, the stimulus of its self-development, where the metaphysician sees only an external contradiction resulting from a more or less accidental collision of two internally non-contradictory things.

Dialectics requires in this case that external contradiction of two things be interpreted as a mutually necessary manifestation of the inner contradiction of each of them. The external contradiction emerges as an inner identity of mutually exclusive moments mediated through a relation to something else and reflected through something else, as an internally contradictory relation of a thing to itself, that is, as a contradiction in one relation and at one and the same moment of time. Marx proceeds from an external manifestation of a contradiction to establishing the inner basis of this contradiction, *from the appearance to the essence* of this contradiction, whereas the metaphysician always tries to act in a precisely reverse manner, refuting the theoretical expression of the essence of a thing from the standpoint of external appearance, which he believes to be the only reality.

That is Bailey's mode of reasoning in the above. That is the mode of reasoning of a metaphysician, who always assumes that the true interpretation of a contradiction is its interpretation as a contradiction in different relations. And it always leads to a destruction of the elementary theoretical approach to things.

Marx regards value as the *relation of a commodity to itself*, rather than to another commodity, and that is why it emerges as a living, unsolved and insoluble inner contradiction. This contradiction is not resolved because on the surface of phenomena it appears as a contradiction in two different relations, as two different transformations—as buying and selling. The entire significance of Marx's analysis consists in showing that the contradiction of value is insoluble in principle within the framework of elementary commodity exchange, and that value inevitably appears here as a living antinomy in itself, no matter how much one specifies concepts, or how deeply one examines, or reflects upon value.

A commodity as an embodiment of value cannot simultaneously assume both of the mutually exclusive forms of value; yet it actually does assume both these forms simultaneously when the exchange according to value *is* performed.

This theoretical antinomy expresses nothing but the real impossibility which the movement of the simple commodity market continually encounters. An impossibility is an impossibility. It does not disappear if it is present in theory as a possibility, as something uncontradictory.

The movement of the real market leaves behind the form of direct exchange of a commodity for another commodity. In considering extensive empirical data expressing this movement, Marx proceeds to the theoretical analysis of those more complex forms by which the market realises and at the same time resolves this contradiction. Therein lies the necessity of the transition to money.

Looking at this matter from the philosophical viewpoint, we shall see that that is an expression of the *materialist* nature of Marx's method of resolving contradictions in the theoretical expression of objective reality. In this method, the contradiction is not resolved by its elimination from the theory. On the contrary, this method is based on the assumption that contradiction in the object itself cannot be and is never resolved in any other way than by the development of the reality fraught with this contradiction into another, higher and more advanced reality.

The antinomy of value finds its relative resolution in money. But then again, money does not eliminate the antinomy of value—it merely creates a form in which this antinomy is realised and expressed as before. This mode of theoretical presentation of a real process is the only adequate logical form in which the dialectical development of the object, *its self-development through contradictions*, may be expressed in theory.

The *materialist* nature of the method by which Marx resolved theoretical contradictions in the definition of the object, was well expressed by Engels in his review.

'With this method we begin with the first and simplest relation which is historically, actually available.... Contradictions will emerge demanding a solution. But since we are not examining an abstract mental process that takes place solely in our mind, but an actual event which really took place at some time or other, or which is still taking place, these contradictions will have arisen in practice and have probably been solved. We shall trace the mode of this solution and find that it has been effected by establishing a new relation, whose two contradictory aspects we shall then have to set forth, and so on.'[17]

It is the objective impossibility of solving the contradiction between the social nature of labour and the private form of appropriating its product through direct exchange of one commodity for another without money that is theoretically expressed as an antinomy, as an insoluble contradiction of the elementary form of value, as an insoluble contradiction of its theoretical definitions. That is why Marx did not even try to get rid of the contradiction in the definition of value. Value remains an antinomy, an unresolved and insoluble contradiction, a direct coincidence of mutually exclusive theoretical definitions. The only real method of the resolution of this antinomy is a socialist revolution eliminating the private nature of the appropriation of the product of social labour, appropriation through the commodity market.

The objective impossibility of resolving the contradiction between the social nature of labour and the private form of appropriation of its products, given the daily need for realising the social exchange of matter through the commodity market, stimulates the search for natural means and methods of doing so. It is this factor that ultimately leads to the emergence of money.

In the same way as money emerges in the real movement of the commodity market as a natural means of resolving the contradictions of direct commodity exchange, the theoretical definitions of money in *Capital* are worked out as a means of resolving the contradiction in the definition of value. Here we are dealing with the most important element of Marx's dialectical method of ascent from the abstract to the concrete, with the dialectical materialist deduction of categories. The stimulus of theoretical develop-

---

[17] Karl Marx, *A Contribution to the Critique of Political Economy*, pp. 225-26.

ment, the motive force behind the unfolding of a system of theoretical definitions of a thing, is the theory's *inner contradiction*. It performs this function precisely because and precisely in those cases when it *directly* reflects the inner contradiction of the object that is the inner stimulus of its development, of the growth of its complexity and development of its forms of existence. The theoretical expression of this stimulus in the concept is naturally preceded by extensive and thorough work on the selection and analysis of empirical data characterising the development of these forms.

From this viewpoint, the entire logical structure of *Capital* emerges in a new light that is of fundamental interest: the entire movement of theoretical thought in *Capital* proves to be locked in between two originally established poles of the expression of value.

The first concrete category following value, money, emerges as a real method of mutual transformation of the poles of expression of value, as that metamorphosis through which the two poles of value, gravitating towards each other and at the same time mutually excluding each other, must pass in the process of their mutual transformation.

This approach objectively orientates reasoning, when it faces the task of establishing the universal and necessary theoretical definitions of money: in considering the entire totality of the empirical, concrete sensual data, only those characteristics are singled out and registered which are necessarily posited by the transformation of value into use-value and vice versa, whereas all the empirical features of the money form which do not necessarily follow from this mutual conversion or cannot be deduced from it, are left aside.

The fundamental difference between dialectical materialist deduction of categories and abstract intellectual deduction comes to light here.

The latter is based on abstract general or generic concept. A particular phenomenon is subsumed under it, and in considering this phenomenon, the traits are discerned that constitute the distinctive features of the given species. The result is mere appearance of deduction. For instance, the Orlov trotter breed is included in the abstraction 'horse in general'. The definition of this particular breed includes those features which permit to distinguish an Orlov trotter from any other breed of horses. It is quite clear, however, that the specific features of an Orlov trotter are by no means included in the abstraction 'horse in general', and they therefore can in no way be deduced from it. They are tacked on to the definitions of the 'horse in general' in a purely mechanical way. Because of this, formal deduction offers no guarantees that these specific differences are discerned correctly, that they *necessarily* belong to the breed in question. It may well be that these specific traits of an Orlov trotter are found in something that it has in common with a trotter from the state of Oklahoma.

The same is the case, as we have seen, with Ricardo's theoretical definitions of money. In his conception the specific differences of the money form are in no way deduced from value. It is for this reason that he cannot distinguish between the really necessary economic characteristics of money as such and those properties that the empirically observed money possesses because of the fact that it embodies the movement of capital. And it is for this reason that he sees the specific definitions of money in the characteristics of quite a different phenomenon—the process of circulation of capital.

Marx's approach was quite different. The fact that in his theory value was understood in the movement of opposites, and that theoretical definition of value in general contains a contradiction, allowed him to discern in the empirically observed phenomena of money circulation *exactly those* and *only those* features which are necessarily inherent in money as money and *exhaustively* define money as a specific form of the movement of value.

Marx includes in the theoretical definition of money only those features of money circulation which are necessarily deduced from the contradictions of value, being necessarily generated by the movement of elementary commodity exchange.

That is what Marx calls *deduction*. It is easy to state here that this kind of deduction becomes possible only if its major premise is not an abstract general concept but a *concrete universal* one interpreted as unity or identity of mutually transforming opposites, as a concept reflecting the real contradiction in the object.

It should be stressed again and again that this theoretical deduction is based on a most detailed and all-sided consideration of a system of empirical facts and phenomena constituting the economic reality that is the object of theory.

That was the only way in which genuinely complete and *meaningful* rather than formal abstractions could be obtained which reveal the specific essence of the money form. Marx obtained theoretical definitions of money by considering the process of circulation *abstractedly*, 'that is, *apart from circumstances not immediately flowing from the laws* of the simple circulation of commodities'.[18]

The circumstances flowing from the immanent laws of simple commodity circulation are precisely the products of the inner contradiction of value as such, of the simple form of value.

The dialectics of the abstract and the concrete is here manifested in a most apparent and graphic form: precisely because money is considered in the abstract, *concrete* theoretical definitions are obtained expressing the concrete historical nature of money as a particular phenomenon.

A football, the planet Mars, a ballbearing can all easily be included in the abstract general concept of the spherical, but no effort of logical thought will deduce the form of a football, of the planet Mars or of a ballbearing from the concept of the spherical in general, for none of these forms *originate* in the reality reflected in the concept of the spherical in general, that is, in the actual similarity or identity of all spherical bodies.

But the economic form of money is deduced, in a most rigorous manner, from the concept of value (in its Marxian interpretation), exactly because the objective economic reality reflected in the category of value in general contains a real objective necessity of generating money.

This necessity is nothing but the inner contradiction of value insoluble in the framework of the simple exchange of one commodity for another. Marx's category of value is a *concrete* universal category exactly because it comprises in its definitions an inner contradiction, being a unity, an identity of mutually exclusive and at the same time mutually assuming theoretical definitions.

The concreteness of the universal concept is in Marx's approach intimately linked with the contradiction in its definition. Concreteness is in general *identity of opposites*,

---

[18] Karl Marx, *Capital*, Vol. I, p. 156 (italics ours—*E. I.*).

whereas the abstract general is obtained according to the principle of bare identity, identity without contradiction.

If one considers closely the movement of Marx's thought from commodity and value in general to money, comparing it to the similar movement of Ricardo's thought, the result will be a clear picture of the difference between dialectics and metaphysics on the question of the motive forces of the unfolding of a system of categories.

Ricardo is stimulated in his progress by the contradiction between the incompleteness, poverty, and one-sidedness of the universal abstraction (value in general) and the richness, fulness, and variety of aspects of the phenomena of money circulation. Including money (just as all the other categories) in the sphere of application of the universal formula of the law of value, Ricardo sees that money is, on the one hand, included in this sphere (money is also a commodity) but, on the other, it possesses many other properties that are not expressed in the abstraction of value in general. In short, he sees that money, apart from the general features registered in the category of value, possesses specific distinctions which he proceeds to establish. In this way he handles all of the developed categories. We have already seen what that entails: empirical data are assimilated in a theoretically undigested form.

Marx's results are different. In *Capital*, the progress of thought towards new definitions is not stimulated by any contradiction between 'incomplete abstraction' and 'fulness of the sensually concrete image' of reality. Such a conception of the motivating contradiction of theory would not take us a single step beyond the Lockean comprehension of theoretical interpretation of reality, fully identifying the methods of Marx and of Ricardo. The theoretical development of categories in *Capital* is based on a more concrete understanding of the contradiction stimulating the progress of thought. Reasoning is here guided by the following principle: *an objective contradiction is reflected as a subjective, theoretical or logical contradiction and poses in this form a theoretical problem or logical task for reasoning, which may only be solved through further study of empirical facts, of the sensual data.*

This further consideration of empirical facts is not done blindly but in the light of a rigorously and *concretely formulated* theoretical task or problem, the latter being formulated each time as a *logical*, that is, formally insoluble, *contradiction*.

We have already analysed the transition from the consideration of value to the consideration of money, establishing that in the real empirically given phenomena of developed money circulation Marx singles out only those and exactly those definitions which make money understandable as a means of relative resolution of the inner contradiction of commodity exchange. Then thought faces a new theoretical contradiction, a new *theoretical problem*: analysis of commodity-*money* circulation shows that this sphere does not comprise in itself any conditions under which circulation of value could generate new value, surplus-value.

'Turn and twist then as we may, the fact remains unaltered. If equivalents are exchanged, no surplus-value results, and if non-equivalents are exchanged, still no surplus-value.' [19]

This generalisation, however, is in the relation of mutually exclusive contradiction with another not less obvious fact—namely, that money put into circulation fetches profit. This also remains a fact, 'turn and twist as we may', and a very ancient fact, the same age as money-lending, and the latter is as old as money itself. In other words, analysis of the commodity-money sphere has resulted in the conclusion that usurious capital is impossible. But, far from being impossible, it remains a pervading fact not only under capitalism but in all the earlier systems, too—under the slave-owning system and feudalism.

This new antinomy, the contradiction of the theoretical thought to itself, contained a *formulation of the problem*, of the theoretical task which Marx was capable of solving, for the first time in the history of economic thought, exactly because he was the first to formulate the problem correctly.

He who has formulated the problem correctly has half the answer to it. Old logic, as is well known, did not in general study the question as a logical form, as the necessary form of the logical process. Idealism skillfully speculated on this drawback of old logic. Thus Kant stated that nature answers only those questions that we ask it, making this an argument in favour of his a priori conception of theoretical cognition: the answer to a question essentially depends on

[19] Karl Marx, *Capital*, Vol. I, pp. 160-61.

the manner of formulating it, and the formulation is done by the subject.

The ability to ask the right question and to formulate the problem correctly is one of the most important tasks of dialectical materialist logic. Marx concretely showed in *Capital* what it meant to formulate a *concrete* question and how to find a concrete answer to it.

Marx's logic is brought into relief in the way he formulated and answered the question of the origin of surplus-value. The question is formulated here not arbitrarily but on the basis of an objective analysis of the laws of commodity-money circulation, and in a form that brings the study of the immanent laws of commodity-money circulation to a *theoretical contradiction.*

'It is therefore impossible for capital to be produced by circulation, and it is equally impossible for it to originate apart from circulation. It must have its origin both in circulation and yet not in circulation.... These are the conditions of the problem. Hic Rhodus, hic salta!' [20]

This formulation of the problem by Marx is not accidental and is by no means only an external rhetorical device. It is linked with the very essence of dialectics as a method of concrete analysis, as a method that follows the analysed reality as it develops through contradictions.

As the development of the reality occurs through the emergence of contradictions and their resolution, so does thought occur as it reproduces this development. This feature of the dialectical method makes it possible not only to ask the right question but also to find its theoretical solution.

An objective inquiry into the commodity-money circulation has shown that this sphere does not contain in it any conditions under which an obvious, unquestionable, and omnipresent economic fact is possible, nay necessary: the spontaneous growth of value. Thought is thus directed at defining that real economically necessary condition in the presence of which commodity-money circulation becomes *capitalistic* circulation of commodities.

This result that we need must satisfy a number of rigorous conditions, it must be correlated with them. These conditions of the theoretical task are established by the study

[20] Karl Marx, *Capital,* Vol. I, p. 163.

of the commodity-money circulation as the universal foundation of the capitalistic commodity system. In this respect, thought moves deductively in the full sense of the term—from the universal to the particular, from the abstract to the concrete, which makes it goal-directed.

Marx formulates the task in the following way: the only condition on which surplus-value is possible without violating the law of value is 'to find, within the sphere of circulation, in the market, a commodity, whose use-value possesses the peculiar property of being a source of value, whose actual consumption, therefore, is itself an embodiment of labour, and, consequently, a creation of value'. [21]

This point sharply marks the fundamental opposition between the dialectics of Marx, that is, materialist dialectics, and the speculative idealist dialectics of Hegel, his method of constructing reality out of a concept.

The axiomatic and unquestionable principle of Hegelian dialectics is that the entire system of categories must be developed from the immanent contradictions of the basic concept. If the development of commodity-money circulation into capitalistic commodity circulation had been presented by an orthodox follower of Hegelian logic, he would have had to prove, in the spirit of this logic, that the immanent contradictions of the commodity sphere generate by themselves all the conditions under which value becomes spontaneously growing value.

Marx adopts the reverse procedure: he shows that commodity-money circulation, however long it may go on within itself, cannot increase the overall value of commodities being exchanged, it cannot create by its movement any conditions under which money put into circulation would necessarily fetch new money.

At this decisive point in the analysis, thought goes back again *to the empirics* of the capitalistic commodity market. It is *in the empirics* that the economic reality is found which transforms the movement of the commodity-money market into production and accumulation of surplus-value. Labour-power is the only commodity which, at one and the same time, is included in the sphere of application of the law of value and, without any violation of this law, makes surplus-

---

[21] Ibid., p. 164.

value, which directly contradicts the law of value, both possible and necessary.

Here we again see the enormous theoretical importance of the fact that commodity was revealed by Marx to be a direct unity, an identity of the opposites of value and use-value.

The essence of labour-power as commodity is also revealed in *Capital* as a direct identity of mutually exclusive definitions of value and use-value: the use-value of labour-power, its specific property, consists only in the fact that in the course of its consumption it is transformed into its counterpart—value.

The economic definitions of labour-power within the capitalistic commodity system of conditions of production derive from this unity of mutually excluding opposites, from their antinomical combination in one and the same commodity, the use-value of which exclusively consists in its ability to be transformed into value in the act of consumption itself.

When labour-power figures as use-value (the act of its consumption by the capitalist), it emerges at the same time as value materialised in the product of labour. That is again a contradiction in one and the same relation—in relation to the process of production and accumulation of surplus-value, an inner contradiction of the capitalist process.

From the logical point of view, one most significant circumstance must be noted here: *any* concrete category of *Capital* emerges as one of the forms of *mutual transformation* of value and use-value, that is, of those two mutually exclusive poles that were established at the beginning of the research, in the analysis of the 'cell' of the organism under study, of those two poles which in their antagonistic unity constitute the content of the basic universal category underlying the entire subsequent deduction of categories. The whole deduction of categories emerges from this angle as a complication of the chain of mediating links through which both poles of value must pass in their transformation into each other.

The formation of the capitalist organism emerges as the process of growing tension between the two poles of the original category. The transformation of the opposites of value and use-value into each other becomes ever more complicated. In simple exchange of one commodity for another, the mutual transformation of value and use-value is performed as a direct act, whereas with the emergence of money each of the poles must first become money and only later its own counterpart. Labour-power emerges as a new mediating link of the mutual transformation of forms of value, as a new form of its realisation.

The poles of value gravitating towards each other remain two extreme points between which ever new economic forms emerge. Any new economic reality assumes a meaning and significance only if it serves the mutual transformation of value and use-value, if it becomes a form of realisation of value as a living antagonistic unity of its inner opposites.

Value becomes the supreme judge of all the economic destinies, the highest criterion of the economic necessity of any phenomenon involved in its movement. Man himself, the subject of the production process, becomes a passive plaything, an 'object' of value, the latter assuming 'an automatically active character ... being the active factor in such a process'.[22]

'In simple circulation, C-M-C, the value of commodities attained at the most a form independent of their use-values, i.e., the form of money; but that same value now in the circulation M-C-M, or the circulation of capital, suddenly presents itself as an independent substance, endowed with a motion of its own, passing through a life-process of its own, in which money and commodities are mere forms which it assumes and casts off in turn'[23]—that is what Marx says of the role of value in the capitalistic commodity mode of production.

It is not difficult to discern here a concealed polemics with the very essence of Hegelian philosophy, its fundamental substantiation in *The Phenomenology of the Spirit.* In this work, containing the whole secret of Hegelian philosophy, the idealist dialectician propounded this requirement to be imposed on science: 'to conceive and to express the truth not as substance but in the same degree as a subject.'[24]

For Hegel, the subject is tantamount to reality developing through contradictions, to the self-developing reality. The whole point is, however, that Hegel did not recognise this as a property of the objective reality existing outside the

---

[22] Karl Marx, *Capital*, Vol. I, p. 152.

[23] Ibid., pp. 152-53.

[24] G. W. F. Hegel, *Phänomenologie des Geistes,* hrsg. von Georg Lasson, 2. Auflage, Verlag von F. Meiner, Leipzig, 1921, S. 12-13.

spirit and independently from it. For him, the only self-developing substance is the logical idea, and it is therefore assumed and substantiated that the requirement to conceive and express the truth not as substance but in the same degree as a subject can only be realised in the science of thought, only in philosophy and in objective idealist philosophy at that.

Using Hegel's terminology in *Capital*, Marx emphasises thereby the fundamental opposition of his philosophical standpoint to that of Hegelianism, demonstrating a model of *materialist* dialectics as the science of development through inner contradictions.

The essence of the Marxian upheaval in political economy may be expressed in philosophical terms in the following manner: in Marx's theory, *not only the substance* of value, labour, was understood (Ricardo also attained this understanding), but, for the first time, value was simultaneously understood *as the subject* of the entire development, that is, as a reality developing through its inner contradictions into a whole system of economic forms. Ricardo failed to understand this latter point. To attain such an understanding, one had to take the standpoint of *conscious materialist dialectics*.

Only on the basis of this conception of the objective laws of development as development through contradictions can one understand the essence of the logic of inquiry applied in *Capital*, the essence of the method of ascent from the abstract to the concrete.

At first sight, viewed from the external form, that is pure deduction, movement from a universal category (value) to particular ones (money, surplus-value, profit, wages, etc.). The external movement of thought resembles very much traditional deduction—money (and subsequently surplus-value and other categories) appears as a more concrete image of value in general, as specific being of value. At first glance, value may seem to be the generic concept, the abstract general, while money and the rest, species of value.

Analysis reveals, however, that there is no genus-to-species relation here. Indeed, the content of 'value in general' is revealed as a directly contradictory unity of value and use-value. As for money and particularly paper money, it does not have use-value, realising in its economic function only one of the two definitions of value in general—that of the universal equivalent. Value in general proves to be richer in content than its own species, money. The universal category has a feature that is not present in the particular category. Money thus realises the two-fold nature of value only in a one-sided (abstract) way. Nevertheless money is a more concrete, more complex, historically derivative economic phenomenon than value. From the standpoint of the traditional conception of deduction that is a paradox, not deduction but something else.

Indeed, that is not deduction in the sense of old logic, but rather movement of thought which combines in an integral manner both the transition from the universal to the particular and vice versa, from the particular to the universal, the movement from the abstract to the concrete and from the concrete to the abstract.

All economic realities reflected in the categories of *Capital* (commodity, money, labour-power, surplus-value, rent) represent both the concrete and the abstract—objectively, independently from their theoretical interpretation. Each of these categories reflects quite a concrete economic formation or phenomenon, and at the same time each of them reflects a reality which is merely a one-sided (abstract) implementation of that whole of which it is an integral part, being a disappearing moment in the movement of this whole, its abstract manifestation.

Deduction reproduces the real process of the formation of each of these categories (that is, of each real economic formation) as well as of their entire system as a whole, disclosing real genetic links, genetic unity, where on the surface there appear a number of seemingly unconnected phenomena and even those which contradict each other.

Hence the fundamental difference between formal-logical, syllogistic deduction and the method of ascent from the abstract to the concrete.

The basis or the major premise of the former is an abstract general, generic concept, the least meaningful in content and the broadest in extent. This concept applies only to those particular phenomena which do not contain a feature contradicting the properties of the universal concept. Apart from that, this concept does not apply to phenomena in which at least one feature included in the definition of the content of the universal concept *is absent*. This phenomenon will be evaluated from the standpoint of old logic as belonging to some other system, to another genus of phenomena.

The axiom of old deduction reads: each of the particular phenomena to which an abstract general concept may apply must possess *all* the features contained in the definition of the universal concept, and must not possess any features contradicting the features of the universal concept. Only phenomena consistent with this requirement are recognised in old deduction as belonging to the genus of phenomena defined by the universal concept. The universal concept here functions as a criterion for selecting phenomena which should be taken into account in considering a certain type of phenomena and, in logical parlance, predetermines from the outset the plane of abstraction, the angle from which things are viewed. But, as soon as we apply this axiom to the categories of political economy, we clearly see its artificial and subjective nature.

Thus, money does not possess an attribute of value in general—use-value. Capitalistic commodity circulation comprises in itself a feature that directly contradicts the law of value, the law of exchange of equivalents—the ability to create *surplus*-value, to which the category of value cannot apply without a contradiction. Surplus-value therefore begins to seem a phenomenon of some other world, not the sphere of the movement of value.

Paradoxes like this confused the bourgeois economists who did not recognise any logic other than formal logic or any deduction other than syllogistic one.

The theoretical task posed by the development of pre-Marxian political economy was this—to show that phenomena directly contradicting the labour theory of value become not only possible but also necessary on the basis of the law of value and without any violations of it.

We have already shown in sufficient detail that this task is absolutely insoluble as long as value is understood as an *abstract general, generic concept*, and that it can be solved rationally if value is interpreted as a *concrete universal category* reflecting quite a concrete economic reality (direct exchange of one commodity for another) containing a contradiction.

This conception of value gave Marx a key to the solution of all those theoretical difficulties that always present an obstacle to theoretical analysis of living reality developing through contradictions.

Marx's analysis discovers in value itself, in the basic category of theoretical development, the possibility of those contradictions which emerge in an explicit form on the surface of developed capitalism as destructive crises of overproduction, as a most acute antagonism between excess of riches at one pole of society and unbearable poverty, at the other, as direct class struggle ultimately resolved only through revolution.

Theoretically presented, this emerges as the inevitable result of the development of that very contradiction which is contained in simple commodity exchange, in the 'cell' of the whole system—value, as in an embryo or kernel.

It now becomes clear why value in the course of theoretical development of the categories of capitalist economy proves to be a rigorous guideline permitting to single out abstractly only those features of analysed reality which are linked with it as its attributes, being universal and necessary forms of the existence of the capitalist system. The theoretical presentation of this system incorporates only those generalisations to which the definitions of value can apply. However, this inclusion of the categories in the sphere of value, as it is performed in *Capital*, is essentially alien to the formal subsumption of concepts under other concepts. Labour-power, for instance, is included in the category of value, but that directly reflects the actual formation of the capitalist system of relations.

Analysis of this system has shown that commodity-money circulation forms the universal basis, the elementary universal and necessary condition without which capitalism cannot emerge, exist, or develop. The theoretical definitions of commodity-money circulation are thus shown to be reflections of those objective universal conditions that must be satisfied by any phenomenon to be included at any time in the movement of the capitalistic commodity organism.

If a phenomenon does not satisfy the conditions dictated by the laws of commodity-money circulation, that means that it could not and in general cannot be included in this process, it cannot become a form of the capitalistic commodity metabolism in society.

Definitions of value thus become for theoretical thought a rigorous criterion of discerning and selecting those phenomena and economic forms that are inherent in capitalism.

Only that which *actually*, independently of thought, satisfies the conditions dictated by the immanent laws of the commodity-money sphere, only that which may be assimilated by this sphere and may assume the economic form of value, may become a form of movement of the *capitalist* system. Therefore reasoning, which abstracts from the boundless ocean of empirical facts only that concrete historical definiteness of these facts which they owe to capitalism as an economic system, is justified in abstracting only those features of the analysed reality which are included in the definitions of value.

If a certain fact does not satisfy these definitions and requirements established in the analysis of the commodity-money sphere and theoretically expressed in the category of value, that is a clear and categorical indication that, objectively, it does not belong to the kind of facts the generalisation of which must serve as the basis for constructing a theory, a system of concrete historical definitions of capital. Everything that cannot assume the form of value, cannot become capital either.

The entire significance of the category of value in Marx's theory is contained in the fact that it reflects the universal and necessary element, a 'cell' of *capital*, constituting the universal and most abstract expression of the specific nature of capital, and simultaneously quite a concrete economic fact—direct exchange of a commodity for another commodity.

Extremely indicative in this light is the theoretical transition from the consideration of the commodity-money sphere to the analysis of the production of surplus-value.

What is the basis for the strictest logical necessity of this transition?

It is founded, first of all, on the fact that the analysis of production of surplus-value is approached from the definitions established by the analysis of the commodity-money sphere. Second, what is *analytically studied here is a real fact*—the fact that money put in *capitalist* circulation, passing through all of its metamorphoses, brings a return—surplus-value. Then one has to go back to establish the conditions which make this fact possible. One of the conditions of this possibility, and an absolutely necessary one, is already established by the analysis of the commodity-money form. It is the law of value, with regard to which it has been shown that, on the one hand, it is an absolutely universal law of the analysed whole and, on the other, that it does not contain all the necessary conditions under which surplus-value is objectively necessary.

A certain necessary condition of the analytically studied economic fact is still missing. Thought is then *purposefully* directed at finding this missing condition, the necessary condition of the possibility of surplus-value.

The task is formulated in this form: the unknown quantity must be found not by logical construction but *among a number of real economic facts, in the empirical reality of developed capitalism.* We do not yet know what that fact is. At the same time we know something very important about it. It must in any case be a commodity, that is, an economic reality entirely subject to the law of value, to its indisputable requirements. This commodity, however, must possess one specific feature: its use-value must consist exactly in its ability to be transformed into value in the act of consumption itself. This second requirement imposed on the unknown quantity is, as is easy to see, an analytically established condition of the possibility of *surplus-value*, of capital.

Empirical consideration of developed capitalistic commodity circulation shows that only one economic reality satisfies these conditions, namely, labour-power. The logically correctly formulated question here yields the only possible solution: the unknown quantity satisfying the theoretically established conditions is labour-power.

This conclusion, this theoretical generalisation of *actual facts* has all the merits of the most perfect induction, if the latter is to be interpreted as generalisation proceeding from actual facts. This generalisation, however, simultaneously satisfies the most stringent demands of the adherents of the deductive character of scientific theoretical knowledge.

The mode of ascent from the abstract to the concrete permits to establish strictly and to express abstractedly only the absolutely necessary conditions of the possibility of the object given in contemplation. *Capital* shows in detail the necessity with which surplus-value is realised, given developed commodity-money circulation and free labour-power.

The totality of all the necessary conditions appears in this method of analysis as a real and *concrete* possibility, while developed commodity-money circulation is shown as an *abstract* possibility of surplus-value. For logical reasoning, however, this abstract possibility appears as *impossibility*: analysis of the commodity-money sphere shows that its immanent laws are in *mutually exclusive contradiction* to surplus-value. In the same way, the study of the nature of labour-power as such reveals that it cannot be considered as a source of surplus-value. Labour in general creates a product, a use-value, and by no means value.

The scientific theoretical conception of surplus-value is in this methodological framework focused on discovering the necessary conditions which make it possible only in their *concrete historical interaction*. Each of them, considered abstractedly, outside concrete interactions with others, rules out in principle the very possibility of surplus-value. In thought, this appears as a mutually exclusive contradiction between the law of value (as an abstract possibility of a fact) and the fact itself—surplus-value.

Only *concrete* possibility is *real*, only the totality of *all* the necessary conditions of the being of a thing in their concrete historical mutual conditioning. A real solution of the contradiction between the universal law and the empirical form of its realisation, between abstraction and concrete fact, can only be found through revealing this concrete totality of conditions. The abstractly expressed universal law inevitably stands in relations of mutually exclusive contradiction to the fact under study. From the standpoint of dialectical logic, there is nothing to be afraid of here. On the contrary, logical contradiction is in this case only an indication and feature of the fact that the analysed object is understood abstractedly and not concretely, that not all the necessary conditions of its being are as yet discovered. The logical contradictions necessarily arising in cognition are thus solved in the unfolding of the concrete system of categories reproducing the object in the entire fulness of its necessary characteristics, of the objective conditions of its being.

But concrete understanding does not completely eliminate all contradictions. On the contrary, it shows in detail that these contradictions are logically correct forms of reflection of the objective reality developing through contradictions. Concrete theoretical knowledge shows the necessity of the fact that phenomena directly contradicting the universal law emerge on its basis without violating, changing, or transforming it in any way.

In this cognitive process, all the necessary conditions of the possibility of the analysed phenomenon are not simply listed or juxtaposed but conceived in their concrete historical interaction, in the genetic links between them.

The mere mechanical sum of the conditions of surplus-value (developed commodity-money circulation and labour-power) does not yet constitute its real, concrete nature. Surplus-value is the product of organic interaction between the two, a qualitatively new economic reality, and its concrete understanding is not simply made up of the characteristics that could be obtained from the consideration of commodity-money circulation and labour-power. Labour-power becomes a factor in the production of surplus-value only on condition that it commences to function in that social form which was developed by the movement of the commodity-money market—in the form of a commodity. But the economic form of commodity also becomes a form of the movement of capital only if it dominates the movement of labour-power. The interaction of the laws of commodity-money circulation and of labour-power gives birth to a certain new economic reality not contained in either of them taken separately, outside their concrete interaction.

Therefore the movement of logical reasoning reproducing the necessary moments of the development of surplus-value cannot consist in the formal combination or synthesis of the theoretical definitions obtained in the analysis of its constituents, that is, of the definitions of the commodity-money sphere, on the one hand, and labour-power as a commodity, on the other. Further movement of thought in which a conception of surplus-value is formed can only proceed through *new* analysis of *new* facts—those of the movement of surplus-value as a specific economic phenomenon that cannot in principle be reduced to its constituents.

On the other hand, this further *theoretical* consideration of the movement of surplus-value could not have taken place in the absence of categories developed in the study of the laws of the movement of the commodity-money market and of the specific features of labour-power as commodity. Unless these categories are previously developed, theoretical analysis of the empirical facts of the movement of surplus-value is impossible. In this case, only abstract characteristics of the production of surplus-value will be obtained, reflecting merely the external appearance of this process rather than concrete theoretical definitions.

Theoretical analysis directly coinciding with the theoretical synthesis of the abstract definitions of surplus-value established earlier does not express the abstract superficial forms of its movement but rather the necessary changes that take place in the movement of the commodity-money market when this movement involves such an unusual commodity as labour-power. This commodity introduces in the movement of commodity-money circulation precisely those changes which transform the commodity-money circulation into the sphere of production of surplus-value.

Labour-power itself is not here regarded as an eternal characteristic identical for all formations but in its concrete historical definiteness *as commodity*. That means that the first thing that is discovered in it (and recorded in a concept) is the *historically definite* form which it assumes only in the sphere of commodity-money circulation.

That is what distinguishes *scientific theoretical reproduction* of the creation of surplus-value from an *abstract description* of this process, from a mere abstract expression of its superficial phenomena.

To understand and *express in concepts* the essence of capitalist production,/ of labour producing surplus-value, one must first establish the entire totality of the necessary conditions on the basis of which *such* labour becomes possible in general, and further trace the changes it introduces into the very conditions of its realisation.

Analysis of changes introduced by labour-power in commodity-money circulation, in the production of value, therefore assumes preliminary analysis of the conditions *that* undergo these changes, that is, analysis of the production of value—the process which *wage* labour finds in existence. Without this, the *origin* of surplus-value is in principle impossible to understand.

This method of interpreting phenomena permits more than a mere description of the aspect in which they emerge before direct contemplation on the surface of the developed stage in their existence—it permits to *reproduce*, in the full sense of the term, their origination, to trace their emergence and development into the present state through the strictly necessary stages.

The method of ascent from the abstract to the concrete is founded at this point on the real circumstance that the actually necessary and universal conditions of the *origin and development* of the object are retained at each given moment as forms of its *existence*. That is why thought can discern, in the analysis of a developed object, its sublated history. A historical approach to the study of an object cannot be realised other than by the method of ascent from the abstract to the concrete.

Therefore the picture presented in the most abstract parts of the theory (e.g., the first chapter of *Capital*) differs most radically from the picture as it appears in the direct contemplation and in the notions of the developed stage of the process. Contrariwise, the greater the number of law-governed influences, tendencies, and stimuli taken into account in the ascent from the abstract to the concrete and the more concrete the picture, the closer it comes to complete coincidence with the picture given in direct contemplation and notion.

As a result, Marx's *Capital* shows more than the 'economic skeleton' of the social organism, more than its inner structure. Lenin believed it to be a great advantage of Marx's method that, in '*explaining* the structure and development of the given formation of society *exclusively* through production relations, he nevertheless everywhere and incessantly scrutinised the superstructure corresponding to these production relations and clothed the skeleton in flesh and blood'. *Capital*, as Lenin pointed out, 'showed the whole capitalist social formation to the reader as a living thing—with its everyday aspects, with the actual social manifestation of the class antagonism inherent in production relations, with the bourgeois political superstructure that protects the rule of the capitalist class, with the bourgeois ideas of liberty, equality and so forth, with the bourgeois family relationships'.[25]

Capital also shows that these actual relations cannot be other than they are, as long as the entire social life is based on privately owned capitalistic commodity economy, just as a person with a curvature of the spine cannot be graceful. It is only the grave that can correct these actual relations. As long as the law of surplus-value works, both crises

[25] V. I. Lenin, What the 'Friends of the People Are' and How They Fight the Social-Democrats, *Collected Works*, Vol. 1, 1960, pp. 141-42.

and unemployment are inevitable, for they are merely the external forms of manifestation of the deepest essence of the capitalistic commodity organism—the contradictions of the accumulation of surplus-value. These contradictions are inherent in capitalism in the same way as protein metabolism is inherent in a living body. They are not spots on the surface but an expression of its very essence. That is exactly what *Capital* shows, and that is what its method is used for—the method of attaining a comprehension of phenomena from their universal essence, the method of ascent from the abstract to the concrete.

Having accepted Marx's method, it is impossible not to accept all the conclusions of *Capital*. That is why it is so hated by the apologists of modern capitalism. It proves that the crises of overproduction, the existence of a reserve army of the unemployed and all the other similar forms of bourgeois 'wealth' are universal and absolute forms of production and accumulation of surplus-value, its integral forms, not only the consequences but also the necessary conditions of this process.

For this reason, bourgeois philosophers and logicians have long tried to discredit Marx's method, calling it 'speculative construction', 'the Hegelian form of reasoning', allegedly adopted by Marx without due criticism, etc., although, as we have taken pains to show, the resemblance to the Hegelian method is purely external and formal. The deduction performed by Marx is merely a synonym of the materialist method, a method of explaining the spiritual-ideological, political, legal, moral, and other relations from the material relations, from the relations of production.

In *Capital,* Marx indicated this fact quite unequivocally: 'It is, in reality, much easier to discover by analysis the earthly core of the misty creation of religion, than, conversely, it is, to develop from the actual relations of life the corresponding celestial forms of those relations. The latter method is the only materialistic, and therefore the only scientific one.'[26]

That is the method which insists that the task of scientific cognition of money does not lie in grasping the fact that money is also a commodity, but in tracing the reasons and the manner in which commodity becomes money. That is a

---

[26] Karl Marx, *Capital*, Vol. I, p. 352.

much more difficult but also a surer way. This method shows the relations of real life which are reflected in the well-known ideological forms and, moreover, it explains why the given, rather than some other, ideological, political, legal, and scientific forms have developed. All of these forms are literally 'deduced' from the relations of real life, from its contradictions. Herein lies the profound difference between the Marxian and the Feuerbachian critique of the forms of religious consciousness. Therein consists the principal advantage of the dialectical method of Marx, Engels, and Lenin, and at the same time, its materialistic nature, in application to any field of inquiry—from political economy to epistemology and esthetics.

* * *

Marx's *Capital*, is indeed the highest type of school for theoretical thinking. A scientist specialising in any field of knowledge can use it as a source of most valuable ideas with regard to the theoretical method of research. Philosophers and logicians must make this treasury more accessible. Of course, a single author and a single book can solve this task to a very limited extent only. In view of the complexity and the amount of work involved, this task will require a whole series of studies.

NAME INDEX

SUBJECT INDEX